Jakarta
a Lonely Planet city guide

Peter Turner

Jakarta
1st edition

Published by
Lonely Planet Publications
Head Office: PO Box 617, Hawthorn, Vic 3122, Australia
Branches: 155 Filbert St, Suite 251, Oakland,
CA 94607, USA
10 Barley Mow Passage, Chiswick,
London W4 4PH, UK
71 bis rue du Cardinal Lemoine,
75005 Paris, France
Printed by
Colorcraft Ltd, Hong Kong

Photographs by
Glenn Beanland (GB), Peter Turner (PT)

Front cover: Wayang golek puppets (GB)
Front gatefold: Top: Golek puppets (GB)
Bottom: Shop front, Glodok (GB)
Back gatefold: Top: Chillis (GB)
Bottom: Local man from Cikini (GB)

First Published
July 1995

Although the authors and publisher have tried to make the information as accurate as possible, they accept no responsibility for any loss, injury or inconvenience sustained by any person using this book.

National Library of Australia Cataloguing in Publication Data

Turner, Peter
Jakarta city guide

1st ed.
Includes index.
ISBN 0 86442 290 3.

1. Jakarta (Indonesia) – Guide-books.
I. Title (Series: Lonely Planet city guide).

915.98220439

text & maps © Lonely Planet 1995
photos © photographers as indicated 1995
climate charts compiled from information supplied by Patrick J Tyson, © Patrick J Tyson, 1995

Peter Turner

Peter Turner was born in Melbourne and studied engineering and then arts before dropping out on the overland trail through Asia. He returned to study Indian and Indonesian studies, before again setting off to Asia. Since his first extended trip through Indonesia in 1978, he has returned to Indonesia six times, travelling through the archipelago. He joined Lonely Planet in 1986 as an editor, and worked in the field on *Malaysia, Singapore & Brunei* and *Singapore* city guide. Now a full-time travel writer, he has also contributed to *South-East Asia* and *Indonesia*, and is the author of *Java*. For the research of this book he was accompanied by his wife, Lorraine, and three-year-old daughter, Ruby. The birth of their second daughter, Madeleine, will add a new dimension for researching travel with children.

From the Author

Of the many people that assisted with this guide, special thanks must go to the staff of the Jakarta City Tourism Office, and Yuni Syafril in particular. Thanks to Drew, and Andreas, for hospitality, company out on the town, and information on living in Jakarta. Above all, thanks to Lorraine for braving the onslaught of Jakarta, help with research, manuscript suggestions and keeping it all together.

From the Publisher

This book was edited at the Lonely Planet head office in Melbourne, Australia, by Kristin Odijk and was proofread by Sharan Kaur and Linda Suttie. Thanks to Sue Galley for suggestions. The maps were drawn by Andrew Tudor who also designed and laid out the book. The cover was designed by Valerie Tellini. Thanks also to Glenn Beanland for travelling to Jakarta and taking the photographs.

Warning & Request

Things change – prices go up, schedules change, good places go bad and bad places go bankrupt – nothing stays the same. So if you find things better or worse, recently opened or long since closed, please write and tell us and help make the next edition better. Your letters will be used to help update future editions and, where possible, important changes will also be included in a Stop Press section in reprints.

We greatly appreciate all information that is sent to us by travellers. Back at Lonely Planet we employ a hard-working readers' letters team to sort through the many letters we receive. The best ones will be rewarded with a free copy of the next edition or another Lonely Planet guide if you prefer. We give away lots of books, but, unfortunately, not every letter/postcard receives one.

Contents

Introduction

Jakarta is all Indonesia rolled into one huge urban sprawl of nearly nine million people. Indonesians come from all over the archipelago to seek fame and fortune, or just to eke a living. Bataks and Minangkabau from Sumatra, Ambonese from Maluku, Dani from Irian Jaya, Minahasans from Sulawesi, Balinese, Madurese and Timorese are all united by Bahasa Indonesia and a desire to make it in the capital. For it is in Jakarta that the latest styles and thoughts are formed, the important political decisions made. Jakarta is the main centre for the economy, the place to do deals and court government officials.

Over the last decade or so, Jakarta has undergone a huge transformation. Once, its miserable poverty and crumbling infrastructure made it one of the hell holes of Asian travel. Now the city's face is being changed by the constant construction of more skyscrapers, flyovers, hotels and shopping malls.

The showpiece of the prosperous new Jakarta is the central business district bound by Jalan Thamrin/Sudirman, Jalan Rasuna Said and Jalan Gatot Subroto. The 'Golden Triangle' as it is known is crammed with office towers, luxury hotels and foreign embassies. Viewed from here, Jakarta has all the appearances of a prosperous Asian boom city. Move away from the city centre, and it becomes obvious that Jakarta is a big city vortex that sucks in the poor, often providing little more than the hope of hard work at low pay.

Jakarta is primarily a city of business not a tourist destination, but the old part of the city is not to be missed. Kota is the heart of the 17th-century Dutch town of Batavia, centred around the cobbled square of Taman Fatahillah. From the fine old Dutch architecture of Kota, you can wander north to the old schooner dock of Sunda Kelapa, the most impressive reminder of the age of sailing ships to be found anywhere in the world. Taman Mini Indonesia Indah is one of Jakarta's most popular attractions. The all-Indonesia theme park provides an informative and interesting look at all the regions of Indonesia. Dunia Fantasi (Fantasy World) on the coast at Ancol is Jakarta's answer to Disneyland and a must for the kids. The city also has a few interesting museums, oversized monuments and good shopping possibilities to keep visitors amused.

Jakarta is the most expensive city in Indonesia, the most polluted and the most congested, but if you can withstand its onslaught and afford to indulge in its charms, then it can also be one of Indonesia's most exciting. For this is the 'big durian', the foul-smelling exotic fruit that some can't stomach but others can't resist.

Facts about Jakarta

HISTORY

Sunda Kelapa

Though evidence exists of human habitation in Jakarta from pre-historic times, it was not until the 12th century that a settlement at the mouth of the Ciliwung River rose to prominence. The Hindu-Buddhist Pajajaran kingdom, whose capital of Pakuwan was upriver near present-day Bogor, established the port of Sunda Kelapa as a trading centre. Like many ports in the archipelago, through trade it came in contact with influences from India, China and Arabia, and the religions of Hinduism and Buddhism and then later of Islam.

Though it was a minor port compared with mighty Malacca on the Malay peninsula, Sunda Kelapa grew in importance after the Portuguese took Malacca in 1511 and the Muslim trade went elsewhere. Yet the Pajajaran kingdom was keen to counter the growing Islamic influence that was sweeping Java. In 1522, Pajajaran signed a treaty with the Portuguese in the hope of staving off the power of the growing Muslim sultanates on Java.

Under the terms of the treaty, the Portuguese would build a fort and godown on the coast, but by the time the Portuguese returned it was too late. The Muslim state of Demak conquered Banten, Pajajaran's other main port to the west of Sunda Kelapa, and then in 1527 the Banten sultanate sent an army under the command of Fatahillah to conquer Sunda Kelapa. Fatahillah not only took Sunda Kelapa but he then attacked and defeated a Portuguese landing, prompting him to rename the city Jayakarta, meaning 'Great Victory'. The date has been ascribed to 22 June 1527, which Jakarta celebrates as its anniversary.

Jayakarta & the Spice Trade (1527-1619)

Jayakarta was overshadowed by Banten, which became a major trading centre in the region. Banten's main trading commodity was pepper, and it attracted merchants from Arabia to China, making Banten a cosmopolitan port. The lucrative spice trade also attracted European interest and armed merchant ships from Holland and Britain came to compete with the Portuguese and Spanish.

Both the British and the Dutch established East India companies, and these government monopolies soon became the main competitors to secure the spice trade. Like other traders, the Europeans sought commerce but, unlike other traders, the Europeans quickly set about trying to establish a monopoly through force.

By 1605, the Dutch company, the United East India Company or Vereenigde Oost-Indische Compagnie (VOC), defeated the Portuguese and Spanish in the Moluccas, the important spices islands to the east, with reserves of cloves and nutmeg. The VOC established themselves at Ambon but needed a base closer to the important shipping lanes of the Malacca and Sunda straits.

The sultanate of Banten had granted the Dutch, along with British, the right to set up godowns in Banten, but the Dutch wanted their own headquarters. The Dutch looked to Jayakarta, still a vassal state of Banten, where the ruler, Prince Jayawikarta, sought to extend his own influence. He granted permission for the Dutch to build a warehouse in 1610, but creative Dutch builders modified and extended the original design to the extent that by 1618 a fully fledged Dutch fort, called Mauritius, occupied a strategic position at the head of the river on the east bank. Opposite, on the other side of the river, was the prince's customs post and a small British post on the site now occupied by the old watchtower.

The dominance of the Dutch in Indonesia can be attributed to the far-sighted but ruthless Governor-General Jan Pieterzoon Coen, who laid the foundation for a Dutch empire. He constantly petitioned his masters in Holland for more men and firepower, as relations between the Dutch and the English came to the boil and his own grandiose plans of Dutch domination grew. After the English seized a Dutch ship at Banten, Coen burned the English post at Jayakarta in 1618. The English, who had signed a pact with the prince of Jayakarta, sent a fleet to Jayakarta and the Jayakartans laid siege to the Dutch fort. Vastly outnumbered, Coen set sail to the VOC post in the Moluccas to gather reinforcements.

That the Dutch survived at Jayakarta was due not so much to heroics but to disunity among the enemy. Banten, angered that the vassal Jayakartans had signed a pact with the British, sent its own fleet to oversee the situation and ensure that the British would not dominate. The siege became a standoff much to the relief of the Dutch. In celebrations in March 1619, the VOC personnel holding out in their fortified post decided to rename the fort 'Batavia' after an ancient Germanic tribe, the ancestors of the Dutch.

Coen returned in May 1619, promptly razed the town and the prince's kraton. All reminders of the old town disappeared, and Batavia became the headquarters of the Dutch in the East Indies.

Batavia (1619-1730)

Coen set about strengthening his empire. In the Moluccas, Coen ensured soaring profits for the company by slaughtering resistance, and granting concessions to

City Walls, Museum Bahari (Maritime Museum), Kota (GB)

planters, who increased spice production with the help
of slave labour.

Batavia was further fortified, and in its early years the
town lived under constant threat of attack. In 1628,
Sultan Agung of the Central Javanese kingdom of
Mataram sent a fleet of 60 ships and 10,000 men to attack
Batavia. They laid siege to the fort, but the Javanese army
was poorly provisioned and had to retreat.

Sultan Agung tried again the following year with an
even bigger army, but the fleet that was sent to supply
the army was easily defeated by superior VOC ships,
and Mataram's starving troops were again forced to
retreat. During the siege, Coen died aged 42, probably
of cholera. Mataram did not try to attack Batavia again,
but Banten continued to harry the Dutch, and the city
grew within thick walls, which were constructed from
1634 onwards.

The walled city grew up on both sides of the river and
the Dutch set about creating an Amsterdam of the East,
complete with canals to drain the swampy coastal low-
lands. They built tall stuffy houses and, just as in
Holland, the most desirable houses fronted the canals.
In 1652, with booming trade, a row of warehouses were
built near the entrance to the port, and these survive
today as the Museum Bahari.

All the while the VOC moved closer to its goal of
monopolising the spice trade. Batavia's position
attracted ships that used the Sunda Strait rather than the
Malacca Strait, and superior Dutch maritime might was
used to blockade Malacca and Banten, the VOC's main
trade rival and the primary base for the British. The
Malacca trade declined and the Dutch eventually took
Malacca in 1641.

Meanwhile on Java, Mataram and Banten vied for
power. The VOC played one off against the other, first
supporting Mataram against Banten and then gleefully
coming to Banten's aid in 1682 after a dispute over the
succession to the sultanate. For their help, the Dutch
demanded and were granted a garrison in Banten,
monopoly of the pepper trade and the British expelled.
It was the beginning of the end for Banten.

Batavia was a company town, and though it tried to
attract more European residents, the labourers, artisans
and many of the traders were Asian. Europeans were
almost exclusively employees of the company and the
largest group of immigrants were the Chinese, which by
1650 comprised nearly 30% of the population and built
their temples in the Glodok and Ancol areas. The largest
group were slaves that the VOC imported from India,
Sulawesi and other Indonesian islands.

The Mardijkers were another significant group that came mostly from the Portuguese territories of Malacca and India captured by the VOC. The Mardijkers were freed slaves that had converted to Christianity, and they spoke a Portuguese patois, hence they were also called the 'black Portuguese'. Many worked for the company or became shopkeepers and enjoyed a relatively high status.

Batavia continued to grow dramatically as the VOC realised its goal of becoming the dominant European power in the region. By the early 17th century Batavia was by all accounts a prosperous and handsome city. Greater public works were undertaken and a new town hall, now the Jakarta City Museum on Taman Fatahillah, was built in 1710. Settlements began to spread beyond the walls of the city and Batavia began to feel growing pains.

Decline of the VOC & Batavia (1730-99)

By 1730, 20,000 people lived within the small walled city and 15,000 lived outside the walls. In terms of company profits, it was a golden age for both Batavia and Holland, but disease was to tarnish Batavia's gloss. The canals, while providing a touch of home for the Dutch, were never completely effective at draining the city and proved to be stinking cesspits in the dry season, and a breeding ground for vermin and malarial mosquitoes. Batavia's water supply came from wells, but the water was undrinkable and easily contaminated.

Batavia went from being a Dutch showpiece to a Dutch graveyard. Typhoid, cholera and malaria mowed down Batavia's population, with disease taking at least one in four Europeans well up into the 1800s. Disease was attributed to 'bad air' in the old city and more residents moved outside the walled city. The south-east became a fashionable European district.

Chinese migration continued and the Chinese became one of the driving forces of the colony, providing much of the labour and many of the services. Wealthy Chinese businesses multiplied and well-to-do Chinese lived throughout the old city, and helped to develop the areas outside the city.

Chinese coolies continued to pour into Batavia, despite high unemployment and extreme hardship among new arrivals. When Chinese gangs formed outside the city the government embarked on a pro-gramme to deport Chinese labourers to Ceylon. On 8 October 1740, the increasingly desperate Chinese

Boat moored at Sunda Kelapa, Kota (GB)

rebelled by attacking outposts and marching on the city.
Though the rebels were crudely armed, the good citizens
of Batavia panicked. The following day Europeans and
Indonesians went berserk and attacked and plundered
Chinese houses within the city. At least 5000 Chinese
were massacred, while the government did nothing to
stop the slaughter. In one incident, 500 Chinese held in
the city hall were brought out one by one and butchered
in the courtyard. The surviving Chinese fled the city and
the VOC government banned them from returning to
reside within the city walls. Relations with the Chinese
were never the same, and Batavia's fortunes declined.

Despite the ills of the city it continued to grow, and in
1750 the population numbered 100,000, with Europeans

numbering less than 2000. Outside the walled city, the large markets of Pasar Senen and Pasar Tanah Abang were connected by main thoroughfares, and wealthy Dutch citizens built large country houses, such as the present-day National Archives building on Jalan Gajah Mada. Batavia grew farther south towards Bogor and Batavia's environs were major sugar-cane production areas. The Priangan district in the highlands south-west of Batavia towards Bandung had important coffee and tea plantations as more roads pushed into the interior.

Towards the end of the 17th century, the spice trade declined and the VOC relied increasingly on plantations to prop up falling profits. The 1784 Treaty of Paris ended the Dutch-English war but also put an end to the Dutch trading monopoly, while inefficiency and expensive military campaigns all helped to bankrupt the company. The Dutch government stepped in and took control, and the VOC was finally dissolved in 1799, issuing in a new era of direct colonial government.

Colonial Administration (1799-1811)

By the beginning of the 19th century, the disease-ridden old city and its walls had fallen into disrepair and most of the administration and military were inland in the Weltevreden district, around present-day Lapangan Banteng. Weltevreden (meaning 'well content') was a country estate purchased in 1767 and many Europeans settled the area in the latter half of the 18th century. Weltevreden officially became the seat of the governor-general in 1797, but it was Governor-General Daendels in 1808 who made the area the official seat of government. Napoleon had conquered Holland in 1795 and installed his brother on the Dutch throne in 1806. In 1808 the government sent pro-revolutionary Daendels with the task of reorganising the colony and defending it against the British, who were in effect blockading Batavia's harbour.

Daendels decided that the old city was indefensible and much of it was levelled, including the old fort and the city wall, and the building materials were carted off to develop Weltevreden. As well as building roads and reshaping the city, Daendels reformed the civil service and attacked corruption. He started work on a new palace, now the Department of Finance building on Lapangan Banteng, though he preferred to escape to the palace at Buitenzorg (present-day Bogor) as much as possible. Buitenzorg became the official seat of the governor-general from this time on.

English Rule (1811-16)

In 1811, after Napoleon's official annexation of Holland, the French flag was raised in Batavia, to the consternation of Dutch residents. Daendels was recalled, and later that year a British force invaded Batavia. The English met little resistance from Dutch troops forced to fight for France.

The English were to rule the Dutch East Indies for the next five years, and Sir Stamford Raffles was appointed lieutenant-governor of Java from 1811 to 1816. A far-sighted and progressive thinker, he set about trying to reform the colony, instituting agricultural reform, abolishing slavery and reorganising the civil service. Though ambitious and well intentioned, Raffles was not always an efficient administrator. At the end of the Napoleonic wars in 1816, Britain returned Dutch colonies before Raffles had the chance to make a large impact on the colony. Raffles' *History of Java* is a lasting contribution to Indonesian scholarship, as were his efforts in encouraging the excavation and study of Hindu-Buddhist archaeological remains in Java. Raffles is best known as the father of Singapore, where he founded a British trading post in 1819 to counteract the resurgence of the Dutch trading monopoly. Singapore went on to become the main entrepôt port in South-East Asia, displacing Batavia in importance in the late 19th century.

19th-Century Batavia (1816-1900)

The returning Dutch administration continued on where they had left off before the British interregnum, developing Java as the centre of their empire in the Dutch East Indies.

From 1825 the Dutch had to fight a five-year guerrilla war led by Prince Diponegoro of the Yogyakarta sultanate. After the war, Dutch control of Java was almost complete.

In 1830, Governor-General van den Bosch introduced the 'Culture System' in a determined effort to improve profits and make the colony pay for itself through export crops. Under this system, instead of land taxes, peasants had to either cultivate government-owned crops on 20% of their land or work in the government plantations for nearly 60 days of the year. Much of Java became a Dutch plantation, and coffee and sugar exports became the mainstay of the colonial economy, generating great wealth in the Netherlands. For the Javanese peasantry, this forced-labour system brought hardship and resentment, while the Javanese aristocracy became effete figureheads. For the Dutch it involved a much more direct role in Java, and colonial settlement in the interior spread rapidly. After a public outcry in the Netherlands about the treatment and suffering of Indonesians under the colonial government, the so-called Liberal Policy was introduced by liberals in the Dutch parliament, trying to reform and eliminate the excesses of the Culture System.

In the 18th century, large tracts of East Java and Central Java were under direct colonial rule. Batavia was overtaken in size by Surabaya and other cities such as Buitenzorg and Bandung also grew in importance. As a consequence, Batavia's growth was less vigorous and more easily controlled. Part of the reason for the lower growth in Batavia was the ever-present health problems. Though towards the end of the century, Batavia was no longer a graveyard for the Dutch, as they moved away from the old city to the spacious and graceful new city. By the end of the 19th century, Batavia was undoubtedly a fine city and was referred to as the 'Queen of the East'.

Throughout the 19th century, Batavia grew as an elongated escape from the unhealthy coastal swamp towards the hills. It stretched over 10 km from the coast along the road to Buitenzorg, and consisted of two main cities – the Batavia/Kota district and the new city around Weltevreden – with settlements straggling along the main road between.

In the new city, the Koningsplein was a large square of grass used for army exercises and though never a fine park, it was, and still is, an open lung in the middle of the city. Nearly one km square, it survives as Merdeka Square.

Large public buildings were erected around the perimeter of the Koningsplein, though the smaller, more attractive Waterlooplein (now Lapangan Banteng) just to the east served more as the centre of the colonial district of Weltevreden. With its churches and classical buildings, such as the Witte Huis (White House – Daendels palace that was finally completed in 1828), the Waterlooplein was a fashionable area to stroll and be seen. To the north of the square were the suburbs of Noordwijk and Rijswijk, which contained Dutch clubs, the most famous being Harmonie, patronised by influential colonials. The fashionable residential suburbs were those farther to the south and east, such as Kramat, Kebon Sirih and Parapatan. These quiet leafy suburbs contained Dutch residences, the more wealthy living in large houses with enormous numbers of servants, each having a specialised duty.

Dutch Architecture, Kota (GB)

Weltevreden was connected to the old city by the Molenvliet, the main road heading to the old town. From 1869 horse trams plied this street and a few years later trains covered the stretch from Kota to Weltevreden with the building of the railway to Buitenzorg. Old Batavia was still an area of commerce but Europeans abandoned it as a residential area. The old port had troubles accommodating the growing marine traffic, and Tanjung Priok to the east eventually became the main, deep-water port in 1886. Old Batavia's importance dropped further.

Chinese immigration continued steadily but not dramatically, and the well-established Chinese community prospered and settled all around the old town. Indonesian immigration grew more dramatically in the latter half of the century, as Indonesians from all over the archipelago came to settle in Batavia. Balinese, Bugis, Ambonese, Malays etc all formed their own kampungs around the town, but intermingling soon saw the emergence of a distinct Batavian identity, and Indonesians from Batavia were known as Orang Betawi (Betawi People). The Betawi were united by Islam and they developed their own dialect of Malay. Though there was no singular Betawi culture, it was a mixture of cultures that produced a particular style and some unique expressions, such as *rebana* and *keroncong* music, and the *ondel-ondel* dances of giant puppets.

Early 20th Century (1900-42)

By 1900, Batavia's population numbered 116,000, and the profits of the colony flowed through the city. Batavia, which had lagged behind the rapid development of other cities such as Surabaya, expanded greatly over the next thirty years. Immigration increased across the board, and with a new influx of Chinese and Indonesians, kampungs sprung up around the city. The European population also increased substantially to around 10% of Batavia's population of nearly 250,000 in the '20s.

The 20th century also heralded a new approach to colonial government as the Ethical Policy was introduced in 1901. Under this policy it became the Dutch government's duty to further the welfare of the Indonesian people with health, education and other social programmes. A limited degree of involvement in the political process was given to Batavia's Asian population when the Batavia Municipal Council was formed. Voting was limited to the wealthier, Dutch-speaking, male tax payers, but it allowed some Asians to vote and stand for office. The council was a forerunner of the Volksraad (People's Council), formed in 1918 under the charter of the Ethical Policy to give non-Europeans a voice, albeit a token one.

The Ethical Policy gave greater education possibilities for Indonesians, though only to a small elite. The vast majority of Indonesians were illiterate and Dutch education was there to inspire the sons of the Indonesian aristocracy to assume positions in the Dutch administration. But Western education also brought with it Western political ideas of freedom and democracy. The seeds of Indonesian nationalism were sown, and Batavia as a centre of government and education contributed to the independence movement.

A kampung near Jalan Jaksa (GB)

In 1908, students from Batavia's STOVIA medical school in Weltevreden formed the Budi Utomo organisation. Often seen as the first nationalist organisation, Budi Utomo sought to promote economic and social advancement for Indonesians.

Of greater note, Sarekat Islam was an early, premodern nationalist movement, inspired more by Islamic and Javanese mysticism than by intellectual notions of independent self-rule. It rallied Indonesians under the traditional banner of Islam, in opposition to Dutch influence, but had no national agenda and was often more anti-Chinese than anti-colonial. Sarekat Islam had a large membership and provoked a few easily crushed demonstrations and outbursts of anti-government violence.

The Indonesian Communist Party (PKI) on the other hand was a fully fledged, pro-independence party inspired by European politics. It was formed in 1920 and developed a following amongst workers in the more industrial cities of Indonesia. The PKI was somewhat ahead of its time and presumptuously decided to start the revolution in Indonesia in 1926. An armed uprising in the Tangerang and Meester Cornelis districts around Batavia resulted in the brief occupation of a telephone exchange, and obliteration of the PKI. The panicked and outraged Dutch government arrested and exiled hundreds of communists, effectively putting them out of action for the rest of the Dutch occupation.

The nationalist movement was not destroyed however, and in an historic announcement in Batavia, the All Indonesia Youth Congress proclaimed its Youth Pledge in 1928, adopting the notions of the one fatherland (Indonesia), one united country and one language (Bahasa Indonesia). A year earlier in Bandung, Soekarno had founded the Indonesian Nationalist Party (PNI), which grew quickly to become the main nationalist party, resulting in Soekarno's arrest in 1929.

By 1930, Batavia's population was 325,000, and most of the population was born outside the city settling new kampungs with regional affiliations, which helped to fragment Betawi culture. The Dutch developed their own suburbs, often by clearing out the kampungs, and large bungalows sprung up in spacious new districts such as Menteng and Gongdangdia.

Batavia was hard hit by the depression of the 1930s and attracted work-seeking villagers who often ended up homeless and destitute. Though government health campaigns had epidemics under control, the death rates for the Indonesian and Chinese populations was still one of the highest in Asia.

Nationalist sentiment remained high in the 1930s, though with many nationalist leaders such as Soekarno and Mohammed Hatta in jail or exiled, the hope of independence seemed a long way off. Even when Germany invaded the Netherlands in May 1940, the colonial government declared its support for the Dutch government in exile in London and was determined to continue its rule in the East Indies. The local population was exhorted to help the war effort, though the war was a continent away and it seemed that South-East Asia would be spared bloodshed. The Japanese made threatening noises, but no one really believed they would attack and pit themselves against British and American military might.

That was to change when the Japanese attacked Pearl harbour on 7 December 1941 and then conquered most of South-East Asia in less than two months. When supposedly impregnable Singapore fell easily to the Japanese in February 1942, the colonial government abandoned Batavia. Many Europeans fled to Australia, while the army withdrew into Java, leaving the Japanese to take the city unopposed.

Japanese Rule (1942-5)

The Japanese imperial army marched into Batavia on 5 March 1942, carrying the red-and-white Indonesian flag along side that of the rising sun. The city's name was changed to Jakarta, Europeans were arrested and all signs of the former Dutch masters eliminated. The Dutch language was banned in the city, Jan Pieterzoon Coen's statue was removed from Waterlooplein and streets were renamed with Japanese and Indonesian names.

It soon became clear, however, that Indonesian independence was not to be and the Japanese wanted to institute their own form of colonisation. Japanese language and customs were taught in schools and Indonesians were expected to bow towards Tokyo on official occasions. The Japanese were keen to impress their superiority on the Indonesian population and soon developed a reputation as cruel masters.

Though greeted initially as liberators, public opinion turned against the Japanese, especially as the war wore on and Indonesians were expected to endure more hardship for the war effort. Undoubtedly though, the Japanese gave Indonesians more responsibility and participation in government, even if only because of its inability to devote a large Japanese presence to Indonesia. The very top administrative positions were held by Japanese, but Indonesians from the top down ruled themselves for the first time. The Japanese also gave prominence to nationalist leaders, such as Soekarno and Hatta, and trained youth militia to defend the country. Apart from giving Indonesia a military psyche that has endured in Indonesian politics, these militia gave rise to the *pemuda* (youth) of the independence movement and would later form the independence army.

Battle for Independence (1945-9)

As the war ended, the nationalist leadership of Soekarno and Hatta was pressured by radical youth groups to immediately declare Indonesia's independence before the Dutch could return. On 17 August 1945, Soekarno proclaimed the independence of the Republic of Indonesia from his Jakarta home at Jalan Pegansaan Timur 56.

Indonesian flag (GB)

Welcome Statue, a view from the Hyatt Hotel, Menteng (GB)

Indonesians throughout the archipelago rejoiced, but the Netherlands refused to accept the proclamation and still claimed sovereignty over Indonesia. Dutch forces were in no position to return immediately, so the job of accepting the surrender and disarmament of the Japanese was given to British troops, which entered Jakarta in October 1945. Under British auspices, Dutch troops gradually returned to Indonesia and it became obvious that independence would have to be fought for.

The republican government, with Soekarno as president and Hatta as vice-president, tried to maintain calm and order in the volatile situation. They needed to impress on the world that a responsible, organised government was in power in Jakarta and the Dutch had no rightful claims on Indonesia. On the other hand, youth groups advocating armed struggle saw the old leadership as prevaricating and betraying the revolution. While Jakarta remained orderly, outbreaks occurred across the country. In Surabaya, the youth groups fought a pitched battle with British troops. The brutal retaliation of the British and the spirited defence of Surabaya by the republicans galvanised Indonesian support and helped turn world opinion against Dutch reoccupation.

Jakarta immediately after WW II was rundown and overcrowded with the population exceeding 800,000. As the Dutch returned, the battle for independence began, though it was always a mixture of diplomacy and warfare. The British government permitted and sponsored Dutch seizures of property, and the city came under the order of three governments: the overseeing

British government, and the Dutch and Republican governments which controlled different areas of the city. The Republicans eventually moved their main headquarters to Yogyakarta, where the independence movement flourished more freely.

The British departed Indonesia in 1947 after sponsoring an agreement that left the Dutch and Republican governments as joint rulers of Indonesia. Like other partition-style agreements that the British were fond of, it solved nothing and the battle for independence escalated. Dutch troops invaded Republican territory and in July 1947, they took Republican positions in Jakarta and the city again became Batavia.

The Dutch reclaimed their clubs and restaurants and set about ruling the city as they had done for centuries. The city's growth had put great pressure on housing and the Dutch developed the new suburb of Kebayoran Baru, which developed as a wealthy, middle class suburb and did nothing to eliminate the growing shanty towns.

The rest of Indonesia became the real battleground for independence, and the United Nations (UN) stepped in to broker a peace. The Dutch launched a full-scale attack on the Republicans in February 1948, breaking the UN agreement and turning world opinion. Under pressure from the USA, which threatened to withdraw its postwar aid to the Netherlands, and a growing realisation at home that this was an unwinnable war, the Dutch were forced to negotiate for independence with the Republicans. On 27 December 1948 the Indonesian flag was raised at Jakarta's Istana Merdeka (Freedom Palace) as power was officially handed over.

Soekarno Years (1949-65)

Soekarno took up residence in the Istana Merdeka (previously the Dutch governor-general's palace), the Koningsplein was renamed Lapangan Merdeka (Independence Square) and the government set about building a nation.

Jakarta's problems were already multiplying as thousands of new immigrants arrived in search of work. In 1950, the city boundaries were redrawn to include much of the surrounding districts, and Jakarta's population was 1.8 million. The public transport system was falling apart, the telephone network was totally inadequate and Jakarta's housing crisis deepened. In 1952, it was estimated that Jakarta had 30,000 shanties.

Yet despite its shabbiness and the grinding poverty of many of its residents, Jakarta still provided more opportunities than the countryside. Indonesia's wealth was concentrated in Jakarta and the city received the lion's share of investment.

Across the nation, political and economic uncertainty accompanied the early independence years. The fledgling nation had to contend with secessionist movements in the outer islands, powerful Muslim opposition to the secular state and an unstable government as seven cabinets came and went up to 1955. The economy stagnated and foreign investment went elsewhere, while inflation and corruption increased dramatically.

It was not all bad news for Indonesia though, as the government pressed ahead with social programmes providing greater access to education and health services for the majority of Indonesians.

In 1955, Indonesia held its first elections with Soekarno's PNI becoming the largest party in a split parliament. By 1957, the country was still in turmoil and without clear government. Soekarno declared martial law and issued in his era of 'Guided Democracy'.

In this new era, both the city and national governments tackled Jakarta's problems with greater authoritarianism. Soekarno personally took an interest in developing Jakarta towards his vision of a great world city. He ordered the construction of grand monuments and modern skyscrapers. The new boulevard of Jalan Thamrin led south from Lapangan Merdeka and was the showpiece of Soekarno's new city, much of it built for the Asian Games of 1962. Soekarno oversaw new projects such as the Hotel Indonesia, Sarinah department store (named after his nursemaid), the Istiqlal Mosque and the National Monument (Monas), which was begun in 1961. The marble and gold National Monument was the greatest extravagance and most monumental of all Soekarno's edifices glorifying the revolution and his reign.

As Soekarno began to shape his dream city, his politics became increasingly strident. He ranted against Western imperialism and its allies in Asia, notably the Dutch in West Irian Jaya and emerging Malaysia. Huge demonstrations took place in Jakarta as the confrontation against Malaysia heightened. In 1963, the embassy of Malaysia's imperialist backers, the British, was burned.

All the while Soekarno held power in a presidential balancing act, as the PKI and the army emerged as the main forces in Indonesian politics. By 1965, political uncertainty spiralled, matching an inflation rate of 500%.

New Order (1965-)

On the night of 30 September 1965, six of Indonesia's top generals were taken from their Jakarta homes and executed in an attempted coup. Led by Colonel Untung and backed by elements of the armed forces, they surrounded the presidential palace and seized the national radio station. They claimed that they had acted against a plot organised by the generals to overthrow the president.

The army, led by General Soeharto, quickly crushed the rebellion and Soeharto orchestrated a counter coup. The army maintained that the Untung coup was organised by the PKI, and an anti-communist pogrom was unleashed. Across the country, hundreds of thou-

Istiqlal Mosque, near Merdeka Square (GB)

sands of communists, suspected communists and Chinese were slaughtered, though the strong army presence in Jakarta meant that the city was spared the worst excesses.

Soekarno was to remain president for two more years, but it was now Soeharto and the armed forces that called the shots. After suppressing opposition and consolidating power, Soeharto was officially appointed president in 1967 and issued in his 'New Order' era. Indonesia turned away from its isolationist stance and Western educated economists set about balancing budgets, controlling inflation and attracting foreign investment.

Jakarta took on a new lease of life as improving economics were reflected in the city. Ali Sadikin was appointed by Soekarno as Jakarta's governor in 1966, and the former army man and cabinet minister was the greatest shaper of Jakarta since Daendels. He took a number of tough decisions, clearing out the shanty towns and seeing through big new development projects.

Sadikin completed Soekarno's projects, such as Istiqlal Mosque, the National Monument and the large Ancol recreation area. Taman Ismail Marzuki cultural centre (TIM) was built on the site of the zoo, which was moved to the southern outskirts. Taman Mini was also begun during Sadikin's tenure, and the Taman Fatahillah area in old Batavia had been restored.

The Jakarta Master Plan, long a drawing board dream, was finally put into action in 1967 and specified green belts and industrial areas such as Pulo Gadung to the east of the city. Major highways, flyovers and ring roads were begun as the city enjoyed unprecedented funding.

Sadikin's vision of a cultural, hi-tech Jakarta proved enormously popular with the elite. He also set about cleaning up the kampungs, improving roads, pavements and water supplies. On the other hand, his land clearance brought great hardship to the poor, as the shanties were levelled to make way for large developed projects.

At the same time Sadikin's views of what was compatible with a modern city resulted with the loss of work for tens of thousands. Sadikin started the campaign against the *becak* (trishaw), which were found all over the city and numbered over 100,000 in 1970. Through non-renewal of licences and zone restrictions, the becak population dwindled. Street hawkers were also subject to arrest and campaigns were implemented to remove them, cutting off an avenue of income for thousands of poor Jakartans. Sadikin also introduced identity cards for permanent residents in 1970, and 'illegal' residents were deported from the city.

By the time Sadikin left his position in 1977, the city had changed significantly. It had come to reflect the changing fortunes of Indonesia, as the economy boomed. Huge oil reserves had saved Indonesia from destitution and Soeharto's main legacy was political and economic stability. Yet disparity of wealth was growing and it was no more obvious than in Jakarta. Visitors to Jakarta in the '70s could see the effects of new development such as the new hotels and office towers down Jalan Thamrin, but also on Jalan Thamrin was Kebun Kacang, a kampung of shanties stretching along a stinking canal. Jakarta was, and still is, the wealthiest city in the country, with large numbers of its citizens enjoying sumptuous lifestyles while many others live in crushing poverty.

The '80s saw even more development in Indonesia as foreign investment poured in, most of it channelled into industrial Jakarta. This imbalance only brought more people from the countryside as the population approached six million. In 1980, Kebun Kacang, the greatest eyesore in the showpiece central business district, was demolished, and the city government's clean-up campaigns of the later '80s were even more ruthless. Governor Suprapto finally banned the becak and they were simply rounded up and thrown in the sea. Shanty clearances increased, and though public housing was built, it was always unaffordable for the very poor. Another, infamous clean-up campaign was also conducted in the '80s, as the bodies of executed underworld figures started turning up around the city, rumoured to be the work of the armed forces.

In the '90s, Jakarta is booming. Jakarta still receives a disproportionate amount of foreign investment, which is growing rapidly as the government deregulates the economy, lowers tariffs and reduces the restrictions on foreign companies. Jakarta also receives a disproportionate amount of the national budget as the government tries to create a great world city, a showpiece for modern Indonesia.

The 'Golden Triangle' – the central business district bounded by Jalan Thamrin/Sudirman, Jalan Rasuna Said and Jalan Gatot Subroto – is a mass of skyscrapers and luxury hotels. It bears no resemblance to the Jakarta of 30 years ago, or even 10 years ago. But you don't have to venture far away to see glimpses of the old Jakarta. The poverty is still there, though the worst slums are mostly on the outskirts of the city now. As Jakarta approaches the 21st century, and the population nears the nine million mark, its biggest task will be to reconcile the chasm between rich and poor, and to keep improving the lot of the majority of its citizens.

GEOGRAPHY

The Special Territory of Jakarta is 661 sq km in area, including the Pulau Seribu islands. The city is bound to the north by the Java Sea, to the south by Bogor district, to the west by Tangerang and to the east by Bekasi, and all these districts lie within the province of West Java. The city boundaries blend imperceptibly into the neighbouring districts, where much of the city's industry is being developed and large numbers of the workforce are located. This greater Jakarta conurbation is known by the acronym Jabotabek.

Jakarta is built on a flat coastal plain, washed by the rivers that flow from the mountain range from the south. The plain can be divided into two areas: the flood prone swampy area bordering the coast which has been built up with mud from the rivers, and the alluvial plain of red soil farther inland, which slopes gently towards the hills. The southern outskirts of the city lie at an elevation of around 100 metres above sea level.

The main river and for long the main artery running though the centre of Jakarta is the Ciliwung, though the extensive canal system first built by the Dutch has changed the river's course near the coast.

CLIMATE

Lying near the equator, Jakarta is hot and humid year-round. The long rainy season falls between late October and early May, though rain occurs throughout the year, averaging 1791 mm. Rains tends to come in short heavy bursts, but even during the rainy season it doesn't rain every day. It rains on only a handful of days during the dry season from July to September.

Afternoon humidity averages around 70%, but is higher during the morning. Temperatures are fairly even throughout the year, averaging nearly 30°C maximum and 23°C minimum. Jakarta gets a steady supply of 12 hours daylight throughout the year, though it is often filtered through cloud cover. In the dry season the skies are clearer, though Jakarta's pollution and the dust haze along the coast means that clear blue skies are rare. Mornings are sunnier than the afternoons.

Jakarta's heat is legendary among its inhabitants, especially the expatriate community, though it is no

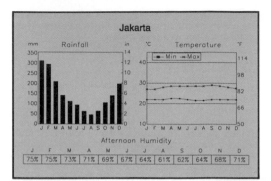

Views from National Monument (Monas), Merdeka Square (GB)

hotter than most other Indonesian cities. It is more a case that the frustrations and clamour of the city are made more intolerable by the heat. The heat and humidity certainly makes it bothersome getting around the city, and walking can reduce all but the most acclimatised to sweating jelly in no time. Jakarta is hotter in the evenings than the inland cities, with the city trapping much of the heat.

ENVIRONMENT

By world standards, Jakarta is an environmental nightmare. The city has no sewerage, a large, ever-increasing automobile population, and mounting air and water pollution.

Jakarta's flat topography and the difficulty in draining the city has long posed a problem for city planners. Its canals were partly responsible for the disease that afflicted the city in its early years, and still pose health problems. Also, because the land is so close to the water table, water pumped from wells, which supply much of the city's water supply, is easily contaminated by sewerage and waste.

Jakarta is one of the world's largest cities, but lacks an efficient public transport system, relying on diesel buses and motorised transport rather than a low polluting rail network. A proposed mass rapid transport system is still years away. Much of the city's planning involves building freeways and flyovers to cope with the already massive traffic jams. The government is aware of environmental problems and has controls in place, but industrial and car pollution is inadequately monitored. As the city grows into an even larger industrial complex, Jakarta's pollution will increase.

GOVERNMENT

Politically, Indonesia is divided into 27 provinces, including Jakarta which is classed as a special territory with a provincial level of government. Jakarta has its own political legislature, headed by a governor, with extensive powers to administer the province.

Jakarta is further broken into five municipalities (*kotamadya*): Jakarta Pusat (Central Jakarta), Jakarta Selatan (South Jakarta), Jakarta Utara (North Jakarta), Jakarta Barat (West Jakarta) and Jakarta Timur (East Jakarta). Each of these is headed by a mayor (*walikota*). Each municipality is comprised of a number of *kecamatan*, headed by a *camat*, and each kecamatan is divided into *kelurahan* or 'village' level. For example, in the Central Jakarta kotamadya, the Menteng kecamatan is the area bounded by Jalan Thamrin to the west, Jalan Kebon Sirih to the north, the Ciliwung River to the east and the Kali Malang to the south. Within the Menteng kecamatan, Kelurahan Kebon Sirih is the area around Jalan Jaksa, Kelurahan Gongdangdia is immediately south of Kebon Sirih, Kelurahan Menteng is farther south again around the Menteng shopping centre and Kelurahan Cikini lies to the east.

In many ways Jakarta is still just a collection of villages, with neighbourhoods providing the basic services such as garbage collection and security. This is organised by the Rukun Tetangga (RT – Neighbourhood Head), who is an unpaid, elected official and carries out a number of duties. The RT system was a legacy of the Japanese occupation and was designed around the Japanese *tonari gumi* neighbourhoods. A neighbourhood usually consists of around 20 households, and the RT is the head of this neighbourhood watch system, carrying out registrations for residents and visitors, and keeping records on births, deaths and marriages for the government. This is the most basic and immediately important level of government. A group of RT neighbourhoods form a Rukun Warga (RW), which is the next level below kelurahan.

House numbers in Jakarta, as in the rest of Indonesia, display RT and RW numbers, as well as the kelurahan and kecamatan.

ECONOMY

Indonesia is part of the world's fastest developing economic region, and the Indonesian economy is bounding along with an annual growth rate over 6%, a rate it has averaged for over 20 years. Jakarta is the centre for this economic boom and the signs of wealth are stamped all over the city – towering new office developments, freeways, multistorey shopping centres, thousands of imported luxury cars and horrendous traffic jams.

Away from the glossy business centre, Jakarta also has the worst slums in the country and most of the city is without sewerage and a decent water supply – and therein lies the dilemma of Indonesia's economy. The economy is booming, but with its huge population and the strain on resources, Indonesia is still one of the poorest countries in South-East Asia. The economy needs to grow much faster just to absorb the growing workforce and its unemployment rate of over 30%. Furthermore, while the statistics show that life for the average Indonesian is getting better each year, the dis-

parity between rich and poor grows even faster.
Indonesia's middle class, earning over US$30,000 per
year, is estimated to number over 20 million people, but
many workers – those lucky enough to have a job – earn
less than US$2 per day and average per capita income is
still only US$650.

The mainstay and saviour of the Indonesian economy
for many years has been oil and gas. During the '70s and
early '80s, the majority of export earnings came from oil,
but the mid-80s slump in oil prices saw a concerted effort
to increase non-oil exports, particularly manufacturing.
Oil and gas exports still account for over US$10 billion
annually, about one-third of all exports. Other major
exports are timber and wood products, tin, coal, copper
and bauxite, and substantial cash crops like rubber,
coffee, copra and fishing. Helped by increased foreign
investment, Indonesia has a rapidly developing light
industrial base and is now a major producer of textiles
and clothing, and is a growing exporter of footwear,
chemicals, fertilisers, cement and glassware. The tourist
dollar is also a growth industry, with Indonesia looking
to increase the three million plus visitor number to five
million within the next few years.

From the late 1980s onwards there has been a change
in attitudes and deregulation is the word. The banking
industry was thrown open to foreign joint ventures,
helping to spur investment. Import monopolies have
been mostly eliminated, resulting in lower prices to
consumers and export-oriented manufacturers. Rules
on stock trading were liberalised in 1989, and 100%
foreign ownership in now allowed in some industries.
As a result, foreign money has started pouring in, much of
it to Jakarta, Java and the island of Batam, a free-trade zone
20 km south of Singapore. The government still controls
many enterprises, but privatisation is gaining speed.

Jakarta, including the neighbouring districts, is
Indonesia's most important industrial zone and the
recipient of over 30% of all foreign investment over the
past 25 years. Most foreign capital has come from the
following countries (in order): Japan, Hong Kong,
Taiwan, South Korea, USA, UK, the Netherlands, Singapore, Germany and Australia.

POPULATION & PEOPLE

Jakarta's population is around nine million people,
while the population of greater Jakarta, known as
Jabotabek, is 17 million and expected to reach 30 million
by the year 2010. The government has a permit system
in place, designed to restrict the flow of the poor to the

Top :   Young man in a kampung near Jalan Jaksa (GB)
Bottom :   Natrabu restaurant staff, Jalan Jaksa area (GB)

city but periodical campaigns to eject those without permits are rarely effective.

The residents of Jakarta are collectively known as the Orang Betawi (Betawi people), the name derived from the Malay for Batavia. It originally referred to Indonesians born in the city, and the Betawi developed their own dialect, customs and culture. In the 19th century, when the city grew only marginally and a large percentage of the population was born in the city, the Betawi identity was at its strongest. Various waves of migrations since, not least the huge growth after independence, have helped to fragment Betawi culture but Jakartans as a whole identify themselves as Betawi and identify with Betawi traditions.

Surrounded by the 110 million people who live on Java, the biggest percentage of Jakarta's population comes from Java. Java has three main groups, each speaking their own language: the Javanese of Central and East Java, the Sundanese of West Java and the Madurese from Madura Island off the north-east coast. But as the melting pot of Indonesia, people from all over the archipelago have settled in the city, and Jakarta also has a sizeable Chinese population. They are all united by the national language, Bahasa Indonesia, the only place in the country where it is the first language of communication.

Orang Betawi

From its earliest days under the VOC, Batavia grew as a cosmopolitan city. In the 17th century, Europeans were a small minority as Chinese, Javanese, Malays, Bugis and others settled in kampungs outside the original city walls.

One of the largest groups was the Mardijkers, who came from the former Portuguese colonies in India and Malacca captured by the Dutch. Many were former slaves granted freedom upon their conversion to Christianity (Mardijker means 'free' and is related to the Indonesian word for freedom, 'merdeka'). Also known as the 'Black Portuguese', they spoke Portuguese and were a strong influence in the city. Their patois became one of the main languages of the colony and many Portuguese words survive in modern Bahasa Indonesia. The Mardijkers settled the Tugu district of Jakarta from 1661, and though they have now been assimilated into Indonesian society, their influence survives in Tugu where the Mardijker church still stands, Portuguese surnames are in evidence and Mardijker music, keroncong, is still played in the city.

The many groups from all over Indonesia that settled in Batavia formed their own kampungs (eg, Kampung Bali in Tanah Abang), though the ethnic barriers began to break down in the 19th century as the population stabilised and intermingled. Many of the Indonesians in the city were born in Batavia, and from this time a distinctly Betawi identity developed. Javanese, Sundanese, Makassarese, Balinese and other cultures, including Chinese and Dutch, combined to produce distinctly Betawi music, dance, architecture and customs. The Betawi developed their own dialect of Malay which, though widely used in trade throughout the archipelago, was vastly different from the Sundanese used outside the city. They were also united by Islam, and the Betawi had a reputation as the most devout Muslims.

In the early 20th century, new waves of immigrants began to outnumber the Betawi, who were only in the majority in isolated pockets around the city. As well as the influx from Java, greater numbers from the other islands came to the city.

Since independence, the immigration boom to the city and national programmes designed to stress an Indonesian identity have helped to obscure the original Betawi culture. In the '50s, artists and intellectuals wrote in Betawi dialect and worked with traditional Betawi art forms, such as theatre, and in the '70s, Governor Ali Sadikin was keen to develop and preserve Betawi traditions. Though as Jakarta continues to grow, and Jakartans try to define themselves, the term Betawi is either an historical one or something that is evolving into a new identity. Traditional Betawi music and theatre are still performed in the city, but are more ceremonial than living traditions. The Orang Betawi of Jakarta today are not so easy to define, as the city absorbs more changes and still more people.

Sundanese

The greatest single ethnic group in Jakarta are the Sundanese, who come from the surrounding province of West Java. Their culture and traditions have much in common with the Javanese, and Sundanese is also a hierarchical language of high and low forms, but Islam has taken stronger root in Sunda and the people are earthier, more direct and more egalitarian. The Sundanese of West Java are likewise less concerned with the flourishes and hierarchies of Central Java. Yet even in this more Islamic atmosphere, the older traditions remain, and evidence of Hindu and pre-Hindu traditions remain.

Javanese

The Javanese, from Central and East Java, are the single largest ethnic groups in Indonesia and the most dominant. Both Soekarno and Soeharto, and many of the top generals and politicians are Javanese. The Javanese syncretist world view has shaped the country's policies and philosophy, and their economic and political dominance is a cause for resentment in many other parts of the archipelago.

Today the Javanese are Muslim. Though many are *santri* (or devout) Muslim, and Java is slowly becoming more orthodox, Javanese culture owes much to pre-Islamic animism and Hinduism. The Javanese cosmos is composed of different levels of belief, stemming from older and more accommodating mysticism, the Hindu court culture and a very real belief in ghosts and numerous benevolent and malevolent spirits.

Indirectness is a Javanese trait, and stems from an unwillingness to make anyone else feel uncomfortable or ashamed. It is impolite to point out mistakes, embarrassments, sensitive or negative areas, or to directly criticise authority. Even the Javanese language reinforces this deference to authority. Javanese has 'high' and 'low' forms; different words are used when speaking to superiors, elders, equals or inferiors. This underlines differences in status, rank, relative age and the degree of acquaintance between the two people talking.

Madurese

While the southern and central part of East Java shows a greater Hindu influence, the north coast is the stronghold of Islam, and much of the population is Madurese. From the hot dry island to the north, the Madurese are a blunt, strong and proud people that migrated to the north-east coast and then farther into East Java. The Madurese have settled all over Java, particularly East Java, and also in Jakarta.

Chinese

Jakarta has always had a high Chinese population, particularly in the early days of Batavia, and have played a huge part in developing the city. Today the Chinese make up only around 10% of Jakarta's population but their importance in the economic life of the city and the country far outweighs their numbers.

The Chinese in Indonesia have long suffered repression and even slaughter, the most notable incident in Jakarta's history being the massacre of 1740. In post-independence Indonesia the Chinese are seen as an overly privileged group, and their own culture has been discriminated against by law. Chinese characters were banned, and in Jakarta Chinese schooling was forbidden to Indonesian citizens, thus those Chinese who had chosen citizenship were forced to drop their language. The issue of citizenship is also a contentious one, with

Men outside Vihara Dharma Bhakti temple, Glodok (GB)

the ever-changing government policies making it hard
for Chinese to gain Indonesian citizenship.

Thus the Chinese in Jakarta have tended to be divided
into two camps. The Totok Chinese are more purely
Chinese, speak Chinese and adhere strongly to Chinese
beliefs and customs, and the Peranakan Chinese who
have adopted Indonesian language and blended more
readily into Indonesian society. Peranakan Chinese have
absorbed Indonesian influences, and have intermarried
with the broader Indonesian community. They have
their own traditions and have developed their own
patois, a mixture of Indonesian with Chinese dialects
such as Hokkien, or they simply speak Bahasa Indonesia.

Other Ethnic Groups

The Sumatran influence is noticeable, with large numbers of Minangkabau and Batak migrating to the city, especially from the early 20th century onwards, when Sumatran music and dance became fashionable in the city. Apart from that there are small numbers of people from all over Indonesia who have come to the capital in search of work.

Jakarta also has a high foreign-worker population, mostly managerial and technical staff employed by foreign companies. Americans and Japanese are the largest foreign nationalities.

ARTS

As a microcosm of Indonesia, Jakarta is the place to see the arts from all over the country. The city has continually changing cultural performances, with music, dance and theatre from all over Indonesia, and Jakarta is the intellectual capital of the country, with influential writers and painters making a contribution.

Wayang golek puppets, Jalan Surabaya Antique Market (GB)

Indonesia has an astonishing array of cultures and all express themselves in different ways. The most readily identifiable arts are from Java, which has provided the greatest cultural influence on Jakarta. No travel documentary on Indonesia is complete without scenes of a *wayang kulit* (shadow puppet) performance performed to the haunting gongs and drums of the *gamelan* orchestra. Java is the home of wayang and gamelan, and Jakarta offers plenty of opportunity to sample these traditional art forms.

As well as the arts from Java and the other islands, Jakarta also has its own unique traditions, the folk theatre, music and dance of the Orang Betawi.

Theatre

If Jakarta is your only stop in Indonesia, then it is worth trying to catch a wayang performance. If your Indonesian is good enough, then Jakarta also has a number of playwrights producing modern works in Bahasa Indonesia. Another bonus for Indonesian speakers is that some regional performing arts may be performed in Bahasa Indonesia, rather than original languages which are more obscure or difficult.

Taman Ismail Marzuki is the showcase for theatre (modern, traditional and imported), Taman Mini is a good venue for performances from all over the archipelago, while the Wayang Museum features wayang performances on Sunday mornings.

Wayang Javanese culture is a product of pre-Hindu, Hindu and Islamic influences. The rise of the 16th-century Islamic states brought a rich new cultural heritage but the Hindu heritage also managed to continue its influence. Javanese wayang theatre has been a major means of preserving the Hindu-Buddhist heritage in Java. The most well-known form is the wayang kulit, the shadow-puppet theatre using puppets made of leather *(kulit* means leather), most popular in Central Java and Bali. In the shadow-puppet theatre, perforated leather figures are manipulated behind an illuminated cotton screen. The stories are usually based on the Hindu epics, the *Ramayana* and the *Mahabharata*, although other purely Javanese stories are also performed. The characters in wayang are brought to life by the *dalang*, the puppeteer, who manipulates the many puppets and directs the gamelan orchestra. The dalang recounts events spanning centuries and continents, improvising from the basic plot a complex network of court intrigues, great loves, wars, philosophy, magic, mysticism and comedy.

Other forms of wayang include *wayang golek*, most popular amongst the Sundanese of West Java, which uses three-dimensional wooden puppets, while *wayang klitik* are flat wooden puppets popular in East Java. *Wayang orang* is a dance drama in which real people dance the part of the wayang characters. *Wayang topeng* is similar to wayang orang but uses masks. The two forms of dance drama were cultivated at varying times in the courts of Central Java.

Betawi Theatre Betawi traditions have given Jakarta some unique theatre forms. The influence of TV and movies have taken their inevitable toll on traditional theatre forms, as have the growing influx of other Indonesian cultures, but there have been concerted efforts to preserve Betawi theatre, which is performed mostly on special occasions.

Lenong folk theatre shows a variety of influences and owes much to Javanese folk theatre, such as *ketoprak*, wayang and *ludruk*. It was performed by travelling troupes, or often local performances were put on by amateurs. Lenong is 'market' theatre – crude, improved plays, often critical of authority and the rich – and it is thought to have been first performed in the market districts such as Tanah Abang. Traders and stall holders from the city and surrounding villages would set up overnight and amuse themselves with music, joking and play acting.

Lenong is traditionally performed in the Betawi dialect and accompanied by a *gambang kromong* (orchestra of gongs), xylophone, drums, Chinese fiddles etc, or a more European-style *tanjidor* (band). Performers wear elaborate costumes and the stage with its painted backdrops has a table and chairs as the only props. Traditionally, performances start in the evening around 8 pm and go until the following morning at around 4 am. The story is often based on the Arabian nights or other Islamic traditions and is loosely scripted, involving much improvisation and joking. The plot is usually set in Jakarta and concerns the trials and tribulations of the poor as they battle landlords and authority.

A favourite hero in Betawi lore is Si Puting, a pious Muslim who is expert in *pencak silat*, the Indonesian self-defence art form. Possessing supernatural powers, he was a protector of the poor and oppressed, battling Dutch overlords and Chinese moneylenders – a Betawi Robin Hood.

Traditional dance, Cikini (GB)

Other theatre forms have tended to fall by the wayside. The Betawi have their form of wayang kulit, but other theatre has tended to die out in the 19th and 20th centuries. One such theatre form was *Stambul*, which showed European, Arabic, Indonesian and Chinese influences and was performed in Malay with songs set to Western dance tunes.

Dance

If you spend much time in Jakarta, you could be forgiven if you thought that disco was Indonesia's traditional folk dance. But if you get out past the skyscrapers and tourist traps, you'll soon find that Indonesia has a rich heritage of traditional dance styles.

In Jakarta you can see everything from Sulawesi wedding dances to a Balinese *barong* dance. Jakarta also has endemic dance traditions, many based on Javanese dances but with a Betawi flavour. The *topeng* mask dances are popular in Java, but Betawi-style topeng is faster and shows more of a Balinese influence in the dance and accompanying gamelan.

In Dutch times, *ronggeng* dances were performed by women at private parties, and even topeng dances were performed by women, much in the style of Cirebon in West Java. In the 19th century, Eurasians performed Portuguese-style *dangsu* dances while Peranakans also developed their own music and theatre forms. Peranakans, or Indies-born Chinese, absorbed many Indonesian customs and beliefs. *Cokek* dances are performed by girls in Chinese-style dress, often accompanied by *gambang kromong* orchestras.

Ondel-ondel puppets, Jalan Jaksa Street Fair (PT)

Ondel-ondel street dances are performed by young boys inside giant puppets. Brilliantly coloured with spangled hair, the puppets whirl about Dervish style to the accompaniment of gongs, drums and whatever else is at hand. The ondel-ondel puppets are the most easily identifiable expression of Betawi culture, and perform on National Day and other Jakartan celebrations.

Music

Indonesians love music, though popular music tends to be dominated by sentimental ballads whose lyrics rely heavily on the word *cinta* (love). Of the more traditional music forms, gamelan is of course the most famous and accompanies many dance/theatre performances from Java and Bali, or you will come across it in hotel lobbies.

A gamelan orchestra is composed of gongs, drums and the *saron*, a xylophone with bronze bars struck with a wooden mallet, which provides much of the melody. Other gamelan instruments are the *suling*, or flute, the only wind instrument in the gamelan orchestra, and the *rebab*, a two-stringed bowed instrument of Arabic origin.

The Mardijkers, or 'Black Portuguese', gave Jakarta their unique *keroncong* music. Mardijkers came from the former Portuguese colonies captured by the Dutch, and though the Mardijkers have assimilated into modern Indonesian society, small keroncong orchestras still perform their Portuguese-influenced music. The music is traditionally sung in a mixture of Portuguese, Dutch and Malay, and accompanied by groups of keroncong, ukulele-type musical instruments. Traditionally, male keroncong performers wear batik trousers and plain tops while women wear sarong and long kebaya. As keroncong music became popular in Jakarta with non-Mardijkers it turned into a more sentimental, mainstream popular music.

Other traditional Betawi music includes Malay *dendang* singing groups, Arab *gambus* (lute) music and *rebana* singing accompanied by a tambourine. Of more lasting contribution are the *gambang kromong* orchestras which accompanied Betawi theatre. Showing Javanese and Chinese influences, these orchestras included a *gambang* (wooden xylophone), *kromong* (bronze bowls), Chinese fiddles, gongs, bamboo flutes, drums and rattles. Another interesting musical style is the *tanjidor* bands, which use European brass and wind instruments such as clarinets, flutes and trombones. Influenced by Dutch military bands, they were popular street performers.

Dangdut music is a very popular Indonesian modern music, characterised by wailing high vocals and a strong beat. Though often attributed to Islamic Arabic influences, its roots lie in Indian pop music popularised by Hindi films. This is the music of Jakarta's kampungs, and is sometimes strongly Islamic in content. Seen as somewhat low class, it was popularised by performers such as Rhoma Irama back in the early '80s. Its popularity has continued to grow and has spread across the nation. Radio stations and clubs around town play nothing but dangdut music.

Western rock music is also very popular in Jakarta – both modern and vintage stuff from the 1960s. Jakarta gets some top-name overseas acts from time to time, and Michael Jackson and the Rolling Stones have given concerts to packed audiences at the Senayan football stadium in South Jakarta.

Literature

Jakarta has produced a number of leading lights in Indonesian literature, and though many have come from outside the capital, Jakarta has been home at some stage or provided inspiration for many of Indonesia's writers.

Chairil Anwar is regarded as one of Indonesia's greatest poets. Originally from Sumatra, he settled in Jakarta in 1940 and lived through the Japanese occupation and became involved with the youth groups that were instrumental in the independence movement. W S Rendra is perhaps Indonesia's greatest living playwright and poet. He has lived and worked in Jakarta, and continues to write despite running foul of the government.

The most famous novel about Jakarta is *Twilight in Djakarta* by Mochtar Lubis, a stinging attack on corruption and oppression of the poor. It has been on and off the banned list since its publication in 1957. Another famous novelist that has fallen foul of the New Order regime is Pramoedya Ananta Toer. A leading intellectual and writer in post-war Jakarta, along with other left-wing and progressive intellectuals he was arrested after the 1965 coup and spent the next 14 years in jail. Javanese by descent, Pramoedya Ananta Toer is most famous for his quartet of novels about life in colonial Indonesia: *This Earth of Mankind*, *Child of All Nations*, *The Fugitive* and *House of Glass*, available in English.

Painting

Indonesia has a thriving art scene, with painters from all over the country exploring modern and traditional styles and media.

One of Indonesia's most celebrated painters is Raden Saleh, a Javanese nobleman, educated in the Netherlands in the 19th century. After many years in Europe he returned to Indonesia in the 1850s and lived in Batavia, where he built a mansion in Cikini. His realist, Western-style paintings are on display in museums in the city.

Since independence, Indonesian painters have used batik and painted in traditional style, but influences include everything from cubism to post-impressionism. Some of the more well-known artists are Affandi from Yogyakarta and Ida Bagus Made from Bali, and their works can be seen at the Balai Seni Rupa in Kota, a showcase for modern Indonesian painting. One of the most striking paintings here is Dede Supria's *Wajah Metropolitan*, a super realist self-portrait with Jakarta's slums as a backdrop. Taman Ismail Marzuki also features a gallery and rotating exhibits feature top Indonesian artists.

Architecture

Jakarta's architecture is a sprawl of old, modern and ramshackle. Modern buildings dominate the skyline in the Golden Triangle business district, and though some are pleasing most of it is utilitarian and designed with rising real estate prices more than aesthetics in mind. Like cities in most developing countries, low-rise concrete blocks dominate much of the city.

That said, Jakarta does have a few notable pieces of architecture. A lot of Dutch architecture remains, though there is little in the way of complete colonial areas and streetscapes. The area around Taman Fatahillah in Kota is noted for 17th-century Dutch architecture, while the

Top :   Art for sale, Ancol (GB)
Bottom : Modern Indonesian art by local artist Munadi,
          Ancol (GB)

Merdeka Square/Lapangan Banteng area has some fine examples of 19th-century colonial architecture. The quiet residential streets of Menteng are lined with early 20th-century bungalows and mansions, and much of the suburb is preserved as the Dutch left it.

Soekarno was an architecture student before he found his calling in nationalist politics and he tried hard to inflict modern architecture on the city. The towering National Monument is Jakarta's most well-known symbol, and the Senayan stadium is a huge sweep of '60s architecture, though most other buildings from the period are forgettable. Of the new architecture around the city, a personal favourite is the Museum Purna Bhakti Pertiwi, a strange but innovative grouping of futuristic, conical buildings.

SOCIETY & CONDUCT

Jakarta is a mixture of societies and customs, with the traditional living side by side with the modern. On the whole, Indonesians hold strongly to traditional values of the family and religion. The head of the family is accorded great respect and children always acquiesce to their parents and elders. Beyond the extended family, the main social unit is the village, and even in Jakarta village units operate with their values of *golong royong*, or mutual cooperation. In Indonesian society, the concerns of the individual are of less importance than those of society, and Western notions of individualism are seen as odd or selfish.

Indonesians are generally a very courteous and hospitable people, and great importance is placed on making sure that offence is not given and a mutual feeling of well being is promoted in dealings with others. 'Keeping face' is extremely important to Indonesians and criticisms are not spoken directly. It is very bad form to shout at, contradict or embarrass someone in public. Refinement and politeness are highly regarded, and loud displays of emotion are considered bad manners.

Avoiding Offence

Indonesians make allowances for Western ways, especially in more cosmopolitan Jakarta, but there are a few things to bear in mind when dealing with people.

Never hand over or receive things with the left hand. It will cause offence – the left hand is used to wash after going to the toilet and is considered unclean. To show great respect to a high-ranking or elderly person, hand something to them using both hands. Talking to someone with your hands on your hips is impolite and is considered a sign of contempt, anger or aggressiveness. Hand shaking is customary for both men and women on introduction and greeting. It is customary to shake hands with everyone in the room when arriving or leaving.

The correct way to beckon to someone is with the hand extended and a downward waving motion of all the fingers (except the thumb). It looks almost like waving goodbye. The Western method of beckoning with the index finger crooked upward won't be understood and is considered rude. It is fine to point at something or to indicate direction, but rude to point at someone – gesture with the whole hand.

When entering someone's house, it is customary to take off your shoes. It is polite to make a gesture to remove your shoes, though more often than not your host will insist you leave them on. Hospitality is highly regarded, and when food or drink is placed in front of you, you should wait until asked to begin by your host, who will usually say *silahkan* or 'please'. It is impolite to refuse a drink, but not necessary to drink it all.

While places of worship are open to all, permission should be requested to enter, particularly when ceremonies are in progress, and you should ensure that you're decently dressed. Always remove footwear before entering a mosque.

Indonesians will accept any lack of clothing on the part of poor people who cannot afford them; but for Westerners, thongs, bathing costumes, shorts or strapless tops are considered impolite, except perhaps around Western-style beach resorts. Elsewhere you should look respectable and revealing dress is not appropriate. Women are better off dressing modestly – revealing tops are just asking for trouble. For men, shorts are considered low class and only worn by boys.

RELIGION

Indonesia is overwhelmingly Muslim, but large communities of Christians, Hindus and Buddhists live in Indonesia. While the Muslim lobby is strong, the government protects the right to freedom of religion, which is enshrined in the state philosophy, Pancasila. The government is very wary of religious extremism in multi-ethnic, multi-religious Indonesia.

Muslims in Jakarta have always been seen as more devout than in other parts of Java, though mysticism and ritual associated with pre-Islamic Java are also in evidence. Jakarta has a large Chinese community, with temples scattered around the city, a considerable Christian population, whose church services can cause traffic jams on Sunday, and a small number of Hindus, mostly from Bali.

Islam

Indonesia first came in contact with Islam through Muslim traders, primarily from India, who introduced a gentler, less orthodox form of Islam than that of Arabia. Today it is the professed religion of 90% of Indonesians and its traditions and rituals affect all aspects of their daily life. Like Hinduism and Buddhism before it, Islam also had to come to terms with older existing traditions and customs. Islam on Java is rooted in Hindu-Buddhism, *adat* (traditional law) and animism.

Customs in Indonesia often differ from those of other Muslim countries. Muslim women in Indonesia are allowed more freedom and shown more respect than their counterparts in other Muslim countries. They do not have to wear facial veils, nor are they segregated or considered to be second-class citizens.

Like other Muslims, Indonesian Muslims practise circumcision. The laws of Islam require that all boys be circumcised and in Indonesia this is usually done somewhere between the ages of six and 11.

One of the most important Islamic festivals is Ramadan, a month of fasting prescribed by Islamic law, which falls in the ninth month of the Muslim calendar. Traditionally, during Ramadan people get up at 4 am to eat and then fast until sunset. During Ramadan many Muslims visit family graves and royal cemeteries, recite extracts from the Koran, sprinkle the graves with holy water and strew them with flowers. Special prayers are said at mosques and at home. At the end of Ramadan, mass prayers are held in the early morning and these are followed by two days of feasting. Extracts from the Koran are read and religious processions take place; gifts are exchanged and pardon is asked for past wrongdoings in this time of mutual forgiveness.

Friday afternoon is officially decreed as the time for believers to worship and all government offices and many businesses are closed as a result. All over Indonesia you'll hear the call to prayer from the mosques, but the muezzin of Indonesia are now a dying breed – the wailing will usually be performed by a cassette tape.

Street-side shop owner, Cikini (GB)

LANGUAGE

Over 300 languages are spoken throughout Indonesia, but the national language, Bahasa Indonesia, is spoken throughout the archipelago and the first language of communication is Jakarta. *Bahasa* means 'language', so Bahasa Indonesia is simply the 'language of Indonesia'.

Bahasa Indonesia is derived from Malay. Pure Malay, as spoken by the Malaysians, is confined in Indonesia to Sumatra but it has long been the common language of the Indonesian archipelago, having been the language of inter-island trade for centuries. The Orang Betawi, the original Indonesian inhabitants of the city in Dutch times, used Malay as the common language of communication. The Betawi developed their own dialect, but many Betawi words were incorporated into Bahasa Indonesia, and Jakartan slang is still adding new words to the language.

Communicating

Bahasa Indonesia has its simplified colloquial form and its more developed literate language. For the visitor who wants to pick up just enough to get by, basic Indonesian is very easy to learn and pronounce. It has a standardised pronunciation, no verb conjugations, no genders, and often one word can convey the meaning of the whole sentence. Plurals are usually indicated by context or you just say the word twice. There are no obscure rules and none of the tonal complications that

Street vendors, Blok M (GB)

make some Asian languages, such as Thai and Chinese, difficult. Finally, the use of Roman script makes learning to read a simple task for most Westerners.

Some of the basics of the language are shown here. For a more comprehensive overview, try Lonely Planet's *Indonesian phrasebook* or *Indonesian CD Audio pack*. They're set out with a view to enabling you to communicate easily, rather than just listing endless phrases.

An English/Indonesian and Indonesian/English dictionary is also very useful. They're sold quite cheaply in Indonesia, and you can also get bilingual dictionaries in French, German, Dutch and Japanese.

Pronunciation

Most sounds are the same as English, although a few vowels and consonants differ. Most of the sounds are pronounced the same every time.

a	like the 'a' in 'father'
e	like the 'e' in 'bet' when unstressed, as in *besar* (big). Sometimes it's hardly pronounced at all, as in the greeting *selamat*, which sounds like 'slamat' when spoken quickly. When stressed it is more like the 'a' in 'may', as in *becak* (rickshaw). There is no general rule as to when the 'e' is stressed or unstressed.
i	like the 'ee' sound in 'meet'
o	like the 'o' in 'boat'
u	like the 'u' in 'flute'
ai	like 'i' as in 'line'

au   like a drawn out 'ow' as in 'cow'
ua   at the start of a word, like a 'w' – such as *uang* (money), pronounced 'wong'

The pronunciation of consonants is very straightforward. Most sound like English consonants except:

c   like the 'ch' in 'chair'
g   like the 'g' in 'garden'
ng   like 'ng' in 'singer'
ngg   like 'ng' in 'anger'
j   like the 'j' in 'join'
r   like Spanish trilled r, achieved by rolling your tongue. *Apa kabar?* (How are you?) is pronounced 'apa kabarrr'
h   like English 'h', but a bit more strongly (as if you were sighing), though almost silent at the end of a word
k   like the English 'k' except when it appears at the end of the word, in which case you just stop short of actually saying the 'k'
ny   is a single sound like the beginning of 'new', before the 'oo' part of that word

Stress

There is no strong stress in Indonesian, and nearly all syllables have equal emphasis, but a good approximation is to stress the second-last syllable. The main exception to the rule is the unstressed 'e' in words such as *besar* (big), pronounced be-SARRR.

Grammar

Articles are not used in Indonesian – there's no 'the' or 'a'. The verb 'to be' is not used before an adjective. Thus, where we would say 'the room is dirty' in Indonesian it is simply *kamar kotor* – 'room dirty'. To make a word plural in some cases you double it – thus 'child' is *anak*, 'children' *anak anak* – but in many other cases you simply use the same singular form, and the context, or words such as 'many' *(banyak)*, indicate the plurality.

Probably the greatest simplification in Indonesian is that verbs are not conjugated, nor are there different forms for past, present and future tenses. Instead words like 'already' *(sudah)*, 'yesterday' *(kemarin)*, 'will' *(akan)* or 'tomorrow' *(besok)* are used to indicate the tense. *Sudah* is the all-purpose past tense indicator: 'I eat' is *saya makan* while 'I have already eaten' is simply *saya sudah makan*.

Except for the adjectives 'all' *(semua)*, 'many' *(banyak)* and 'a little' *(sedikit)*, adjectives follow the noun. Thus a 'big bus' is *bis besar*.

Pronouns

I	*saya*	we	*kita/kami*
you (sing)	*anda*	you (pl)	*saudara*
he/she/it	*dia/ia*	they	*mereka*

Pronouns are often dropped when the meaning is clear from the context.

Speaking to an older man (especially anyone old enough to be your father) or to show respect, it's common to call them *bapak*, 'father' or simply *pak*. Similarly, an older woman is *ibu*, 'mother' or simply *bu*.

Tuan is a respectful term, like 'sir', and is often used to address officials. *Nyonya* is the equivalent for a married woman and *nona* for an unmarried woman. When in doubt, these forms can be used to avoid causing offence.

Mas (older brother) is widely used in Java for men of roughly the same age, and *mbak* is the female equivalent. *Kamu* and *engkau* are used only among friends or to address children. *Saudara* is a more formal, less-used word for people of roughly the same age or status who you do not know well. *Anda* is the egalitarian form designed to overcome the plethora of words for the second person. It is often seen in written Indonesian and is becoming more common in everyday speech between equals.

Greetings & Civilities

Good morning. (until 11 am)	*Selamat pagi.*
Good day. (11 am to 3 pm)	*Selamat siang.*
Good afternoon. (3 to 7 pm)	*Selamat sore.*
Good night.	*Selamat malam.*
Good night. (to someone going to bed)	*Selamat tidur.*
Welcome.	*Selamat datang.*
Goodbye. (said by the person who is leaving to the person who is staying)	*Selamat tinggal.*

Goodbye.	*Selamat jalan.*
(said by the person who is staying to the person who is going)	

Morning is *pagi* and extends from about 7 to 11 am. Pagi pagi is early morning before 7 am. *Siang* is the middle of the day, around 11 am to 3 pm. *Sore* is the afternoon, around 3 to 7 pm. Night is *malam* and only really starts when it gets dark.

Thank you.	*Terima kasih.*
Thank you very much.	*Terima kasih banyak.*
You're welcome.	*Kembali.*
Please. (asking for help)	*Tolong.*
Please open the door.	*Tolong buka pinta.*
Please. (giving permission)	*Silakan.*
Please come in.	*Silakan masuk.*
Sorry.	*Ma'af.*
Excuse me.	*Permisi.*
How are you?	*Apa kabar?*
I'm fine.	*Kabar baik.*
What is your name?	*Siapa nama anda?*
My name is...	*Nama saya...*

another, one more	*satu lagi*
good, fine, OK	*baik*
nice, good	*bagus*
Yes.	*Ya.*
Not/No. (the negative)	*Tidak/Bukan.*

The negative *tidak* is used with verbs, adjectives and adverbs, whilst *bukan* is used with nouns and pronouns.

Questions & Comments

What is this?	*Apa ini?*
What is that?	*Apa itu?*
How much?	*Berapa?*
How much is the price?	*Berapa harga?*
How much money?	*Berapa uang?*
expensive	*mahal*
How many kilometres?	*Berapa kilometer?*
Where is?	*Di mana?*
Which way?	*Ke mana?*
I don't understand.	*Saya tidak mengerti.*

this/that	*ini/itu*
big/small	*besar/kecil*
finished	*habis*
open/closed	*buka/tutup*

Getting Around

I want to go to...	*Saya mau pergi ck...*
ticket	*karcis, ticket*
airport	*lapangan udder*
domestic air terminal	*terminal Dalam Negeri*
international air terminal	*terminal Luar Negeri*
bus	*bis*
train	*kereta Api*
ship	*kapal*
motorcycle	*sepeda motor*
station	*stasiun*
here	*di sin*
stop (verb)	*berhenti*
straight on	*terus*
right	*kanan*
left	*kiri*
slow	*pelan-pelan*

Places

bank	*bank*
post office	*kantor Pos*
immigration office	*kantor imigrasi*
tourist office	*dinas parawisata*

Masks and wooden carvings for sale, Jalan Surabaya
Antique Market (GB)

Map Reading

map	*peta*
north	*utara*
south	*selatan*
east	*timur*
west	*barat*
central	*tengah*
beach	*pantai*
big	*besar*
bridge	*jembatan*
church	*gereja*
city	*kota*
garden	*kebun*
island	*pulau*
mosque	*mesjid*
mountain	*gunung*
park	*taman*
province	*propinsi*
district/regency	*kabupaten*
river	*sungai*
road	*jalan*
sea	*laut*
village	*desa, kampung*

Accommodation

price list	*daftar harga*
hotel	*hotel*
room	*kamar*
bath room	*kamar mandi*
towel	*handuk*
bed	*ranjang, tempat tidur*

Please wash my clothes.	*Tolong cucikan pakaian saya.*
I want to pay now.	*Saya mau bayar sekarang.*

Numbers

1	*satu*	6	*enam*
2	*dua*	7	*tujuh*
3	*tiga*	8	*delapan*
4	*empat*	9	*sembilan*
5	*lima*	10	*sepuluh*

After the numbers one to 10, the 'teens' are *belas*, the 'tens' are *puluh*, the hundreds are *ratus* and the thousands *ribu*. Thus:

11	*sebelas*
12	*dua belas*
13	*tiga belas*
20	*duapuluh*
21	*duapuluh satu*
25	*duapuluh lima*
30	*tigapuluh*
90	*sembilanpuluh*
99	*sembilanpuluh sembilan*
100	*seratus*
200	*duaratus*
250	*duaratus limapuluh*
254	*duaratus limapuluh empat*
888	*delapanratus delapanpuluh delapan*
1000	*seribu*
1050	*seribu limapuluh*

A half is *setengah*, which is pronounced 'stengah', so half a kilo is 'stengah kilo'. 'Approximately' is *kira-kira*.

Time

When?	*Kapan?*
tomorrow / yesterday	*besok/kemarin*
hour	*jam*
week	*minggu*
month	*bulan*
year	*tahun*
What time?	*Jam berapa?*
How many hours?	*Berapa jam?*
five hours	*lima jam*
5 o'clock	*jam lima*

Days of the Week

Monday	*Hari Senin*
Tuesday	*Hari Selasa*
Wednesday	*Hari Rabu*
Thursday	*Hari Kamis*
Friday	*Hari Jumat*
Saturday	*Hari Sabtu*
Sunday	*Hari Minggu*

Necessities

battery	*baterei*
candle	*lilin*
chemist/drugstore	*apotik*
flashlight	*senter*
matches	*korek api*

mosquito coil	*obat nyamuk*
postage stamp	*perangko*
sanitary pad and/or tampon	*pembalut wanita*
sanitary pads (Kotex)	*Softex*
soap	*sabun*
sunblock (UV lotion)	*Pabanox*
telephone card	*kartu telepon*
telephone number	*nomor telepon*
toilet	*kamar kecil WC*
	(pronounced 'way say')
toilet paper	*kertas WC*
toothpaste	*pasta gigi*

Emergency

I'm sick.	*Saya sakit.*
hospital	*rumah sakit*
Call the police.	*Panggil polisi.*
Help!	*Tolong!*
Thief!	*Pencuri!*
Fire!	*Kebakaran!*

Facts for the Visitor

ORIENTATION

Jakarta sprawls over 25 km from the docks to the suburbs of South Jakarta, covering 661 sq km in all. The centre of the city fans out from around Merdeka Square, which contains the central landmark of Soekarno's towering gold-tipped National Monument (Monas). Merdeka Square itself is just a barren, deserted field, a product of grand urban planning gone wrong. Jakarta's main problem is that it doesn't really have a centre that can be explored on foot, but a number of centres, all separated by vast traffic jams and heat.

For most visitors, Jakarta revolves around the modern part of Jakarta to the south of the monument. Jalan Thamrin, running from the south-west corner of Merdeka Square down to the Welcome Monument roundabout, is the main thoroughfare containing many of the big hotels and a couple of major shopping centres – the Sarinah department store and the Plaza Indonesia.

Just east of Jalan Thamrin and south of Monas is Jalan Jaksa, the likeable oasis of backpackers' hotels and restaurants – the area at least has some life in the evenings. Immediately south is the fashionable residential area of Menteng and just to the east is Cikini, home to many of Jakarta's mid-range hotels.

North of Monas, the old city of Jakarta has Jakarta's main tourist attractions. It includes the Chinatown area of Glodok, the old Dutch area of Kota and the schooner harbour of Sunda Kelapa. The modern harbour, Tanjung Priok, is several km along the coast to the east past the Ancol recreation park.

The main railway station, Gambir, is just to the east of Monas. The intercity bus stations – Kalideres in the west, Kampung Rambutan in the south and Pulo Gadung in the east – are on the outskirts of Jakarta.

Heading south from Jalan Thamrin, the street becomes Jalan Jenderal Sudirman, home to more hotels, large banks and office blocks. This is the heart of the Golden Triangle business district, bound to the east by Jalan Rasuna Said.

Farther south are the affluent suburban areas of South Jakarta: Kebayoran Baru, Pondok Indah and Kemang, with their own centres and busy shopping districts, such as Blok M in Kebayoran Baru.

MAPS

If you're planning to stay a long time in Jakarta, by far the best reference is the *Jakarta Street Atlas* published by Falk. This detailed street directory also contains plans of Bekasi and Tangerang. The *Falk City Map* by the same company is a good, detailed single-sheet map, and the Nelles map to Jakarta is another good commercial map, available in map shops overseas.

Many free maps are available and quite adequate for short-term visitors. Pick up a copy of the *Jakarta City Map* from the Visitor Information Centre, or the excellent *Jakarta Welcome Map* is a free giveaway available from many of the large hotels.

TOURIST OFFICES

Local Tourist Offices

The Visitors Information Centre (☎ 332067, 364093) is opposite the Sarinah department store in the Jakarta Theatre building on Jalan Thamrin. It can answer most queries and has a good giveaway map of Jakarta, and a number of excellent leaflets and publications, including the *Jakarta Official Guide*, which is stacked with handy information. The office is open every day except Sunday and holidays from 9 am to 4.30 pm. There is a branch office at the airport (☎ 5507088) in the arrival hall of the international terminal.

The headquarters of the Indonesia Tourist Promotion Organisation is the Directorate-General of Tourism (☎ 3103117) at Jalan Kramat Raya 81. This is not the best place to have your travel queries answered but it has some useful publications, including the *Calendar of Events* and the *Indonesia Tourist Map*, and you might be able to squeeze a copy of the useful *Indonesia Travel Planner* out of them. The office is open government office hours only.

Tourist Offices Abroad

There are a number of Indonesian Tourist Promotion Offices (ITPO) abroad where you can get some brochures and information about Indonesia. Abroad, Garuda Airlines offices are also worth trying for information.

Australia
Level 10, 5 Elizabeth St, Sydney, NSW 2000 (☎ (02) 233 3630)
Germany
Wiessenhuttenstrasse 17 D.6000, Frankfurt am Main 1 (☎ (069) 233677)
Japan
2nd floor, Sankaido Bldg, 1-9-13 Akasaka, Minatoku, Tokyo 107 (☎ (03) 3585-3588)
Singapore
10 Collyer Quay, Ocean Bldg, Singapore 0104 (☎ 5342837)
Taiwan
5FL No 66 Sung Chiang Rd, Taipei (☎ (02) 5377620)
UK
3-3 Hanover St, London W19HH (☎ 4930030)
USA
3457 Wilshire Blvd, Los Angeles, CA 90010 (☎ (213) 3872078)

VISAS

Tourist Passes

For many nationalities, a visa is not necessary for entry and a stay of up to 60 days. This includes, but is not limited to, the following countries: Argentina, Australia, Austria, Belgium, Brazil, Canada, Chile, Denmark, Finland, France, Germany, Greece, Iceland, Ireland, Italy, Japan, Liechtenstein, Luxembourg, Malaysia, Malta, Mexico, Morocco, the Netherlands, New Zealand, Norway, the Philippines, Singapore, South Korea, Spain, Sweden, Switzerland, Thailand, UK, USA, Venezuela and Yugoslavia.

If you're from one of these countries, a 60-day tourist pass (which is a stamp in your passport) is issued on arrival, as long as you enter and exit through recognised entry ports. Jakarta is an official entry port and the main gateway to Indonesia. Officially (but not always in practice), you must have a ticket out of the country when you arrive. You cannot extend your tourist pass beyond 60 days.

Make sure to check your passport expiry date. Indonesia requires that your passport has six months' life left in it on your date of arrival.

Study & Work Visas

The main reason you need to obtain a visa is if you will be working or studying in Indonesia, or arriving or leaving via an obscure entry point that is not on the official list of recognised entry/exit ports. Apart from Jakarta, official ports for visa-free entry include: Bali,

Biak in Irian Jaya, Balikpapan and Pontianak in
Kalimantan, Surabaya and Semarang in Java, Ambon in
Maluku, Kupang in Nusa Tenggara, Medan in Sumatra,
Batam and Bintan islands in the Riau Archipelago and
Manado in Sulawesi. More ports are being opened, so
check with an Indonesian embassy before leaving home.

Visas issued on this basis are normally only valid for
one month, not 60 days as for visa-free entry, and can
only be extended for two weeks. Visas must be obtained
from an Indonesian embassy before you enter the county.

Visas for social or study purposes can be arranged if
you have a sponsor, such as an educational institution,
in Indonesia. These are normally one-month visas that
are extended every month for up to six months or more.

Old Dutch warehouses, VOC shipyards, Kota (GB)

If you are contemplating a three or four-month trip to Indonesia and see this as an alternative to a tourist pass, it is rarely worth the trouble of first hassling with an overseas embassy and then with the local immigration office every month. By the time you pay visa fees and possibly bribes, it can be almost as cheap as leaving the country and returning after 60 days. There is a central immigration office (☎ 349811) at Jalan Teuku Umar 1 in Menteng.

Work visas are an almighty hassle to get and should be arranged by your employer. The Indonesian embassy in Singapore is the busiest and most troublesome for issuing working visas – foreign companies usually hire agents who know the ropes.

Cleaning the hull of a pinisi, Sunda Kelapa, Kota (GB)

DOCUMENTS

Travel Insurance

A travel insurance policy to cover theft, loss and medical problems is a wise idea. There are a wide variety of policies and your travel agent will have recommendations. Some policies offer lower and higher medical expenses options, and a mid-range one is usually recommended for Asia where medical costs are not so high. Check the small print to see if it excludes 'dangerous activities' that you may be contemplating, such as scuba diving, motorcycling or even trekking. Check if the policy covers ambulances or an emergency flight home, which may be useful.

Theft is a potential problem in Jakarta so make sure that your policy covers expensive items adequately. Many policies have restrictions on laptop computers and expensive camera gear, or refunds are often for depreciated value, not replacement value.

Driver's Licence

If you plan to drive in Indonesia get an International Driving Permit from your local automobile association. They are valid for one year only. Also take your home driver's licence, even if you won't be driving. A driver's licence with a photo is useful for identification and can be used in lieu of a passport in some instances.

Student & Youth Cards

The International Student Identity Card (ISIC) can perform all sorts of miracles, such as getting you a discount on some international and domestic flights, as well as discounts at a few museums. Small wonder there is a worldwide trade in fake cards, but the authorities have tightened up on the abuse of student cards in several ways. You may be required to provide additional proof of student status – such as having 'student' marked in your passport, or a letter from your university or college stating that you are a student. In addition, there are now maximum age limits (usually 26) for some concessions, and the fake-card dealers have been clamped down on.

A Hostelling International (HI) card is of very limited use in Indonesia, but there are a few hostels which will recognise it and give a slight discount.

EMBASSIES & CONSULATES

Indonesian Embassies Abroad

Australia
> Embassy: 8 Darwin Ave, Yarralumla, ACT 2600 (☎ (06) 2733222)
> Consulates: 236-238 Marcubra Rd, Sydney, NSW 2035 (☎ (02) 3449933); 18 Harry Chan Ave, Darwin, NT (☎ (089) 410048); 72 Queens Rd, Melbourne, Vic (☎ (03) 5252755); Judd St, South Perth, WA 6151, (☎ (09) 3671178)

Belgium
> Avenue de Turvueren 294, 1150 Brussells, Belgium (☎ (02) 7715060)

Brunei
> KG Sungai Hanching Baru, Simpang 528, Lot 4494, Jalan Muara, Bandar Seri Begawan (☎ 330180)

Canada
> Embassy: 287 Maclaren St, Ottawa, Ontario K2P OL9 (☎ (613) 2367403 to 5)
> Consulates in Vancouver and Toronto

Denmark
> Orehoj Alle 12900, Hellerup, Copenhagen (☎ 624422)

France
> Embassy: 47-49 Rue Cortambert 75116, Paris (☎ (1) 45.03.07.60)
> Consulate in Marseille

Germany
> 2 Bernakasteler Strasse, 5300 Bonn 2 (☎ (228) 382990)
> Consular offices in Berlin, Bremen, Dusseldorf, Hamburg, Hannover, Kiel, Munich and Stuttgart

India
> 50-A Chanakyapuri, New Delhi (☎ 602348)

Italy
> 53 Via Campania, Rome 00187 (☎ 4825951)

Japan
> 9-2 Higashi Gotanda 5 Chome, Shinagawa-ku, Tokyo (☎ (03) 34414201)

Luxembourg
> Ave Guillame 62, L-1650 Luxembourg (☎ 455858)

Malaysia
> Embassy: 233 Jalan Tun Razak, Kuala Lumpur (☎ (03) 9842011)
> Consulates: 467 Jalan Burma, Penang (☎ (04) 374686); 5A Pisang Rd, Kuching, Sarawak (☎ (082) 241734); Jalan Karamunsing, Kota Kinabalu, Sabah (☎ (088) 219578); Jalan Apas, Tawau, Sabah (☎ (089) 765930)

Netherlands
> 8 Tobias Asserlaan, 2517 KC Den Haag (☎ (070) 3108100)

New Zealand
> 70 Glen Rd, Kelburn, Wellington (☎ (04) 4758669)

Norway
> Inkonitogata 8, Oslo 2 (☎ (2) 441121)

Papua New Guinea
    1 & 2/140, Kiroki St, Sir John Guise Drive, Waigani, Port
    Moresby (☎ 253116, 253118, 253544)
Philippines
    Embassy: 185/187 Salcedo St, Legaspi Village, Makati,
    Manila (☎ (2) 855061 to 7)
    Consular office in Davao
Singapore
    7 Chatsworth Rd (☎ 7377422)
Spain
    13 Caile del Cinca, Madrid (☎ 4130294)
Sweden
    Strandvagen 47/V, 11456 Stockholm (☎ (08) 6635470)
Switzerland
    51 Elfenauweg, 3006 Bern (☎ 440983)
Thailand
    600-602 Petchburi Rd, Bangkok (☎ 2523135 to 40)
UK
    38 Grosvenor Square, London W1X 9AD (☎ (0171)
    4997661)
USA
    Embassy: 2020 Massachussetts Ave NW, Washington DC
    20036 (☎ (202) 7755200)
    Consulates in Los Angeles, Honolulu, Chicago, Houston,
    New York and San Francisco

Foreign Embassies in Jakarta

Some of the embassies include:

Australia
    Jalan Rasuna Said, Kav 15-16 (☎ 5227111)

Scene of domesticity in a kampung near Jalan Jaksa (GB)

Austria
   Jalan Diponegoro 44 (☎ 338090)
Belgium
   Wisma BCA, Jalan Jenderal Sudirman, Kav 22-23
   (☎ 5710510)
Brunei
   Wisma BCA, Jalan Jenderal Sudirman (☎ 5712180)
Canada
   5th floor, Wisma Metropolitan I, Jalan Jenderal Sudirman,
   Kav 29 (☎ 5250709)
Denmark
   Bina Mulia Bldg, 4th floor, Jalan Rasuna Said, Kav 10
   (☎ 5204350)
Finland
   Bina Mulya Bldg, 10th floor, Jalan Rasuna Said, Kav 10
   (☎ 5207408)
France
   Jalan Thamrin 20 (☎ 3142807)
Germany
   Jalan Raden Saleh 54-56 (☎ 3849547)
India
   Jalan Rasuna Said 51, Kuningan (☎ 5204152)
Italy
   Jalan Diponegoro 45 (☎ 337445)
Japan
   Jalan Thamrin 24 (☎ 324308)
Malaysia
   Jalan Rasuna Said Kav X/6/1-3 (☎ 5224947)
Myanmar (Burma)
   Jalan H Agus Salim 109 (☎ 3140440)
Netherlands
   Jalan Rasuna Said, Kav S-3, Kuningan (☎ 511515)
New Zealand
   Jalan Diponegoro 41 (☎ 330680)
Norway
   Bina Mulia Bldg, 4th floor, Jalan Rasuna Said, Kav 10
   (☎ 5251990)
Pakistan
   Jalan Teuku Umar 50 (☎ 3144009)
Papua New Guinea
   6th floor, Panin Bank Centre, Jalan Jenderal Sudirman 1
   (☎ 7251218)
Philippines
   Jalan Imam Bonjol 6-8 (☎ 3100345)
Poland
   Jalan Diponegoro 65 (☎ 3140509)
Russia
   Jalan Thamrin 13 (☎ 327007)
Singapore
   Jalan Rasuna Said, Block X, Kav 2 No 4 (☎ 5201489)
South Korea
   Jalan Jenderal Gatot Subroto 57 (☎ 5201915)
Spain
   Jalan Agus Salim 61 (☎ 331414)

Sri Lanka
    Jalan Diponegoro 70 (☎ 3161886)
Sweden
    Bina Mulia Bldg, Jalan Rasuna Said, Kav 10 (☎ 5201551)
Switzerland
    Jalan Rasuna Said, B-1, Kav X-3 (☎ 516061)
Taiwan
    Chinese Chamber of Commerce to Jakarta, Jalan
    Banyumas 4, (☎ 351212)
Thailand
    Jalan Imam Bonjol 74 (☎ 3904055)
UK
    Jalan Thamrin 75 (☎ 330904)
USA
    Jalan Merdeka Selatan 5 (☎ 360360)
Vietnam
    Jalan Teuku Umar 25 (☎ 3100357)

CUSTOMS

Customs allow you to bring in a maximum of two litres
of alcoholic beverages, 200 cigarettes or 50 cigars or 100
grams of tobacco, and a 'reasonable' amount of perfume
per adult. Bringing narcotics, arms and ammunition,
cordless telephones, TV sets, radio receivers, pornogra-
phy, fresh fruit, printed matter in Chinese characters and
Chinese medicines into the country is prohibited. The
rules state that 'film, pre-recorded video tape, video
laser disc, records, computer software must be screened
by the Censor Board', presumably to control pornogra-
phy. You are permitted to bring in one radio or cassette
recorder as long as you take it out on departure. Officially, your personal goods are not supposed to have a
value exceeding US$250, but in effect customs officials
rarely worry about how much gear tourists bring into
the country – at least if you have a Western face. Personal
effects are not a problem.

MONEY

Cash & Travellers' Cheques

US dollars are the most widely accepted foreign currency in Indonesia, but you can change all major
currencies in Jakarta. If you intend travelling farther
afield in Indonesia then bring US dollars – either in cash
or travellers' cheques (safer) from a major US company
such as American Express (the most widely accepted),
Citicorp or Bank of America – or you'll be sorry. If you
bring other than US dollars, be prepared to put in more

legwork – first to find a bank that will accept them and secondly to find one that gives a good rate.

Jakarta banks offer some of the best rates in the country. The rate for US dollars rarely varies by more than 5% but other currencies can vary more. Banks sometimes give a slightly better rate for travellers' cheques but overall you usually get a slightly better rate for cash.

ATMs

Many Indonesian banks have ATMs, but these are available mostly for domestic accounts only. Banks are just starting to link up to the international banking networks, such as Cirrus and Maestro, allowing withdrawals from overseas savings accounts via ATMs. Check with your bank at home before you leave to see if you can use this facility, and also check to see what charges apply. As yet, cash advances on credit cards are not available through ATMs in Indonesia.

Credit Cards

Credit-card outlets are limited in Jakarta, but most mid-range and all top-end hotels, expensive restaurants and shops accept them, and they are very useful for major purchases like airline tickets.

Credit cards can be a convenient way to carry your money. You don't have money tied up in travellers' cheques in a currency that is diving, you don't pay commission charges and the interbank exchange rates are often better than those offered by local banks for cash or travellers' cheques. The disadvantages are that interest is charged unless your account is always in the black, and not all banks will give cash advances on a credit card.

Cash advances can be obtained over the counter at most banks. Indonesian banks don't usually charge transaction fees for cash advances on credit cards, but always ask first. Also check with your home bank to make sure they don't charge transaction fees.

Visa and MasterCard are the most widely accepted credit cards, followed by American Express. Indonesian vendors will often give extra discount for cash rather than credit card. Sometimes they will try to pass the 3% transaction fee onto customers, especially if you have bargained a very good price and then pull out your credit card.

Currency

The unit of currency in Indonesia is the rupiah (rp). Coins of 25, 50, 100 and 500 rp are in circulation, both the old silver-coloured coins and the new bronze-coloured coins. The five and 10 rp coins have vanished, as has the new 1000 rp coin, and the 25 rp coin is going the same way. Notes come in 100, 500, 1000, 5000, 10,000, 20,000 and 50,000 rp denominations.

There is no restriction on the import or export of foreign currencies in cash, travellers' cheques or any other form, but you're not allowed to take in or take out more than 50,000 rp.

Exchange Rates

The rupiah has a floating rate, and in recent years it has tended to fall by about 4% a year against the US dollar.

Australia	A$1	=	1623 rp
France	FF1	=	443 rp
Germany	DM1	=	1561 rp
Japan	Y100	=	2359 rp
Malaysia	RM1	=	867 rp
Netherlands	G1	=	1394 rp
Singapore	S$1	=	1535 rp
Switzerland	SFr1	=	1856 rp
UK	UK£1	=	3615 rp
USA	US$1	=	2213 rp

Street vendors (GB)

Changing Money

Jakarta is crawling with banks and moneychangers. Jakarta's banks offer some of the best exchange rates in Indonesia, but it pays to shop around. Banks offer better rates than moneychangers. Banks may charge a transaction fee (ask first), and a 500 rp 'stamp duty' (tax) is payable if changing more than 100,000 rp but some banks absorb this fee. Many foreign exchange banks are found on and around Jalan Thamrin, and most are open from 8 am to 4 pm Monday to Friday, and until 11 am Saturday.

Handy banks to Jalan Jaksa are the Lippobank and Bank Duta on Jalan Kebon Sirih. The Lippobank gives cash advances on credit cards and good (though not necessarily the best) rates for cash and travellers' cheques. Bank Duta on the other side of the street also has good rates.

In the Sarinah department store building, on Jalan Wahid Hasyim, the branch of the BDN bank usually has good exchange rates. The moneychanger inside Sarinah is open until 9 pm and changes foreign cash at below bank rates.

Jalan Thamrin has plenty of banks and many of the hotels have bank branches that offer good exchange rates. The Plaza Indonesia has a selection of banks and Bank Dagang Nasional Indonesia, in the basement of the Sogo supermarket, has a foreign-exchange booth, open every day from 10 am to 9 pm for after-hour transactions. It changes US$ cash at reasonable rates, travellers' cheques and other currencies at poorer rates.

Entrance to Dunia Fantasi, Ancol recreational park (GB)

The American Express Bank (☎ 5501152) head-quarters in Jakarta is at Jalan Rasuna Said Block X-1. Pacto Ltd is the American Express agent throughout Indonesia and handles postal services and American Express cheque and card transactions at their Hotel Borobudur Inter-Continental branch (☎ 3865952).

Costs

Jakarta is the most expensive city in Indonesia, but is still cheap by international standards. How much it will cost to stay in Jakarta is largely up to the individual and depends on what degree of comfort you desire or what degree of discomfort you're prepared to put up with.

The best international standard hotels start at around US$100 per night, though simpler but comfortable mid-range accommodation can be had for US$35 and up. Budget accommodation starts at US$2.50 for dormitory accommodation in the Jalan Jaksa backpackers' enclave, or a basic room starts at US$5, or for US$15 you can get a simple room with air-con.

Food can be very cheap or very expensive. You can get a good meal in a cheap eating house or food stall for US$2 or less, while a top restaurant in one of the big hotels can cost over US$100. In the US$10 to US$20 per person range, Jakarta has plenty of restaurants serving good quality food with high standards of hygiene and service. Indonesian food always tends to be cheaper, and a Indonesian meal in a restaurant of good standard can be had for as little as US$5, though the bill will be much higher in the fanciest Indonesian restaurants. International food is much more expensive, and prices are comparable to restaurants in most major cities around the world.

Transport around the city is cheap, as is entry to most attractions. A short taxi ride will cost less than US$1, and buses are ridiculously cheap, though they can be ridiculously crowded.

Tipping

Tipping is not a normal practice, but is often expected for special service. Jakarta taxi drivers expect (demand?) a tip – the fare is usually rounded up to the next 500 rp. Hotel porters also expect a few hundred rupiah per bag. Tipping in the very cheap restaurants is not expected, and many of the expensive restaurants add a 10% service charge to the bill. In moderate to expensive restaurants where no service charge is added, a tip of a few thousand rupiah is appreciated. Anyone who carries your bags or shopping, parks your car etc, will expect a small tip of a few hundred rupiah.

Bargaining

Many everyday purchases in Jakarta require bargaining. This applies particularly to handicrafts, clothes and artwork but can also apply to almost anything you buy in a shop. Restaurant meals, transport and, often, accommodation are generally fixed in price – restaurants usually have their menus and prices posted, and hotels usually have a price list. Many of Jakarta's more expensive hotels are willing to bend their prices, and it pays to ask about any discounts available. Prices are fixed in department stores, supermarkets, book shops and some of the fancier shops but are open to bargaining in most other retail outlets.

Your first step should be to establish a starting price. It's usually easiest to ask them their price rather than make an initial offer, unless you know very clearly what you're willing to pay. As a rule of thumb your starting price could be anything from a third to two-thirds of the asking price – assuming that the asking price is not completely crazy. Then with offer and counter-offer you move closer to an acceptable price. Don't show too much interest when bargaining, and if you can't get an acceptable price, walk away. You will often be called back and offered a lower price.

A few rules apply to good bargaining. First of all it's not a question of life or death, where every rupiah you chisel away makes a difference. Don't pass up something you really want that's expensive or unobtainable at home because the seller won't come down a few hundred rupiah more. Secondly, when your offer is accepted you have to buy it – don't then decide you don't want it after all. Thirdly, while bargaining may seem to have a competitive element in it, it's a mean victory knocking a poor becak driver down from 500 to 400 rp for a ride.

Bargaining is sometimes fun – and often not. A lot depends on whether you and the vendor are smiling or yelling at each other.

COMMUNICATIONS

Post

The main post office and efficient poste restante is behind Jalan Pos, off to the north-east of Monas. It's a good half-hour walk from the city centre, or you can take a No 12 bus from Jalan Thamrin. Poste restante is open from 8 am to 4 pm Monday to Friday, until 1 pm Saturday. For basic postal services, a few windows are open from 6 am to 10 pm Monday to Saturday (closed 11 am to noon Friday) and from 9 am to 4 pm on Sunday. Mail services are also offered by private post and telephone agencies called warpostels or warparpostels, and business centres in the major hotels.

International airmail rates for letters (up to 20 grams) are 1000 rp to Australia and the Pacific, 1400 rp to Europe and 1600 rp to the USA and Canada. Postcards cost a flat 600 rp. Parcels up to a maximum weight of 10 kg can be sent by sea mail, though rates are high. If you have more than 10 kg, break it up into several parcels.

Letters and small packets bound for overseas or domestic delivery may be registered for an extra fee at any post office branch. There are also two forms of express service available for mail within Indonesia: blue (kilat) envelopes are for regular airmail; yellow (kilat khusus) are for airmail express. These envelopes, plus aerogrammes, can be bought at all post offices.

Telephone

Jakarta's telephone network has a bad reputation, though it is slowly improving. Demand far outstrips supply and telephone lines and switchboards are limited. It can take a long time to get through on the phone, and many businesses list numerous phone numbers. Take a note of them all; you may need them. The 'hunting' numbers are the most useful as they try all lines to find one free.

For international and intercity phone calls, the efficient, government-run Telkom centre is opposite the tourist office in the Jakarta Theatre building. It is open 24 hours. From private booths you can dial direct to anywhere in Indonesia or overseas and then pay at the counter. Dial Home Direct phones are also available. Just press the button for your country (Australia, USA etc) and an operator from that country will come on the line for a reverse-charge or international telephone card call.

Private telecommunications agencies, usually called wartel, warpostal or warparpostel, are also dotted around the city. They may be marginally more expensive but are often more convenient. They are usually open from around 7 am until midnight, but sometimes 24 hours. As a rule, wartels don't offer a collect-call service, or in the rare cases that they do, a first-minute charge may apply. Convenient for those staying around Jalan Jaksa is the privately run RTQ Warparpostel (☎ 326221;

fax 3904503), Jalan Jaksa 25, opposite Nick's Corner Hostel. Operating hours are from 8 am until midnight.

Public pay phones can be found in some post offices, at the airports and in public phone booths. They are blue in colour and take 50 rp and 100 rp coins. Telephone cards *(kartu telepon)* can be used at the phones that accept them *(telepon kartu)*. Cards are available at telephone offices and retail outlets. Local calls cost around 100 rp.

International Direct Dialling (IDD) is available to many countries – dial 001, then the country code, area code (minus the initial zero if it has one) and then the

Telkom sign (GB)

number you want to reach. Public phones rarely support this facility and you'll have to go to a Telkom office or wartel. The country code for dialling Indonesia is 62.

Local telephone calls in the major hotels range from around 200 to 500 rp for three minutes. Surcharges on international calls apply.

Fax, Telex & Telegraph

The Telkom office in the Jakarta Theatre building has fax, telex and telegraph services. Local faxes cost 1500 rp per page, while international faxes range from 4400 rp per page to Malaysia and Singapore, up to 7700 rp for Australia and the USA, and 8800 rp for most European destinations.

Faxes can also be sent from wartels. The RTQ Warparpostel (☎ 326221; fax 3904503), Jalan Jaksa 25, opposite Nick's Corner Hostel, will receive faxes here for 1500 rp per page, and incoming faxes are listed on a noticeboard at the door. Costs for sending faxes are slightly higher per page than Telkom.

Business centres in the major hotels also have fax services. Typical fax charges are around 3500 to 4000 rp per minute for local faxes and 12,000 rp and up for faxes to Europe, USA and Australia.

BOOKS

Guidebooks

The Ganesha Volunteers operate from the National Museum and organise lectures and programmes designed to promote understanding of Indonesian culture. They produce *The Jakarta Explorer*, a detailed guide to areas of historical and cultural interest in Jakarta. Numerous tours are included, and though not all are of interest to short-term visitors, this is an essential guide for someone who wants to explore Jakarta in depth.

The American Women's Association (AWA) produces some excellent publications about Jakarta. *Introducing Indonesia: A Guide to Expatriate Living* gives a complete rundown on living in Indonesia for expatriates, with special reference to Jakarta. It explains Indonesian society and customs and is packed with information on everything from taxation regulations to transporting pets. If you are thinking of living in Jakarta, this book is a must. The AWA also produces the *Jakarta Shopper's Guide*, a comprehensive index to shopping and services in Jakarta. AWA publications are available in bookshops in Jakarta, or from the AWA Center, Jalan Leuser 12, Kebayoran Baru, Jakarta Selatan.

Other guidebooks to Jakarta include *Jakarta* by Times Editions, a thoughtful and well-photographed introduction to Jakarta, and the *Insight Pocket Guide to Jakarta* from APA Publications. For travel farther afield in Indonesia, Lonely Planet has detailed guides to *Java* and *Bali & Lombok*, while *Indonesia* covers the whole country.

History

Jakarta: A History by Susan Abeyasekere provides the best history on Jakarta and is particularly good for the later colonial period and post-independence Jakarta. Scholarly but very readable, it provides an excellent introduction to Jakarta.

Historical Sights of Jakarta by Adolf Heuken SJ is part history, part guidebook to Jakarta's colonial period. It gives a wonderful rundown on Dutch architecture around the city, the history of Batavia and the various groups that populated the city.

General

The most famous novel on the city, *Twilight in Djakarta* by Mochtar Lubis is a scathing attack on corruption and the plight of the poor in Jakarta in the 1950s. The book was banned and the author jailed for this book. Much has changed, but the problems still remain.

MEDIA

The news media is expected to – and does – practise self-censorship. 'Politeness' is the key word, and in typically indirect Javanese style, stories of corruption, wastage of funds and government ineptitude are frequently run, but care is always taken not to point the finger too closely. Most importantly, criticism of Soeharto and his immediate family is not tolerated.

Through the early '90s the press enjoyed greater liberalisation and became increasingly bold. New magazines like *Detik* and *Editor* exposed scandals and corruption and ran articles critical of the government. Government tolerance was seen as a step towards a more open and mature society, until June 1994, when the government banned *Detik*, *Editor* and the long-running and highly respected *Tempo* magazine. The move prompted widespread criticism and demonstrations in Jakarta, to no avail it seems as the government has since announced greater restrictions and non-renewal of licences because 'Indonesia has too many publications' according to the government.

Newspapers & Magazines

Local The English-language press is limited mostly to the *Jakarta Post*, published daily except Sunday. While subject to the same 'self-censorship' as other Indonesian publications, it manages to tell you quite a lot about Indonesia – and the rest of the world – in a roundabout way. It gives a useful run down of what's on, temporary exhibitions and cinema programmes in the city, and is available from hotel kiosks and bookshops, and street vendors in the tourist areas. It usually costs 1000 rp but take a close look at the date. It is not uncommon for street vendors to try to sell old news.

The other English-language newspaper is the *Indonesian Observer*, but its coverage and independence are a long way behind that of the *Jakarta Post*.

Of course, Indonesian-language newspapers are on sale in Jakarta. Two of the leading newspapers are the Jakarta daily *Sinar Harapan* and the Catholic newspaper *Kompas*. *Suara Karya* is the mouthpiece of Golkar, the government political party.

Foreign The *International Herald-Tribune*, *Asian Wall Street Journal* and major Asian dailies are sold in Jakarta. Western magazines like *Time*, *Newsweek*, *The Economist* and the excellent Hong Kong-published *Far Eastern Economic Review* are also available from the large hotels.

Radio & TV

Radio Republik Indonesia (RRI) is the national radio station, which broadcasts 24 hours in Indonesian from every provincial capital. Indonesia also has plenty of privately run stations.

Televisi Republik Indonesia (TVRI) is the government-owned Indonesian-language TV station, is broadcast in every province. It broadcasts on two channels.

Private stations are Rajawali Citra Televisi Indonesia (RCTI), with many shows in English, SCTV (Surya Citra Televisi), Televisi Pendidikan Indonesia (TPI), a government-owned educational station, and AN-TV (Andalas Televisi).

Satellite dishes also pick up uncensored overseas stations transmitting in the region, which has worried some government sources and Islamic groups complaining about moral corruption. Overseas TV can be seen at the large tourist hotels, and while many smaller hotels have satellite dishes, they are not usually interested in tuning them in to programmes in a foreign language they cannot understand. CNN, BBC, Television Australia and Malaysian TV can all be received, though the most popular in the foreign stakes seems to be French TV. Apart from soccer games, French TV occasionally shows kissing and even bare flesh.

FILM & PHOTOGRAPHY

Colour print film is preferred to anything else, so slide film and black & white film are not as readily available. Nevertheless, you can usually find most types of film in Jakarta, even Polaroid film, movie film and video tape. Fuji is by far the most widely available brand for prints and slides, while Kodachrome is rarely seen and has to be sent overseas for developing. Film is cheap.

Developing and printing is quite good and much cheaper than in the West. You can get Ektachrome and Fujichrome slide film developed in two or three days and colour print film can be developed same day through photographic shops. Many of these have machines which churn out prints in 45 minutes, and the quality is usually very good. Camera batteries and other accessories are readily available from photographic shops.

Jalan Agus Salim, between Jalan Jaksa and Jalan Thamrin, has photographic shops for film, developing and equipment. Jakarta Foto at No 35A has a good range and also does repairs. Some of the shops on Agus Salim charge 'tourist prices' and bargaining may be required.

Movie posters, Cikini (GB)

The Plaza Indonesia has a Fuji shop at No 139 on the 1st floor and stocks the full range of Fuji film and provides complete developing services. Otherwise, Jakarta has plenty of places for film developing.

Jakarta tends to be hazy and the pollution and frequent cloud cover are not conducive to great travel photography. Shoot early or late as from 10 am to 1 or 2 pm the sun is uncomfortably hot and high overhead, and you're likely to get a washed-out look to your pictures. On sunny days, a polarising filter helps reduce glare and darken an otherwise washed-out sunlit sky. A lens hood will reduce your problems with reflections and direct sunlight on the lens. Beware of the sharp differences between sun and shade – if you can't get reasonably balanced overall light you may have to opt for exposing only one area or the other correctly, or use a fill-in flash.

Jakarta is a good place to take people photographs. Most Indonesians are pleased to have their photo taken, but not all and it pays to ask first with a smile and gesture with the camera.

Military buildings and installations are sensitive photographic subjects and may be prohibited. Ask if in doubt.

TIME

Jakarta is seven hours ahead of GMT. Allowing for variations due to daylight-saving time, when it is noon in Jakarta it is 5 am in London, 1 pm in Singapore, 3 pm in Melbourne or Sydney, midnight in New York and 9 pm the previous day in San Francisco or Los Angeles.

Indonesia has three time zones. Sumatra, Java, and West and Central Kalimantan are on Western Indonesian Time, which is seven hours ahead of GMT. Bali, Nusa Tenggara, South and East Kalimantan and Sulawesi are on Central Indonesian Time, which is eight hours ahead of GMT. Irian Jaya and Maluku are on East Indonesian Time, which is nine hours ahead of GMT.

ELECTRICITY

Electricity is 220 v, 50 cycles AC. Sockets are designed to accommodate two round prongs of the European variety. Recessed sockets are designed to take earth (ground) facilities, but most appliances and the wiring in many cheap hotels aren't earthed, so take care. Safe adaptors for foreign plugs are hard to find, so bring your own.

Electricity is fairly reliable but blackouts do occur in Jakarta, usually for only a few minutes but they can last longer. Large hotels have backup generators. Power surges also occur, so a surge guard for electrical equipment, such as computers, is recommended.

LAUNDRY

Virtually every hotel – from the smallest to the largest – has a laundry service, and except for the most expensive hotels, this is usually very cheap. About the only thing you need be concerned about is the weather as clothes are dried on the line, so a hot, sunny day is essential. Give staff your laundry in the morning – they like to wash clothes before 9 am so it has sufficient time to dry before sunset.

WEIGHTS & MEASURES

Indonesia has fully adopted the international metric system.

HEALTH

Standards of sanitation in Jakarta are generally poor and tap water is not safe to drink, but with a few precautions and common sense, most visitors don't experience any serious health problems. The main rule is to take care with food and water, and the most you are likely to suffer is a stomach upset.

Immunisations

Indonesia requires no vaccinations to enter the country, apart from yellow fever if you are arriving from a yellow fever infected area within six days. Other vaccinations are optional for a short stay. Recommended vaccinations, especially if you will be travelling to other parts of Indonesia, are:

- Tetanus & diptheria – boosters are necessary every 10 years

- Typhoid – available either as an injection or oral capsules

- Infectious Hepatitis – a new vaccine, Havrix, provides long-term immunity (possibly more than 10 years) after an initial course of two injections and a booster at one year. The second injection should be administered at least three weeks prior to departure. The other alternative is the less-effective gammaglobulin, given as close as possible to departure

Food & Water

The simple rule is don't drink the water unless it has been boiled. Ice can also be a problem if made from unboiled water, though ice and drinks are usually made from boiled water in Jakarta, because everyone knows that the tap water is not safe.

Bottled water is widely available in Jakarta, and is reasonably priced in grocery shops or supermarkets. You can boil your own water if you carry an electric immersion coil and a large metal cup (plastic will melt), both of which are available in department stores and supermarkets in Indonesia. Water can also be sterilised by iodine or by chlorine tablets.

It's a good idea to carry water with you. Dehydration is a potential problem in Jakarta's heat. Bottled fruit juices and soft drinks are safe to drink, as is tea and coffee because the water has been boiled.

When it comes to food, use your best judgement. Have a good look at the restaurant or warung – if it looks dirty, think twice. Street food generally runs a higher risk. If you are only eating at the best restaurants, then the chances of catching diseases such as hepatitis or dysentery from contaminated food are minuscule. To be absolutely safe, everything should be thoroughly cooked – salads and unpeeled fruit can be a problem. Fish, meat and dairy products are generally OK provided they are fresh – if they spoil, you could become violently ill. Fish can also be a problem if they lived in contaminated water, and shellfish is a much higher risk.

Rambutan seller, Blok M (GB)

Other Precautions

Sunburn is also a problem, particularly for those just off
the plane who want to hit the beach. Bring sunscreen
(UV) lotion and something to cover your head. You can
also buy sunscreen in better Indonesian pharmacies –
two popular brands are Pabanox and Parasol.

If you're sweating profusely, you're going to lose a lot
of salt and that can lead to fatigue and muscle cramps
for some people. If necessary you can compensate for
this by putting extra salt in your food (a teaspoon a day
is plenty), but don't increase your salt intake unless you
also increase your water intake.

Medical Problems

Diarrhoea Diarrhoea is often due simply to a change
of diet. A lot depends on what you're used to eating and
whether or not you've got an iron gut. If you do get
diarrhoea, the first thing to do is wait – it rarely lasts
more than a few days.

Diarrhoea will cause you to dehydrate, which will
make you feel much worse. The solution is to drink
water mixed with oral rehydration salts, which are available at pharmacies. The most common brand is Oralit,
but the generic term is *bubuk glukosa elektrolit* (glucose
electrolyte powder). Oralit is also useful for treating heat
exhaustion caused by excessive sweating.

If diarrhoea persists then the usual treatment is
Lomotil or Imodium tablets. Entrostop is a good local
brand. Anti-diarrhoeal drugs don't cure anything, but
slow down the digestive system so that the cramps go
away and you don't have to go to the toilet all the time.
Activated charcoal can also provide much relief.

Malaria & Dengue Fever Jakarta is one of the few
places in Indonesia that has been classified as malaria
free. If travelling farther afield, malarial prophylactics
are recommended. Bali and Java officially fall within the
malarial zone but if you are travelling only to the main
cities and tourist areas the risk is very minimal. Irian Jaya
on the other hand is definitely a high-risk area, as are
some of the more remote parts of the other islands.

Dengue fever does occur in Jakarta, mostly in the
kampung areas of East and North Jakarta. The risk is
slight in the main tourist areas. There is no prophylactic
available for this mosquito-spread disease; the main
preventative measure is to avoid mosquito bites – cover
up in the evenings and use mosquito repellent. Dengue
fever is characterised by a sudden onset of fever and

headaches, and severe joint and muscle pains are the first signs before a rash starts on the trunk of the body and spreads to the limbs and face. After a further few days, the fever will subside and recovery will begin. Serious complications are not common.

Hepatitis Hepatitis A is a potential problem for travellers to Indonesia. Fortunately, long-term protection is available through the new vaccine Havrix. The disease is spread by contaminated food or water.

Hepatitis B is spread through contact with infected blood, blood products or bodily fluids, for example, through sexual contact, unsterilised needles and blood transfusions. Type B is more severe than type A. An effective prophylactic vaccine is readily available in most countries, but requires a course of injections over six months. Vaccination is recommended for anyone who anticipates contact with blood or other bodily secretions, either as a health-care worker or through sexual contact with the local population, particularly those who intend to stay in the country for a long period of time.

Other strains of hepatitis have been discovered, but they are fairly rare (so far) and following the same precautions as for A and B should be all that's necessary to avoid them.

Sexually Transmitted Diseases Sexual contact with an infected sexual partner spreads these diseases. While abstinence is the only 100% preventative, using condoms is also effective. Gonorrhoea and syphilis are the most common of these diseases.

HIV/AIDS Any exposure to blood, blood products or bodily fluids may put the individual at risk. Official HIV figures in Indonesia are pathetically low, though it is widely believed that the real figures are much higher and set to increase significantly unless the promotion of safe sex and hospital practices are improved. The primary risk for most travellers is contact with workers in the sex industry, and in Indonesia the spread of HIV is primarily through heterosexual activity.

HIV/AIDS can also be spread through infected blood transfusions, dirty needles, intravenous drug use, vaccinations, acupuncture, tattooing, ear piercing etc. If you do need an injection, ask to see the syringe unwrapped in front of you, or better still, take a needle and syringe pack with you overseas.

Fear of HIV infection should never preclude treatment for serious medical conditions. Although there may be a risk of infection, it is very small indeed.

Medical Facilities

Jakarta has the best medical facilities in the country.

In South Jakarta, most expatriates use Rumah Sakit Pondok Indah (☎ 7500157), Jalan Metro Duta Kav UE, a perfectly modern hospital that rivals the best hospitals in the West, although it charges modern prices. In South Jakarta there is also the Rumah Sakit Pertamina (☎ 7200290), Jalan Kyai Maja 43, Kebayoran – if your illness doesn't kill you, just wait until you see the bill. Better known hospitals in central Jakarta (near Jalan Jaksa) are the Rumah Sakit Cipto Mangunkusumo (☎ 330808), Jalan Diponegoro 71, a government public hospital (reasonably priced but very crowded), and St Carolus Hospital (☎ 4214426), Jalan Salemba Raya 41, a private Catholic hospital charging mid-range prices.

Also popular is Medical Scheme (☎ 515367, 5201034) in the Setiabudi building, Jalan H Rasuna Said, Kuningan. It's a private practice but it deals with all emergencies, and vaccinations are given to non-members for a small fee. Doctors speak English and Dutch. SOS Medika (☎ 7505980), Jalan Puri Sakti 10, Cipete, is very popular with expats and has English-speaking doctors. It is affiliated with Asia Emergency Assistance International.

The Metropolitan Medical Center (☎ 3140408) is in the Hotel Wisata, Jalan Thamrin, behind the Hotel Indonesia. Opening hours at this practice vary so it's best to ring first. Dr Damiyanti & Associates (☎ 3146823) is at Jalan Lombok 57, Menteng. Some English is spoken and it has branch practices in a number of major hotels.

WOMEN TRAVELLERS

Indonesia is a Muslim society and very much male oriented. Nevertheless, women are not cloistered in Indonesia and generally enjoy more freedom than in Middle East countries. Jakarta is a cosmopolitan city with a large expatriate population, so Western attitudes and lifestyles are less foreign here, especially among the city's educated elite, but traditional values are still strong.

Lots of Western women travel in Indonesia either alone or in pairs – most seem to enjoy the country and its people, and most seem to get through the place without any problems, or else suffer only a few minor hassles with the men. Your genetic make up plays a part – blonde-haired, blue-eyed women seem to have more hassles than dark women. There are some things you can do to avoid being harassed; dressing modestly helps a lot.

Indonesians, both men and women, are generally not comfortable being alone – even on a simple errand they are happier having a friend along. Travelling alone is considered an oddity – women travelling alone, even more of an oddity. Nevertheless, for a woman travelling alone or with a female companion, Indonesia can be easier going than some other Asian countries.

You might spare a thought for Indonesian women, who are given the privilege of doing backbreaking labour and raising children, but never trusted in positions of authority. The whole concept of feminism, equality between the sexes etc, would seem absurd to most Indonesians.

JAKARTA FOR CHILDREN

Indonesians love children and cute Western children usually attract lots of admirers. The attention and special treatment can become a little overwhelming at times, but the care for and acceptance of children make Indonesia a good country to travel with children. Jakarta is hot, crowded and overwhelming, and special care should be taken to avoid dehydration (drink lots of liquids) and to avoid contaminated food. See the Health section earlier in this chapter for details.

School children, Glodok (GB)

Jakarta is not over endowed with family attractions but kids will love Dunia Fantasi (Fantasy World), the Disney inspired fun park at Ancol. It has rides, exhibitions and various 'lands' from Africa to the wild West. Children young and old can easily spend a full afternoon here.

Zoos are an old standby for amusing the kids, and Ragunan Zoo has plenty of animals from Indonesia and around the world. It is a large but not overly attractive zoo. The main problem is that the spacious grounds involve a lot of walking in the heat, but a shuttle does a loop of some of the zoo.

Taman Mini Indonesia Indah is educational and is good for older children (and adults) who want to gain an understanding of Indonesian culture. It also has a few family diversions and rides, such as the cable car across the park.

USEFUL ORGANISATIONS

Cultural Organisations

The Ganesha Society (☎ 360551) at the National Museum is an organisation of volunteer museum workers that holds weekly lectures or films about Indonesia at the Erasmus Huis (☎ 512321) on Jalan Rasuna Said, beside the Dutch Embassy in South Jakarta.

The Indonesian/American Cultural Center (Perhimpunan Persahabatan Indonesia Amerika) (☎ 8583241), Jalan Pramuka Kav 30, has exhibits, films and lectures related to Indonesia each week. The Australian Cultural Centre (Pusat Kebudayaan Australia) at the Australian Embassy, Jalan Rasuna Said, has a good library, and is open from 10.30 am to 3.30 pm Monday to Friday. The British Council (☎ 5223311) also has a good library in the Widjoyo Centre, Jalan Jenderal Sudirman 56. The French Cultural Centre (☎ 3908585) has a French library and screens French films. The Goethe Institut (☎ 8581139) is at Jalan Mataram Raya 23.

National Parks/Nature Reserves

The national parks body, the PHPA, is in the Forestry Department (Departemen Kehutanan) building, Jalan Gatot Subroto. Take bus No 210 or 213 from Jalan Jenderal Sudirman. Entry permits to national parks and/or reserves can be acquired directly from local offices located on site throughout Indonesia.

DANGERS & ANNOYANCES

For a city with such a huge population and obvious social problems, Jakarta is surprisingly safe. Violent crime is very rare, though the normal precautions should be taken.

Theft

Theft can be a problem. Pickpockets are common and crowded buses and market places are favourite haunts. The thieves are very skilful and often work in gangs – if you find yourself being hassled and jostled, check your wallet, watch and bag. 'Pencuri' is the Indonesian word for thief. Most hotels have safes for passports and valuables.

Don't leave valuables unattended, and in crowded places hold your handbag or day pack closely. Always lock your hotel room door and windows at night, and whenever you go out.

If travelling by car, keep your door locked. Many intersections are crowded with hawkers that descend on stationary vehicles. Snatch theft is rare but not unheard of.

Unlike some other Asian cities or even other Indonesian tourist centres, Jakarta is not noted for its scams or con artists. Most people who come up to you on the street simply want to meet and chat to a foreigner. Be suspicious if the conversation turns to some great deal or someone wants to lead you to the best shopping bargains, but chances are they are merely touts who get commission on your purchases from shop keepers.

Pollution & Traffic

Jakarta is noisy, crowded and polluted, and disorienting for the first-time visitor.

Noise is a problem in cheap hotels with paper-thin walls and TVs blaring in the lobby, but if you choose your room carefully, you might be able to avoid the full impact. Another major source of noise is the mosques, which start broadcasting the calls to prayer at 4 am, repeating the procedure four more times during the day. Again, choose your hotel room carefully.

Jakarta is usually covered with a pollution haze, a result of the vast traffic jams and ineffective control of industrial emissions. Those sensitive to pollutants or asthma sufferers may have problems, but Jakarta's pollution is not yet as bad as some other cities, such as Bangkok or even Los Angeles on a bad day.

The traffic is a constant spoiler of appointments and is at its worst during the peak hours in the morning and especially the afternoon, when the traffic stops moving from around 3 to 7 pm or later. Crossing the street is difficult. Overhead pedestrian bridges are in short supply, and often house a contingent of beggars. Pedestrians have no rights.

BUSINESS HOURS

Government offices are variable (sometimes very variable) but are generally open Monday to Thursday from 8 am to 3 pm, Friday until 11 am and Saturday until 2 pm. Go early in the morning if you want to get anything done.

Private business offices have staggered hours: Monday to Friday from 8 am to 4 pm or 9 am to 5 pm, with a lunch break in the middle of the day. Offices are also open on Saturday mornings until about noon.

Banks are open Monday to Friday, usually from 8 am to 3 pm, and on Saturday usually until noon, though some close on Saturday. Moneychangers are open longer hours.

Shops open around 9 am and shopping complexes, supermarkets and department stores stay open until 9 pm, though smaller shops may close at 5 pm. Sunday is a public holiday but many shops and airline offices open for at least part of the day.

PUBLIC HOLIDAYS

The following are the main national holidays as celebrated throughout the country. For those that do not follow the Western calendar and change each year, the likely month they will fall is given.

1 January
New Year's Day
February
Isra Miraj Nabi Mohammed – This celebrates the ascension of the Prophet.
March-April
Good Friday
Lebaran (Idul Fitri) – This marks the end of Ramadan and is a noisy celebration at the end of a month of gastronomic austerity. It is a national public holiday of two days in duration.
Nyepi (Balinese New Year) – This marks the end of the Hindu saka calendar.

April-May

Waisak Day – This marks the Buddha's birth, enlighten-
ment and death.

Idul Adha – This is a Muslim festival commemorating
Abraham's willingness to sacrifice his son, Isaac, and is
celebrated with prayers and feasts.

Islamic New Year

May 24

Ascension of Christ

August

Maulud Nabi Muhammed (Hari Natal) – This is the birthday
of the Prophet Muhammed.

17 August

Independence Day (Hari Proklamasi Kemerdekaan) – On
17 August 1945, Soekarno proclaimed Indonesian independence in Jakarta. It is a national public holiday, and
the parades and special events are at their grandest in
Jakarta.

25 December

Christmas Day

Independence Day on 17 August is celebrated with great
gusto in Jakarta. The president delivers an address to the
nation on the preceding day and then on Independence
Day a flag-raising ceremony is held at Merdeka Palace.
Special events organised on this day include various
carnivals and cultural shows which are well worth
seeing if you are in the city at this time.

The Jakarta Fair is an annual event lasting one month.
It is based around 22 June, the official anniversary date
of the founding of Jakarta, and usually starts a week
earlier and goes though until mid-July. The main centre
of activities is at the Jakarta Fair Grounds in Kemayoran.
As well as trade and industrial exhibits at the convention
centre here, normal fairground rides and activities are
set up, and various cultural events are staged all around
the city.

The Jalan Jaksa Street Fair was inaugurated in 1994
and was such a success that it is scheduled to become an
annual event. Organised by the traders in Jakarta's backpacker centre, it features performances of Betawi dance,
theatre and music, as well as well-known Jakartan
stand-up comics and singers. Street stalls sell food and
souvenirs, and art and photography exhibits are also
staged. It is held for one week in August.

The Jakarta International Cultural Performance (JICP)
is held each year in May. Betawi and Indonesian dance
and music are performed all around the city, and performers from around Asia are also invited.

Top :   View of Jalan Thamrin from Arjuna Statue (PT)
Bottom : Modern Skyscrapers, Jalan Thamrin (GB)

A flower-stall arrangement (GB)

ACTIVITIES

Jakarta is not the place for bicycle riding or roller blading and even walking can take its toll. The largest and most handy recreational park is Ancol, though it is not a really well set up centre for leisure and sporting pursuits and the beach is hardly a tropical paradise. To enjoy such pursuits, head outside Jakarta to the beaches of West Java or Pulau Seribu. Some opportunities for walking can also be had relatively close to Jakarta (see the Excursions chapter later in this book).

Language Courses

A few centres offer Bahasa Indonesia courses, but are mostly long-term courses designed for expatriates, though short intensive courses can be arranged for a price. Some of the cultural centres arrange courses, notably the Perhimpunan Persahabatan Indonesia Amerika, the French Cultural Centre and the Goethe Institut (see Useful Organisations earlier in this chapter).

Private courses are expensive. Schools with a good reputation are the Indonesian Australia Language Foundation (☎ 5213350), Jalan Rasuna Said Kav C6, and Business Communications Services (☎ 8301741), Jalan Dr Sahardjo 107D.

WORK

Jakarta has a high number of foreign workers, most of whom have been transferred by foreign companies that have set up shop in Jakarta. People with valuable technical skills, such as engineers, computer programmers and the like may be able to find jobs with foreign multinational corporations, primarily in Jakarta, though most expats are in managerial positions. By far the best way to arrange employment is through a company overseas. By fronting up in Jakarta and finding work, you may miss out on the benefits that most expats get as standard – accommodation, car and driver etc.

Work visas are hard to get, as the Indonesian policy is to hire Indonesians wherever possible. Travellers have been able to pick up work, usually as English teachers. The best paying jobs by far are in Jakarta. Salaries start at 30,000 rp per hour, and can go as high as 50,000 rp per hour if you teach at banks, five-star hotels and other large companies. It's not quite as good as it sounds though. Most banks and big companies will not offer you full-time work, and you'll have to do some commuting between jobs in Jakarta's insane traffic if you want to work 20 hours a week, which is about as much as most teachers can stand. Also, it takes connections to get the really plumb jobs.

Getting There & Away

AIR

Jakarta is the principal gateway for entry to Indonesia. With its huge tourist trade Bali gets almost as much traffic, and special deals may make it cheaper to get a ticket to Bali with a Jakarta stopover.

Flights from Singapore to Jakarta are cheap, and as it is a major travel hub in the region, it may be cheaper to fly to Singapore, from where you can reach Jakarta by air or ship.

For bargain fares, it is usually better to go to a travel agent than to the airline, as the latter can only sell fares by the book. Budget tickets may come with lots of restrictions. Check for how long the ticket is valid, the minimum period of stay, stopover options, cancellation fees and any amendment fees if you change your date of travel. Plenty of discount tickets are valid for six or 12 months, allowing multiple stopovers with open dates. Make sure you get details in writing of the flights you've requested (before you pay for the ticket). 'Round-the-world' tickets may also be worth looking into.

Fares quoted in this section are an approximate guide only. Fares vary depending on the season (high, shoulder or low) and special deals are often available. Fares can vary from week to week, and it pays to shop around by ringing a variety of travel agents for the best fare and ticket to suit your needs.

Immigration officials at Jakarta airport have a bad reputation for requesting 'gifts' from visiting business people. It is best to stand your ground and resist unless it becomes obvious that you are not going to get anywhere. Tourists are rarely bothered, and Jakarta is one of the few places where it is best to dress down for immigration (put away the brief case and don the Hawaiian shirt).

Departure tax on international flights from Jakarta is 21,000 rp.

Airline Offices

Addresses of some of the international airlines are:
Air Canada
    Jalan Jenderal Sudirman Kav 21, Chase Plaza, ground floor (☎ 5738185)

Air France
 Jalan Jenderal Sudirman Kav 61-62, Summitmas Tower, 9th floor (☎ 5202262)
Air India
 Jalan Thamrin 7 A (☎ 325406)
British Airways
 Jalan Jenderal Sudirman Kav 29, World Trade Centre, 10th floor (☎ 521150)
Canadian Airlines International
 Jalan Riau 19A (☎ 323730)
Cathay Pacific
 Hotel Borobudur Inter-Continental, 3rd floor, Jalan Lapangan Banteng Selatan (☎ 3806664, 3459802)
China Airlines
 Jalan Jenderal Sudirman, Wisma Dharmala Sakti (☎ 5704003)
Delta Airlines
 Jalan Jenderal Sudirman Kav 28, Wisma Dharmala Sakti, 11th floor (☎ 5212340)
Garuda Indonesian Airways
 BDN Bldg, Jalan Thamrin 5 (☎ 2300925). Also at Borobudur Hotel (☎ 2310339), Hotel Indonesia (☎ 2300568), Wisma Dharmala Sakti (☎ 5706155) and Jakarta International Trade Centre (☎ 2600244).
Gulf Air
 Jalan Hasyim Ashari 33B (☎ 3457489)
Japan Airlines
 Jalan Jenderal Sudirman Kav 10-11, Mid Plaza (☎ 5703883)
KLM
 Plaza Indonesia, Jalan Thamrin (☎ 3107666)
Lufthansa
 Panin Centre Bldg, Jalan Jenderal Sudirman 1 (☎ 5702005)

Arjuna Statue, near Merdeka Square (GB)

Malaysian Airline Systems (MAS)
  Hotel Indonesia, Jalan Thamrin (☎ 3142102)
Philippine Airlines
  Hotel Borobudur Inter-Continental (☎ 3810949)
Qantas
  BDN Bldg, Jalan Thamrin 5 (☎ 3450755, 2300655)
Royal Brunei
  Jalan Hasyim Ashari 33B (☎ 5211842)
Sempati
  Hotel Borobudur Inter-Continental (☎ 3805555). Also in
  many of the major hotels, including the Hotel Indonesia
  (☎ 320008), Sari Pan Pacific (☎ 323707), Le Meridien
  (☎ 5711414) and Sahid Jaya (☎ 5704444).
Silk Air
  Jalan Jenderal Sudirman Kav 21, Chase Plaza, 4th floor
  (☎ 5208018)
Singapore Airlines
  Jalan Jenderal Sudirman Kav 21, Chase Plaza, ground
  floor (☎ 5206881)
Thai Airways International
  BDN Bldg, Jalan Thamrin 5 (☎ 3140607)
United Airlines
  Hotel Borobudur Inter-Continental (☎ 361707)

To/From Singapore

Garuda has the most flights between Singapore and
Jakarta, but this route is serviced by many airlines that
offer better discounts. Singapore-Jakarta tickets cost as
little as US$70. Sempati is regularly one of the cheapest
airlines, but Gulf Air and Air India are also cheap.

Singapore is also a good place to buy a cheap air ticket
if you're leaving South-East Asia for the West. Cheap air
tickets from Singapore are available at Airmaster and
Airpower travel agents. Also try STA.

To/From Australia

Bali is the major gateway to Australia, with almost all
flights to/from Jakarta routed via Denpasar. Qantas and
Garuda are the main carriers. The only nonstop flights
to Jakarta from Australia are Perth-Jakarta (Garuda and
Sempati) and Sydney-Jakarta (Qantas and UTA).

Fares vary between the low season (February to
December) and the high season (December and
January). Return tickets are usually limited to 45 or
90-day excursion fares, or Garuda has 12-month return
tickets to Jakarta, and you can add on a Bali stopover for
around A$100. From Melbourne, Sydney or Brisbane to
Jakarta, a 12-month ticket will cost around A$1000
return in the low season and A$1150 return in the high

season, while excursion fares are slightly cheaper. From Darwin or Perth, fares are about A$200 cheaper.

Travel agents are the best place to shop for cheap tickets, but because Bali is such a popular destination discounting on flights to Indonesia is not large. Travel agents to try include the big networks like STA or Flight Centres International, with offices in the main cities, or check the travel pages of the main newspapers. It is also worth ringing the airlines direct. The highest demand for flights is during school holidays and especially the Christmas break, when flights to Jakarta via Denpasar can be full – book well in advance.

To/From New Zealand

Garuda and Air New Zealand have direct flights between Auckland and Denpasar, with connections to Jakarta. Air New Zealand's fares are generally a little lower than Garuda's. The return economy air fare from Auckland to Denpasar or Jakarta is about NZ$1300 to NZ$1500, depending on the season.

Check the latest fare developments and discounts with the airlines, or shop around a few travel agents for possible deals. As in Australia, STA Travel and Flight Centres International are popular travel agents.

To/From the UK

Ticket discounting is a long-established business in the UK and it's wide open – the various agencies advertise their fares and there's nothing under the counter about it at all. To find out what is available and where to get it, pick up a copy of the giveaway newspapers *TNT, Southern Cross* or *Trailfinder*, or the weekly 'what's on' guide *Time Out*. Discounted tickets are available all over the UK, and they're not just a London exclusive. The magazine *Business Traveller* also covers airfare possibilities.

A couple of excellent places to try are Trailfinders and STA Travel. Trailfinders is at 194 Kensington High St, London W8 (☎ (0171) 938 3939) and at 46 Earl's Court Rd (☎ (0171) 938 3366). It also has offices in Manchester (☎ (061) 839 6969) and Glasgow (☎ (041) 353 2224). STA Travel is at 74 Old Brompton Rd, London W7 (☎ (0171) 581 1022) and Clifton House, 117 Euston Rd (☎ 388 2261).

Garuda is one of the main discounters to Indonesia, with flights from around £500 return to Jakarta in the low season, while high season prices are about 30% more. Travel agents also put together cheap tickets via Singapore, or you can do it yourself. Flights from London to Singapore start at around £225 one way, £400 return. From Singapore you can reach Jakarta by boat, or a one-way ticket to Jakarta will cost around £50.

To/From Europe

The Netherlands, Switzerland, Antwerp and Brussels are good places for buying discount air tickets. In Antwerp, WATS has been recommended. In Zurich, try SOF Travel and Sindbad. In Geneva, try Stohl Travel. In the Netherlands, NBBS is a reputable agency.

As well as Garuda and other Asian airlines, KLM and Lufthansa have a number of flights to Indonesia. Usually is it is cheaper to fly to Jakarta than Denpasar. For example, Lufthansa's regular discount fares from Germany are around 1600 DM to Jakarta. The cheapest way to reach Indonesia is often via Singapore, with the East European airlines offering some of the cheapest flights. Aeroflot's flight into Jakarta once a week is also cheap.

Garuda has flight connections between Jakarta and several European cities: Paris, Amsterdam, Zurich, Frankfurt and Rome.

To/From the USA

There are some very good open tickets which remain valid for six months or one year but don't lock you into any fixed dates of departure. For example, there are

Ancol Harbour (GB)

cheap tickets between the US west coast and Singapore with stopoffs in Japan, Korea, Taiwan, Hong Kong and Bangkok for very little extra money – the departure dates can be changed and you have one year to complete the journey. However, be careful during the peak season (summer and Chinese New Year) because seats will be hard to come by unless reserved months in advance.

San Francisco is the bucket shop capital of the USA, though some good deals can be found in Los Angeles, New York and other cities. Bucket shops can be found through the Yellow Pages or the major daily newspapers. The *New York Times*, the *LA Times*, the *Chicago Tribune* and the *San Francisco Examiner* all produce weekly travel sections in which you'll find any number of travel agents' ads. The magazine *Travel Unlimited* (PO Box 1058, Allston, Mass 02134) publishes details of courier and cheap air fares to destinations all over the world from the USA.

Council Travel is the largest student travel organisation and, though you don't have to be a student to use them, they do have specially discounted student tickets. Council Travel has an extensive network in all major US cities and is listed in the telephone book. There are also Student Travel Network offices, which are associated with STA Travel.

From the US west coast, fares to Jakarta cost around US$700/1000 one way/return. Alternatively, Garuda has a Los Angeles-Honolulu-Biak-Denpasar-Jakarta route, which is an extremely interesting back-door route into Indonesia. The return fare from Los Angeles to Jakarta is about US$1100 or US$600 one way in the low season.

To/From Canada

Getting discount tickets in Canada is much the same as in the USA – go to the travel agents and shop around until you find a good deal. Again, you'll probably have to fly into Hong Kong or Singapore and carry on from there to Indonesia.

CUTS is Canada's national student bureau and has offices in a number of Canadian cities, including Vancouver, Edmonton, Toronto and Ottawa – you don't necessarily have to be a student. There are a number of good agents in Vancouver for cheap tickets, CP-Air are particularly good for fares to Hong Kong.

The *Toronto Globe & Mail* and the *Vancouver Sun* carry travel agents' ads. The magazine *Great Expeditions* (PO Box 8000-411, Abbotsford BC V2S 6H1) is useful.

SEA

To/From Singapore

An interesting way to reach Jakarta is from Singapore via Sumatra's Riau Archipelago. The main stepping stone is the island of Bintan, only a short high-speed ferry ride from Singapore's World Trade Centre. Four departures go per day and Bintan is a visa-free entry port.

From Bintan, Pelni, the national passenger line, has two ships, the KM *Rinjani* and KM *Umsini*, calling in every two weeks on their way between Jakarta and Dumai in Sumatra. The problem with the Pelni ships has always been the difficulty of finding out the constantly changing Pelni schedule before arriving in Indonesia, but now there is also another regular twice-weekly service from Bintan to Jakarta. The MV *Bintan Permata* leaves Tanjung Pinang every Tuesday and Friday at 8 am, arriving 6 am the following day. It costs 91,500 rp in economy and 111,500 rp in 1st class. The ship leaves Jakarta on Wednesday and Saturday at 4 pm. Bookings can be made through Primkopal, 18 Jalan Samudra, Tanjung Pinang, or PT Admiral Lines, 21 Jalan Raya Pelabuhan, Jakarta.

TO/FROM OTHER PARTS OF INDONESIA

Jakarta is also a major centre for domestic travel, with extensive bus, rail, air and sea connections.

Air

Most domestic flights operate from the Soekarno-Hatta International Airport. Airport tax is 8800 rp on domestic flights, but is usually included in the ticket. Flights depart from Jakarta to all the main cities in Java and to places all over the archipelago. The main domestic airlines have offices open during normal business hours, and usually Sunday morning as well. Addresses of some of the domestic airlines are:

Garuda (☎ 2300925), BDN Bldg, Jalan Thamrin 5. Garuda also has offices at the Borobudur Hotel (☎ 2310339), Hotel Indonesia (☎ 2300568), Wisma Dharmala Sakti (☎ 5706155) and Jakarta International Trade Centre (☎ 2600244). Garuda flies to the major cities throughout Indonesia.

Merpati (☎ 4247404), Jalan Angkasa 2, Kemayoran. This office
is inconveniently located, but travel agents sell tickets.
Merpati is the main domestic carrier with flights throughout the archipelago.

Sempati (☎ 3805555), Hotel Borobudur Inter-Continental.
Sempati also has offices in many of the major hotels,
including the Hotel Indonesia (☎ 320008), Sari Pan Pacific
(☎ 323707), Le Meridien (☎ 5711414) and Sahid Jaya
(☎ 5704444). Most travel agents can book Sempati.
Sempati has a jet fleet flying to most of the main cities in
Indonesia.

Bouraq (☎ 6295150), Jalan Angkasa 1, Kemayoran. Bouraq has
direct flights from Jakarta to Bandung, Semarang,
Pangkal Pinang, Pontianak, Balikpapan and Banjarmasin
with connections farther afield in the eastern islands.

Mandala (☎ 368107), Jalan Veteran I No 34.

Train

Java has quite a good rail network, though trains often
run over schedule. Trains range from crowded, slow
ekonomi-class cattle trains to comfortable *bisnis* and
eksekutif-class trains, and a couple of luxury trains with
sleepers. The four stations are quite central, making the
trains the easiest way out of the city into Java.

Gambir On the east side of Merdeka Square, conveniently central Gambir is the main station. It handles
most of the trains to the south and east, including Bogor,
Bandung, Cirebon, Yogyakarta and Surabaya.

The best trains to Bogor are the express *Pakuan* (2000
rp, one hour) offering bisnis-class carriages at 7.30, 10.30
am, 2.15 and 4.40 pm. To Bandung, the efficient
Parahyangan express service departs roughly every hour
between 6 am and 8.30 pm, and takes three hours. To
Cirebon, the *Cirebon Express* departs Kota and arrives at
Gambir station at 6.45, 9.45 am and 4.30 pm.

Kota In the old part of the city, Kota is on the same line
as Gambir, and some Gambir trains also leave from or
arrive at Kota. Some only depart from Kota, such as the
deluxe night express trains to Surabaya – the *Bima* (via
Yogyakarta) and the *Mutiara Utara* (via Semarang) – and
these can be booked at the station or through travel
agents. If departing from Kota, allow adequate time to
wend your way through the rush hour traffic snarls.

Pasar Senen Farther east of Gambir, Pasar Senen has
a few ekonomi services to Surabaya via Semarang as
well as Yogya.

Tanah Abang This station, directly to the west of Jalan Thamrin, has trains to Merak, for Sumatra, and a few other ekonomi services. Departures to Merak (1500 rp, four hours) are at 7 am and 2.35 pm, but the buses are much quicker.

Bus

Jakarta has three major bus stations, all a long way from the city centre. In some cases it can take longer getting to the bus station than the bus journey itself, making the trains a better alternative for arriving at or leaving Jakarta. This is especially true for buses to/from Kampung Rambutan bus station.

Kalideres Buses to the west of Jakarta leave from the Kalideres bus station, about 15 km from Merdeka Square. Catch public buses here for Java's west coast destinations, such as Labuhan and Serang.

Kampung Rambutan The big, new Kampung Rambutan terminal handles buses to areas south and south-west of Jakarta. It was designed to carry much of Jakarta's inter-city bus traffic, but it mainly handles buses to West Java, including Bogor and Bandung, though the train is a better option for these two destinations.

Pulo Gadung This wild, crowded station has buses to Cirebon, Central and East Java, Sumatra and Bali. It is

A local bus (GB)

about 12 km to the east of the city centre. Most of the
air-conditioned, deluxe buses operate from here, and
can be booked in advance through agents in town. Jalan
Jaksa agents sell bus tickets and can include travel to the
bus station or bus company depots.

For Bukittingi in Sumatra, two good companies are
ALS and ANS, with luxury buses costing 60,000 rp for
the 30-hour plus journey. To the east, frequent buses go
to Central and East Java and on to Bali. Normal/air-con
buses include: Cirebon (4700/7900 rp, four hours),
Yogya (11,000/18,000 rp, 12 hours) and Denpasar
(28,000/45,000 rp). Deluxe buses to Denpasar cost
around 55,000 rp and take 24 hours.

Intercity Taxis

There are also intercity taxis and minibuses to Bandung
that will pick you up and drop you off at your hotel.
Fares start at 12,000 rp per person; they're fast and
convenient but taxis will only depart when they have
five passengers. Media Taxis (☎ 3140343) are at Jalan
Johar 15, near Jalan Jaksa. The 4848 Taxis (☎ 364488) is
at Jalan Prapatan 34, just beyond the Aryaduta Hotel.
Door-to-door minibus services are also available to
Bandung, Yogya and other destinations, and can be
booked through travel agents.

Boat

Pelni has lots of services out of Jakarta, departing from
and arriving at Pelabuhan or Dock No 1 at the Tanjung
Priok Harbour. Some of the more popular links are from
Jakarta to: Tanjung Pinang (from 37,000 rp economy
class), Padang (from 37,000 rp economy class), Ujung
Pandang (from 55,000 rp economy class), Belawan (from
56,000 rp economy class) and Pontianak (36,000 rp
economy class).

The Pelni ticketing office (☎ 4211921) is at Jalan
Angkasa No 18, to the north-east of the city centre. Pelni
agents charge a small premium but are much more
convenient – try Panintama Tour & Travel (☎ 390 2076)
in the Sarinah department store building on Jalan
Thamrin, near the Jalan Jaksa area.

TRAVEL AGENTS

Jakarta is no ticket discount centre compared with Singapore or Bangkok, but it is the best place to buy
international tickets in Indonesia. Small agents specialising in services for travellers may advertise international

tickets, but you will usually get much better discounts at one of the bigger flight specialists. At travel agencies, you usually save at least 3% if you pay cash rather than using a credit card.

International student-card holders should ask about discounts (up to 25%) if buying international tickets in Indonesia. These discounts are generally available only on overpriced published fares anyway, and not for already discounted tickets.

Heavy discounting on domestic tickets has dropped off since the airlines agreed to collude on prices, and Sempati, the major instigator of discounting, joined the fold. The major ticketing travel agents still offer very small discounts and reasonable deals on return flights. Discounts are often small (5 to 10%) but can be substantial for return tickets (up to 40%). Student discounts are also available on domestic flights.

For international flights, the travel agents on Jalan Jaksa are convenient places to start looking: try Seabreeze Travel (☎ 3902996) at No 38 and Balimaesti near Angie's cafe. Travel International (☎ 3905188) in the President Hotel on Jalan Thamrin is also a good place for cheap tickets, as is Vayatour (☎ 3100720) next door. Other agents worth checking are Natrabu (☎ 331728), Jalan Agus Salim 29A (near Jalan Jaksa), and Pacto Ltd (☎ 3810837) in the Hotel Borobudur Inter-Continental. Both are large operators with offices throughout Indonesia, and they also offer package and tailor-made tours around Jakarta or farther afield.

Indo Shangrila Travel (☎ 6256080), Jalan Gajah Mada 219G, is the STA agent and often has good deals. It also organises tours to Cipanas, Bandung and Cirebon, as well as farther afield in Java and Bali.

Other travel agents for tours around Jakarta include Citra Netrama (☎ 314220) in the Hotel Indonesia on Jalan Thamrin and Vista Express Tours & Travel (☎ 323432), Jalan Cikini Raya 58, which have tours in and around the city, and Metropole Indahwisata (☎ 6905137-9), Jalan Pintu Besar Selatan 38, which has Bogor-Puncak tours among others. See Organised Tours in the following Getting Around chapter for information on Jakarta city tours.

ORGANISED TOURS

Jakarta is not a prime tourist destination, and very few tours are organised just to Jakarta from overseas. Tours to Java will include Jakarta but after a quick look at the sights of Old Batavia and a bit of shopping, tours tend to get out of the city as soon as possible.

Travel agents can usually arrange Jakarta flight and accommodation packages. Garuda has three-day/two-night Jakarta City Holiday packages for a minimum of two people arriving or departing on a Garuda flight. They cost around US$200 per person on a twin share basis, including accommodation in a four or five-star hotel, breakfast, transfers and a half-day city tour.

Travel agents in Singapore arrange short, reasonably priced tours to Jakarta. These tours tend to focus on Dunia Fantasi and Taman Mini.

Getting Around

TO/FROM THE AIRPORT

Jakarta's Soekarno-Hatta International Airport is 35 km west of the city centre. A toll road links the airport to the city and a journey between the two takes 45 minutes to an hour, although it can take longer in the rush hour.

The Damri airport bus departs every 30 minutes between 3 am and 10 pm to Gambir station (near Jalan Jaksa), and continues on to Blok M, Kemayoran and Rawamangun. It costs 3000 rp per person.

A metered taxi from the airport to Jalan Thamrin costs about 24,000 rp, including the airport surcharge (2300 rp, payable from but not to the airport) and toll road charges (4000 rp between the airport and Bandara, and then another 2000 rp into the city centre). Catch metered taxis from taxi ranks outside the terminal, and avoid offers of 'transport' from unregistered drivers unless you want to pay double. At the taxi rank you will be given a card with the number of the taxi written on it. This card lists toll road and airport surcharges, which are paid on top of the metered fare. Anything extra that the driver may request at the end of the journey is a 'tip'.

More expensive luxury taxis (38,000 rp) and limousines can be found at the transport booths inside the airport terminal. Most of the budget hotels on Jalan Jaksa arrange transport to the airport for 25,000 rp per car or minibus, which may be convenient but is no saving, especially if they avoid the toll road.

Soekarno-Hatta International Airport

Jakarta's Soekarno-Hatta airport is spacious, modern and surprisingly efficient but has only a few overpriced food and shopping outlets. Standard duty-free items are on sale at the airport, but local cigarettes are much cheaper than the imported duty-free variety, and there are no great bargains for alcohol either. The airport has a reasonable bookshop, post office, left-luggage and money-changing facilities.

The airport has a domestic terminal and an international terminal, about one km apart. Garuda's domestic flights usually arrive at and depart from the Garuda international terminal. A shuttle bus loops between the terminals about every 15 minutes and costs

1000 rp. Have exact money as no change is given. Taxis waiting on ranks aren't interested in doing the short trip between terminals but private operators will offer for exorbitant amounts of money.

Departure tax is 21,000 rp on international flights, 8800 rp on domestic flights.

BUS

In Jakarta everything is at a distance. It's hot and humid, and hardly anybody walks – you will need to use some form of transport to get from one place to another. Jakarta has probably the most comprehensive city bus network of any major Indonesian city. Its buses, however, tend to be hopelessly crowded, particularly during rush hours. Jakarta's pickpockets are notoriously adept and they're great bag slashers too. So take care. Indeed, if you are carrying a camera or anything else of value, you would be wise to spring for a taxi.

Around town there are lots of big regular city buses charging a fixed 250 rp fare. The big express 'Patas' buses charge 550 rp and the air-con Patas buses cost 1300 rp; these are usually less crowded and by far the best option. These services are supplemented by orange toy-sized buses and, in a few areas, by pale blue Mikrolet buses, which cost between 300 rp and 500 rp.

The Visitor Information Centre in the Sarinah department store on Jalan Thamrin can provide information on the city buses. Some of the more useful Patas buses include:

P11, P10 (air-con)
  Kampung Rambutan to Kota via Jalan Thamrin
P1
  Blok M to Kota via Jalan Thamrin
P14
  Tanjung Priok to Tanah Abang via Jalan Kebon Sirih
P7A
  Pulo Gadung to Kalideres via Jalan Juanda

CAR

Driving yourself around Jakarta is not recommended. The traffic is chaotic, and the traffic jams infuriating. There appear to be no road rules in Jakarta, but a logic does exist, based mostly on the rule of 'might is right'. Bicycles give way to motorbikes, motorbikes to cars, cars to trucks and everyone gives way to the buses, which are driven by maniacs. Pedestrians give way to everything. Everyone pushes in wherever they can, yet astonishingly tempers are rarely frayed and accidents are usually only minor.

It you do want to drive in Jakarta, bring an international driver's licence and your home licence. A good street directory is essential. During the morning peak hours until 10 am the 'three-in-one' traffic restriction applies when only cars with three or more passengers can enter the central business district.

Hire car companies also rent cars with drivers. This is only marginally more expensive than renting a self-drive car, and much more preferable. Rental starts at around US$80 per day for a small car with driver, and minibuses and limousines are also available. Some of the major companies are:

Avis
   Jalan Diponegoro 25 (☎ 3904745) and Hotel Sari Pan Pacific, Jalan Thamrin (☎ 3203707 ext 1281)
Blue Bird
   Jalan HOS Cokroaminto 107, Menteng (☎ 3256073)
Hertz Car Rental
   Mandarin Oriental Hotel, Jalan Thamrin (☎ 3141307 ext 1268), Aryaduta Hotel (☎ 3840606 ext 197) and Soekarno Hatta International Airport (☎ 5505773)
National Car Rental
   Kartika Plaza Hotel, Jalan Thamrin 10 (☎ 3143423)

Private operators can also be hired. Private minibuses or cars often hang around train stations and some hotels, but rather than get someone off the street, ask at your hotel or at travel agents. At big hotels and major travel agents, you'll pay major prices. The cheaper hotels and small travel agents either have cars or minibuses that can be hired, or know of a driver with a vehicle looking for work. Prices have to be negotiated, but are as little as half that of the car rental companies.

TAXI

Taxis in Jakarta are metered and cost 900 rp for the first km and 450 rp for each subsequent km. Make sure the meter is used. Many taxi drivers provide a good service, but Jakarta has enough rogues to give its taxis a bad reputation. Some drivers are helpful and friendly, others are downright sullen and grumble at short fares, but this is probably understandable given Jakarta's traffic. Taxis that wait for a long time at bus and train stations often refuse to take short fares on the meter and will ask the

Magic Knocking

In Jakarta's chaotic traffic, fenders are easily dented. Jakarta has plenty of car-repair specialists for hammering out panels and respraying, but in the tradition of Javanese mysticism, the powerful spirits are called upon to perform unique panel-beating services. Take your car to a *ketok magik bengkel* (magic-knocking workshop), where the shop owner will assess the damage and determine whether the gods can help. If so, a price is quoted and the car owner must pay the exact amount, not a rupiah more or less. Old coins must be found if the figure is something odd like 12,345 rp. Certain conditions may also apply, such as the driver must not drive the car on a particular day, or the accident will be repeated. The car is left in the locked workshop unattended for the prescribed amount of time while prayers are offered. The magic knocking begins and the repairs are 'magikally' effected. Though the repairs have been attributed to human intervention and other devices, such as powerful magnets, the magic knocking workshops have plenty of satisfied customers, and they are cheaper than conventional repairers. ■

earth. If this happens, walk to the nearest main road and hail another one or wait for a taxi that is dropping off a passenger.

Taxi drivers don't carry street directories and don't always know the city well. Carry a map or get good directions and the name of the nearest well-known landmark before you hop in a cab. If a taxi driver asks you which way you want to go, you're in trouble. Either he doesn't know or, more likely, he's trying to find out if you know. If offered alternative routes – via the long, expensive route or the short, normal route – just say *'langsung'* (direct). Most taxis, however, will take you directly, but bear in mind that the most direct route may well be circuitous given Jakarta's system of one-way streets and traffic restrictions.

Tipping is expected, if not demanded, but not obligatory. If good service is provided, it is customary to round the fare up to the next 500 or 1000 rp. Carry plenty of small notes. Jakarta taxi drivers *never* have change under 1000 rp.

Jakarta has a large fleet of taxis and it's usually not too difficult to find one. Bluebird cabs (pale blue) (☎ 3143000, 7999000) have the best reputation and well-maintained cars.

Typical taxi fares from Jalan Thamrin are: to Kota (4000 rp), Sunda Kelapa (5000 rp), Pulo Gadung (6000 rp) and Kampung Rambutan or Taman Mini (12,000 rp).

Taxis can also be rented by the hour, usually for a minimum of two hours, or for trips outside the city. The best way to do this is to ring Bluebird or try to arrange one at the hotel ranks of the big hotels, particularly the Hotel Indonesia and the Hilton.

BAJAJ & OTHERS

Jakarta has all sorts of other weird and wonderful means of getting around. Unfortunately, they all seem destined to become museum pieces as the city government clamps down and banishes them from the city. The campaign to rid the city of the becak began back in the '70s and now becaks have disappeared from the city.

Top :   Traffic along Jalan Medan Merdeka Timur (GB)
Bottom : A bajaj (GB)

Only a few tourist becaks remain at Ancol. Recently the government has announced that it wants to get rid of the *bajaj* and *bemo*, which may not be salubrious, modern transport but provide a necessary service for Jakarta's residents, not to mention employment.

A bajaj (pronounced ba-jai) is nothing less than an Indian auto-rickshaw – an orange three-wheeler that carries two passengers (three at a squeeze if you're all dwarf size) and sputters around powered by noisy two-stroke engines. Short trips – Jalan Jaksa to the post office, for example – will cost about 2000 rp. They're good value, especially during rush hours, but hard bargaining is required. Always agree on the price beforehand. Bajaj

Top :   A local taxi (GB)
Bottom: Boats moored at Sunda Kelapa, Kota (GB)

are not allowed along main streets, such as Jalan Thamrin, so make sure your driver doesn't simply drop you off at the border. Bajaj are good for short trips and for negotiating narrow backstreets.

'Morris' bemos are old English Morris vans that operate around Glodok and other parts of Jakarta. These small public buses have seats down either side of the back and are usually crammed with passengers and shopping.

In the backstreets of Kota, pushbikes with a padded 'kiddy carrier' on the back will also take you for a ride!

The *helicak*, cousin to the bajaj, is a green motorbike contraption with a passenger car mounted on the front. They are found only in the back streets of Menteng. Jakarta also has *ojek*, motorbike riders that take pillion passengers, but weaving in and out of Jakarta's traffic on the back of an ojek is only for the brave.

Scattered around the old city, water ferries still take passengers across the canals for a couple of hundred rupiah. A line is strung across the canal, and a boatman manually pulls the punt from one side of the canal to the other.

WALKING

Jakarta is very spread out and there are few central areas where you can walk around a number of attractions. Some areas are good to explore on foot, such as Old Batavia and Menteng (see the Things to See & Do chapter for some interesting walking tours), but otherwise take a taxi. It's hot, polluted and difficult to cross the street. Only the really destitute walk in Jakarta.

ORGANISED TOURS

Numerous travel agents offer daily tours of Jakarta but they tend to be expensive. Contact the Visitor Information Centre for full details, or they can be booked at major hotels and some travel agents. City Tour (☎ 3856134) and Boca Pirento Tours & Travel (☎ 5664481) have regular city tours, pick up from the major hotels and also organise tours farther afield in Java. Other agents for extended tours include Vayatour (☎ 3800202), Nitour (☎ 346347) and Setia Tours (☎ 6390008). All tour buses pick up from the major hotels, and tour prices and sights are very similar. A four-hour morning city tour, for example, costs US$20 and includes the National Museum, Monas, Sunda Kelapa and Kota. Tour prices are dependent on demand.

If you are the only one wanting a tour, of course the cost will be very high.

There are also a variety of tours to nearby towns in West Java, which basically go to Bogor, the Puncak Pass and Tangkuban Prahu volcano near Bandung. A six-hour tour to the Bogor botanical gardens and zoological museum costs US$35; to the Puncak costs US$40. Tours to Bandung, Banten, Anyer, Pulau Seribu etc are also available.

Things to See & Do

While Jakarta is not packed with tourist attractions, it is Indonesia's most historic city, and its theme parks attract large numbers of domestic and overseas visitors. The main problem with seeing Jakarta is getting to the points of interest. Few attractions are within walking distance of the main city centre around Jalan Thamrin and it is necessary to take taxis or buses to reach many of the sights. From Ancol to Taman Mini can take two hours when the traffic is bad.

HIGHLIGHTS

Jakarta has plenty of different areas to explore, but its most visited and popular attractions for overseas visitors are:

• Kota district
• Sunda Kelapa
• National Monument
• National Museum
• Taman Mini
• Dunia Fantasi

The most interesting part of town is the old city in the Kota district, centred around the cobbled square of Taman Fatahillah. This was the centre of the Dutch city of Batavia and there are many fine examples of Dutch architecture. Just north of Taman Fatahillah is the old schooner dock of Sunda Kelapa, with its impressive collection of sailing ships, and more Dutch architecture. This area is reached by bus or taxi from Jalan Thamrin and is easily explored on foot.

Close to the main tourist accommodation area is Merdeka Square, which also has a few points of interest. In the middle of Merdeka Square is the National Monument (Monas), with fine views from the top of the towering obelisk. Around Merdeka Square are more grand public buildings, such as the Presidential Palace, or Istana Merdeka, and the Istiqlal Mosque, and architectural reminders of the Dutch era, especially around Lapangan Banteng. The National Museum on the west side of Merdeka Square is the finest museum in the country and a must for students of Indonesian history and culture. The area around Merdeka Square can be covered on foot, but it pays to take a taxi or bajaj between some points of interest.

Taman Mini Indonesia is on the southern outskirts of the city, at least an hour from Jalan Thamrin. This all-Indonesia theme park is very well done and it is easy to spend a half a day or more wandering around the various traditional houses and exhibits from all over the archipelago.

Ancol is a recreational park area which also has some of Jakarta's most popular attractions, No 1 being Dunia Fantasi, a Disneyland clone that is great for children. The Pasar Seni art market here is also well worth a browse. Ancol is to the north of the city and can be combined with a visit to Kota and Sunda Kelapa.

Other sights of interest are the Chinatown area in Glodok near Kota, numerous museums and Ragunan Zoo on the southern outskirts of the city, and Jakarta also has a number of interesting markets and shopping possibilities that can be combined with sightseeing. The most interesting areas for shopping and browsing are Jalan Surabaya in Menteng, Blok M in Kebayoran Baru, Pasar Seni at Ancol, Jalan Thamrin and Pasar Baru (see the Shopping chapter later in this book for more details).

Sunday morning is a good time to explore the Kota area. Not only does the reduced traffic make it easy to reach but you can also see puppet performances at the Wayang Museum. Sunday is also a good day for wandering around the Merdeka Square area, but the Sunday queues for the lift at Monas stretch forever. Attractions that are popular with Jakarta residents, such as Taman Mini, Ancol and Ragunan Zoo, are very crowded on Sunday.

It is possible to see the main attractions in a couple of days, but bear in mind that Jakarta's heat can be very tiring and traffic jams can be very time consuming. Because of the difficulties in getting around the city, it is best to divide the attractions up into north and south. In the north of town, three hours is sufficient to explore Kota and Sunda Kelapa. An extra side trip can be made to Chinatown or Ancol from Kota, though during the week, Ancol's main attractions don't really get going until late afternoon or evening.

Closer to the city centre, the Merdeka Square area and National Museum can be explored in a few hours, depending on how much you want to see. From Lapangan Banteng it is a short walk to the Pasar Baru area for interesting shopping. Other good shopping forays in the city centre are to the Jalan Surabaya antique market, Pasar Senen and Jalan Thamrin.

On the southern side of the city, you could see Taman Mini in the morning and then take in the zoo or head west for shopping at Blok M in the Kebayoran Baru area.

The following rundown on sights in Jakarta includes some walking tours. It may seem like a maniacal thing to do in heat-hazed Jakarta, and Jakartans will certainly tell you that it is, but like anywhere else in the world it is only on foot that you can really absorb the atmosphere of a city. The foot tour of Old Batavia is certainly recommended and the only way to see the area. Other walking tours are for those who want to explore the city in depth or who have special interests. Most tours can also be at least partly done by car or taxi, and especially bajaj, which are readily available, instead of walking.

OLD BATAVIA (KOTA)

The old town of Batavia, known as Kota today, at one time contained Coen's massive shoreline fortress, the Kasteel, and was surrounded by a sturdy defensive wall and a moat. In the early 19th century Governor-General Daendels demolished much of the unhealthy city, including the fort and the city walls, but there is still a Dutch flavour to this old part of town. A few of Batavia's old buildings remain in active use, although others were restored during the 1970s and have become museums.

The centre of Old Batavia is the cobblestone square known as Taman Fatahillah, standing in front of the old Dutch city hall. Taman Fatahillah was named after the Banten commander who captured Sunda Kelapa and renamed the city Jayakarta. In Dutch times the square was known as the Stadhuis Plein. A block west of the square is the Kali Besar, the great canal along the Ciliwung River. This was once the high-class residential area of Batavia.

Jakarta History Museum

On the south side of Taman Fatahillah, the museum is housed in the old town hall (Stadhuis) of Batavia, which is one of the most impressive architectural reminders of Dutch rule in Indonesia.

This large bell-towered hall was completed in 1710 and replaced a previous town hall that existed on the site from 1627 to 1707. The design was said to be influenced by Amsterdam's town hall, now the Royal Palace.

The town hall housed a number of administrative functions in colonial Batavia, including the registrar of marriages, trustees of the orphanage, magistrates council, civil court and the jail, with its dungeons forming the main prison compound of Batavia. Those lucky enough to escape cholera and typhoid in the dungeons may have found themselves on the gallows out front in the square, or subject to public torture. Famous prisoners to find themselves imprisoned in the town hall include the Javanese hero Prince Diponegoro, who was held here in 1830 on his way into exile in Manado. Diponegoro was spared the dungeons and he and his retinue were given quarters within the main building.

Apart from the regular public executions, the town hall and square also witnessed gayer events. As well as lavish civic ceremonies, weekly markets and fairs were held in the square.

The town hall was used by the military after WW II, and then by the police until 1974, when the building was renovated and the exhibits from the Museum of Old Batavia, housed in the Wayang Museum across the square, were moved to the new museum. The square itself was a parking lot before restoration.

Today the museum contains lots of heavy, carved furniture and other memorabilia, mostly from the Dutch period. On the ground floor, the main entrance room contains furniture and a Dutch stone lion holding the shield of Batavia. Other rooms contain 17th-century furniture and old weapons, and some house pre-colonial exhibits, including dedications to Fatahillah and replicas of early Hindu inscription stones.

Upstairs are the old court chambers, which were the rooms of the Bench of Magistrates and the Council of Justice. The painting in the main room at the top of the stairs is a triptych by J J de Nijs dating from 1660 and featuring classical scenes of justice, including King Solomon passing judgement on the life of a baby claimed by two women. The best examples of furniture are found upstairs, most dating from the 18th century, though some early 19th-century furniture from the British interregnum is also displayed. A superb carved screen showing the Greek goddess of wisdom, Athena, came from the chamber of the Council of Indies, advisers to the governor-general. Amongst the other exhibits is a series of gloomy portraits of the Dutch governors-general, and early pictures of Batavia. The painting of Jan Peiterzoon Coen is one of the few reminders in the city of the founder of Batavia. Other rooms are dedicated to the Javanese painter Raden Saleh and Diponegoro.

In the courtyard at the back of the building there is a strange memorial stone to one Pieter Erbervelt, who was put to death on 22 April 1722 for allegedly conspiring to massacre the Dutch inhabitants of Batavia. Other displays here include Dutch stone tablets, old horse

Top :   Cannon Si Jagur, Taman Fatahillah, Kota (GB)
Middle : Jakarta History Museum, Kota (GB)
Bottom : Balai Seni Rupa (Fine Arts Museum), Kota (GB)

carriages and becaks. This quiet, pleasant courtyard was also the scene of the most gruesome event in the town hall's history. During the Chinese uprising of 1740, 500 Chinese held in the dungeons afterward were brought out and slaughtered one by one in the courtyard.

This museum is a rarity in Indonesia in that it preserves Indonesia's Dutch heritage, though exhibits are unlabelled and not always well presented. Plans are afoot for proper labelling, but until then it pays to take a guide. Many students, often speaking Dutch as well as English, offer their services and can shed some light on the displays, and a pamphlet on the museum is available. The museum is open every day except Monday, from 9 am to 4 pm Tuesday to Friday, until 1 pm Saturday and until 4 pm Sunday. Entry costs 150 rp, or 100 rp on Sunday and holidays.

Wayang Museum

Facing Taman Fatahillah to the west, this museum is housed in another good example of Dutch architecture and contains the best collection of wayang puppets in Indonesia.

Formerly the Museum of Old Batavia (1938-74), the building was constructed in 1912 on the site of the New Dutch Church of Batavia (1736-1808), which replaced the Old Reformed Church (1640-1732). Dandaels demolished the Dutch Church in 1808, after an earthquake had damaged the building. The present building is a typical early 20th-century Dutch residence.

The top floor and most of the bottom floor are devoted to wayang puppets. At the back courtyard, an inscrip-

Wayang Museum, Kota (GB)

tion on the wall denotes the site of the churches and remembers those buried in the graveyard, including Jan Pieterszoon Coen, founder of Batavia, and 18 of the Dutch governors-general. Excavations in 1938 uncovered Coen's grave, which was previously unknown. He died of cholera in 1629 during the siege of Mataram and was interred at this site in 1634. A number of tombstones are scattered along the wall opposite the inscriptions, including those of Governor-General van Imhoff and VOC officials and their families.

Puppets displayed are not only from Indonesia but also China, Vietnam, Malaysia, India and Cambodia. As well as the more familiar wayang kulit (leather puppets), wayang golek (three-dimensional wooden puppets) and wayang klitik (flat wooden puppets) are on display. Wayang topeng masks and wayang beber scrolls are also featured, and the museum holds musical instruments, historical documents, photographs and maps. One of the finest displays is the Khiyai Intan wayang kulit puppet encrusted with semi-precious stones.

Wayang golek or wayang kulit performances are held upstairs every Sunday from 10 am to 2 pm, and are well worth seeing.

Closed on Monday, the museum is open Tuesday to Thursday and Sunday from 9 am to 3 pm, on Friday until 11 am and Saturday until 1 pm. Entrance costs 150 rp, or 100 rp on Sunday and holidays.

Balai Seni Rupa (Fine Arts Museum)

Built between 1866 and 1870, the Palace of Justice building is now a museum housing a collection of contemporary Indonesian paintings, with works by Indonesia's most prominent painters, including Raden Saleh, Affandi and Ida Bagus Made. The museum also includes a large collection of Chinese ceramics and Majapahit terracottas.

The neo-classical building with its columns is a fine piece of architecture but the museum is run down.

Closed on Monday, the museum is open Tuesday to Thursday from 9 am to 4 pm, Friday until 11 am, Saturday until 1 pm and Sunday until 2 pm. Entrance costs 150 rp.

Cannon Si Jagur

This huge bronze cannon on the north side of Taman Fatahillah is adorned with a Latin inscription, *Ex me ipsa renata sum*, which means 'Out of myself I was reborn'. The cannon tapers at one end into a large clenched fist, with the thumb protruding between the index and middle fingers. This suggestive fist is a sexual symbol in Indonesia and childless women would offer flowers and sit astride the cannon in the hope of gaining children. Si Jagur is a Portuguese cannon brought to Batavia as a trophy of war after the fall of Malacca in 1641, but the Javanese, naturally, have a mystical story to tell.

The legend relates that a king of Sunda had a dream in which he heard the thundering sound of a strange weapon. He ordered his prime minister, Kyai Setomo, to find a similar weapon, threatening him with death if he failed. Kyai Setomo discussed his fateful task with his wife, Nyai Setomi, and they both did some meditation. Days passed and the king grew so impatient that he visited Kyai Setomo's home, only to discover that the couple had been transformed into two large cannons! Sultan Agung then heard about the great weapons and ordered them to be brought to his court at Mataram, but the male cannon, Kyai Setomo, refused to go. Instead he fled at night to Batavia, where he had to remain outside the locked gates of the city. The people of Batavia were of course quite surprised to find a cannon sitting at their gates and came to regard it as holy. They gave it a little paper umbrella as protection from the sun and calld it Kyai Jagur (Mr Fertility).

Gereja Sion

On Jalan Pangeran Jayakarta, near Kota railway station, this church dates from 1695 and is the oldest remaining church in Jakarta. Also known as Gereja Portugis or Portuguese Church, it was built just outside the old city walls for the so-called 'Black Portuguese' – the Eurasians and natives captured from Portuguese trading ports in India and Malaya and brought to Batavia as slaves. Most of these people were Catholics but they were given their freedom on the condition that they joined the Dutch Reformed Church, and the converts became known as the Mardijkers, or 'liberated ones'.

The exterior of the church is very plain, but inside there are copper chandeliers, the original organ and a baroque pulpit. Although in the year 1790 alone, more than 2000 people were buried in the graveyard here, very few tombs remain. One of the most interesting is the ornate bronze tombstone of Governor-General Zwaardecroon, who died in 1728 and, as was his wish, was buried among the 'ordinary' folk.

Top :   Chicken Market Bridge, Kota (GB)
Bottom : Gereja Sion, Kota (GB)

Kali Besar

The Kali Besar is the canal built along the Ciliwung River connecting the port to the old city of Batavia. It once thrived with commerce and boats shuttled goods to and from the port. In the 18th century, it was lined with houses of Batavia's rich and famous, and on the banks of the Ciliwung River overlooking the canal are the last of the big private homes dating from that era. Though some buildings are in need of renovation and the canal is dirty, this stretch of Dutch buildings is the most evocative of Batavia's early heyday, which peaked in the 1730s.

Top :   Kali Besar canal, Kota (GB)
Bottom :   Maintaining the pisini, Sunda Kelapa (GB)

Directly behind the Wayang Museum, along both sides of the canal, are some fine examples of Dutch architecture. The **Toko Merah**, or Red Shop, at Jalan Kalai Besar Barat 11, on the west side of the canal, was formerly the home of Governor-General van Imhoff. Now offices, the building originally comprised two grand homes (the one on the right was van Imhoff's); much of the furniture from the house was taken to Old Batavia Museum before being eventually transferred to the Jakarta History Museum.

Heading north along Kali Besar canal, at Jalan Nelayan Timor, is a small 17th-century Dutch draw-bridge, the last in the city, called the **Chicken Market Bridge**, or Hoenderpasarbrug as it was known in VOC days. Before silting of the river in the mid-18th century, the drawbridge allowed ships to sail farther upriver.

Farther north on Jalan Kakap, the river bank was used by the British before the Dutch founded Batavia. The VOC located their wharfs here and small **shipyards** were in operation until Daendels closed them in 1809. Adjoining the shipyards are the remains of 17th-century Dutch warehouses.

SUNDA KELAPA

Just a 10-minute walk north of Taman Fatahillah, the old port of Sunda Kelapa has more sailing ships, the mag-nificent Makassar schooners called *pinisi*, than you ever thought existed.

At the mouth of the Ciliwung River, Sunda Kelapa (*kelapa* means coconut) was a trading post of the Sundan-ese Pajajaran Empire from the 12th century. It was a minor port until the 16th century, when trade in the region expanded dramatically and European powers came to contest the spice trade. In 1522 Pajajaran signed a treaty with the Portuguese, and the Portuguese erected an inscribed stone, the Padrao stone, at Sunda Kelapa to commemorate the event. This stone was redis-covered in 1918 during excavations at the corner of Jalan Cengkeh and Jalan Nelayan Timur, over half a km south of the present harbour, and is now in the National Museum. The Portuguese were unable to gain a foot-hold at Sunda Kelapa, however, because the Muslim sultanate of Banten took Sunda Kelapa in 1527. The victorious commander, Fatahillah, renamed the city Jayakarta.

Both the Dutch and the English established trading settlements at Jayakarta in the early 17th century. The

British post was never extensive, though the Dutch built their post into a formidable fortress they called the Kasteel, which lay on the east side of the river near the entrance to the dock. In 1619, Jan Pieterzoon Coen took Sunda Kelapa and levelled the settlements outside the Kasteel. The town was renamed Batavia.

The city grew around the Kasteel, and thick walls built from 1634 on surrounded the city. Batavia grew in prominence and grandeur until its decline in the mid-17th century, when the canals that crossed the city became breeding grounds of disease and Europeans moved out and settled a new town to the south-east. From 1809 much of the crumbling, disease-ridden old city was demolished, including the Kasteel and the city walls. The port, however, remained the main artery of trade until the 1880s when the new port of Tanjung Priok was built farther along the coast.

The port is still used by the pinisi schooners. These brightly painted sailing ships are one of the finest sights in Jakarta. Pinisi are still an important means of transporting goods to and from the outer islands. Most of them come from Kalimantan, spending up to a week in port unloading timber and then reloading cement and other supplies for the return journey.

If you get out to the Thousand Islands (Pulau Seribu) in the Bay of Jakarta, you will probably see Makassar schooners under sail.

Entry to the dock is just around from the Museum Bahari and costs 200 rp.

Museum Bahari (Maritime Museum)

At the entrance to the Pasar Ikan, an old Dutch East India Company warehouse built in 1652 has been turned into a maritime museum. Here the Dutch stored their spices and other trade, and this building is the oldest and best preserved from the early boom trade times. Wander around downstairs and then head upstairs and out onto the city walls, which have been incorporated into the building. The historic sentry posts outside are the best preserved remains of the old city wall, which has all but disappeared.

The museum exhibits model craft from around Indonesia and has an interesting collection of old photographs recreating the voyage to Jakarta from Europe via Aden, Ceylon and Singapore. It is open every day except Monday, from 9 am to 3.30 pm Tuesday to Thursday, until 3 pm Friday and Sunday, and until noon Saturday. Admission is 150 rp (100 rp on Sunday).

Watchtower

Just before the entrance to the museum is the old Watchtower, back near the bridge. It was built in 1839 to sight and direct traffic to the port. The Watchtower is situated on the site occupied by the original British trading post, which was burnt in 1618 by the Dutch, whose fort was directly opposite on the other side of the river. In 1645 a bastion, part of the city walls, occupied the site. There are good views over the harbour from the Watchtower, but it is usually locked – if you find the caretaker he can unlock it for you.

Watchtower, Kota (GB)

Top :   Boat moored at Sunda Kelapa, Kota (GB)
Bottom : Shop front Pasar Ikan, Kota (GB)

Old Batavia & Sunda Kelapa Walking Tour

The logical place to start a walking tour of Old Batavia is at Taman Fatahillah, easily reached by bus or taxi from the central Jalan Thamrin area. Most of the attractions are around the square. Start with the **Jakarta History Museum** to get a feel for life in colonial times and then take in the **Wayang Museum** and the **Balai Seni Rupa**. On the north side of the square is the **Cannon Si Jagur** and the wonderful **Cafe Batavia**, which has been restored to its 1920s look and is an excellent place to stop for a meal or drink.

From Taman Fatahillah, head south towards the **Kota Railway Station**, in itself a good example of colonial architecture, and the **Gereja Sion**. Head back to the square and then across to **Kali Besar**. Go north along Kali Besar and admire its fine Dutch houses, such as the **Toko Merah** fish market, then continue to the **Chicken Market Bridge** and the **old shipyards** on Jalan Kakap. If the heat is too much you can always take a taxi or bajaj between some of these attractions for around 2000 rp. Or try Kota's unique transport – bicycles with padded kiddy seats on the back, an improvised becak now that the three wheelers have been banned from the city. You'll find them around Kali Besar and they can take you up towards Sunda Kelapa.

The **Museum Bahari** is a cool break from the heat, and when refreshed you can wander down past the **Pasar Ikan** fish market and explore this small, colourful market. Back towards the main road is the **Watchtower**, which is usually closed unless you can find the caretaker to unlock it for you.

Sunda Kelapa is then a short stroll away around the corner – the entrance is at the end of Jalan Krapu. Wander around and watch the loading and unloading of the old Bugis schooners. There is a small cafe for drinks at the dock. Old men will offer to take you in row boats around the schooners for about 3000 rp. Spend a good half-hour or so rowing around the schooners, avoiding decapitation by mooring ropes and gangplanks and occasionally having rubbish thrown on you from the ships. The boats can drop you off at **Luar Batang**, where you can see the mosque close to the waterfront. Tell your boatman to wait for you and he can take you back to Sunda Kelapa or drop you at Pasar Ikan.

Depending on how long you spend in the museums, this tour can take most of a morning or afternoon and is usually enough touring in one stretch for most people. From Sunda Kelapa it is a short taxi ride to Ancol and its attractions, or you can also take in Glodok to the south. If you want to take in the Glodok walking tour as well, it is best to start at Sunda Kelapa and do this tour in reverse. (See Glodok Tour in the following Glodok section.) ■

Pasar Ikan

Farther along the same street from the museum is the early-morning fish market, Pasar Ikan. Around dawn when the day's catch is sold it is an intense, colourful scene of busy crowds. Later in the day it sells household items and a growing collection of souvenirs.

Luar Batang

Across the small reach of the river north of Pasar Ikan is the kampung of Luar Batang, which has an historic mosque dating from 1739. The mosque contains the grave of an Arab missionary Said Husain Abu Bakar al-Aidrus, which attracts pilgrims. In Dutch times, Luar Batang was a Javanese fishing village, lying outside the city walls and *luar batang* (outside the main river). Boats hired from Sunda Kelapa can take you to Luar Batang.

GLODOK

After the Chinese massacre of 1740, the Dutch decided there would be no repetition and prohibited all Chinese from residing within the town walls, or even from being there after sundown. Glodok, just outside the city walls to the south-west, had long been settled by the Chinese and now became Jakarta's Chinatown, and the city's flourishing commercial centre.

Because of the ban on Chinese characters, Glodok is at first glance like any another busy market area in Indonesia and unlike any other Chinatown around the world. It is reluctant to overtly celebrate its Chinese identity, like the Chinese people who have to blend in as much as possible in the face of anti-Chinese sentiment in Indonesia.

Glodok is bound to the east by Jalan Gajah Mada, a wide road lined with offices, restaurants and modern shopping plazas. But if you walk in from Jalan Pancoran, opposite the Glodok Plaza, you'll find a small part of old Glodok still consists of winding lanes, narrow crooked houses with balconies, slanting red-tiled roofs and tiny obscure shops. This is a fascinating area to wander around and has one of the most interesting traditional markets, with numerous eating places and street hawkers.

Vihara Dharma Bhakti Temple

Just south of Jalan Pancoran is the Vihara Dharma Bhakti Temple, the oldest and most venerated in Jakarta. Built in 1650, it was the chief temple for the Chinese of Batavia

Top & Bottom : Vihara Dharma Bhakti Temple, Glodok (GB)

and was once known for its casino and Chinese wayang kulit. At present this is the largest Buddhist temple in Jakarta and was once also a Buddhist monastery. Though primarily Buddhist, like most Chinese temples it also has Taoist alters and honours various Chinese gods.

In the central courtyard, directly in front of the well-like incense burner, is the main, restored temple. One of the finest in Jakarta, it dates from 1650, though much of it was rebuilt after the Chinese massacre in 1740 and further restored in the 19th century. Always crowded, it fills with incense lit by shafts of light streaming in through the open-roofed section in the centre. The temple contains Buddhist and Taoist images, but Kuan Yin, the goddess of mercy and the most popular deity in South-East Asia, has prime place of importance at the back of the temple. The former monastic cells at the side of the temple also host images of various gods.

Shop front, Glodok (GB)

Glodok Walking Tour

The best place to start a walking tour is the **Pasar Glodok** building on the corner of Jalan Pancoran and Jalan Gajah Mada. This crowded Chinese market is built on two levels – the basement level is crammed with Chinese food stalls, with large sacks of birds' nests, sharks' fins and other Chinese delicacies. The upper level sells all sorts of goods, including batik. Chinese fortune tellers are also found here. From Pasar Glodok, a pedestrian bridge crosses Jalan Gajah Mada to more shops and the Glodok Plaza, a modern shopping mall noted for its electronics, but its shopkeepers are predominantly Chinese and it has a couple of interesting Chinese jewellery and furniture shops.

Emerge from Pasar Glodok on **Jalan Pancoran** past the food stalls and go down the street, where shops spill their goods onto the covered pavement. You can buy everything from gold to traditional Chinese medicine here. The north side of the street is a long string of fruit stalls, with the one of the best selections of seasonal and imported fruit in Jakarta.

From Jalan Pancoran turn left into **Jalan Kemenangan**. This narrow street is a canvas-covered fish market with oddities such as frogs and snakes for sale. Continue through the market and keep heading south until you reach the **Vihara Dharma Bhakti**, the most interesting temple in Glodok (see the entry at the beginning of the Glodok section).

From the southern temple entrance turn right into Jalan Kemangan III, a narrow road crammed with traffic and bajaj that carry local traffic and market shoppers. This road wends right and north past another small Chinese temple at No 48, the **Vihara Dharma Jaya Toasebio**, built in 1751. A little farther on where the street turns west is the **Gledek Medical Hall**, housing a traditional Chinese elixir company dating back to 1868. The building is like many in the area with a Chinese pitched roof, but the facade is a later art deco addition topped with a strange goblin/Garuda statue.

Jalan Kemangan leads to the Kali Krukul canal. Just before the small bridge, turn right down Jalan Petak Sembilan to take you back to Jalan Pancoran. At the bridge, pause to note the row of traditional **Chinese terraces** to the south on the other side of the canal, with tiled roofs and decorative tiles on their fronts – typical of Peranakan Chinese houses.

Just to the west of Jalan Pancoran, the Jalan Pekojan area used to be the Arab Quarter of Jakarta. It has some historic mosques and old houses, but it is a hot walk for relatively little reward. ■

HARMONI

If you're walking from Glodok back along Jalan Gajah Mada, it's worth pausing to have a glance at a couple of old Jakarta buildings along this street. The area south of Kota was known as Rijswijk in Dutch times when a fort was built outside the city walls in the rice paddies, hence the suburb's name, from *rijst* (rice) and *wijk* (area). The fort stood near the present site of the Pelni building before being relocated in 1729 to the corner with Jalan Veteran. Rijswijk became an area of fashionable shops in the 19th century, and the most famous club of the colony, Harmonie, was situated on the Jalan Maja Pahit/Jalan Medan Merdeka Utara corner. The club was torn down to make way for road construction in 1985.

Today Harmoni is a busy office and commercial district with plenty of traffic jams and a few shopping centres, like the big Gajah Mada Plaza. Little remains of its former atmosphere but two buildings are of note.

The **Candra Naya** at Jalan Gajah Mada 188 was once the home of the Chinese 'captain' employed by the Dutch to manage the affairs of Batavia's Chinese community. The building, dating from the 17th century, is one of Jakarta's best examples of Chinese architecture. Since 1946 the building has housed the offices of a social work society, but you may be able to have a short wander inside.

Farther south at No 111, the **National Archives building** (Arsip Nasional) dates from 1760 and was formerly the country house of Governor-General Reinier de Klerk. In the mid-18th century those who could afford to escape the diseased old city did so and settled outside the city walls.

MERDEKA SQUARE

Merdeka Square is the heart of the city, but a dead heart. The one-km square is a vast open stretch of grass dotted with a few trees, dominated by the National Monument, which towers from the centre of the park. Otherwise, it is poorly utilised and almost deserted apart from boys playing soccer, using the 'playing soccer forbidden' signs as goal posts, a few vendors, and itinerants catching a nap during the day. That said, it is at least a large, central area of open space in overdeveloped Jakarta, and stretched all around it are notable reminders of later Dutch rule, and the National Museum.

Merdeka Square began life as the Koningsplein when the new Dutch city of Weltervreden sprung up in the 18th century. The colonial inhabitants moved out of the old city and settled this leafy, healthier area to the south-west and the government administration followed. In the early 19th century, Koningsplein was a parade ground for the army, but as Weltevreden developed it became surrounded by important buildings. Though it was often classed as the centre of the colonial city, the real heart of Weltevreden grew up around Waterloo-plein (present-day Lapangan Banteng) just to the north-east of Merdeka Square. A walking tour around Lapangan Banteng takes in impressive reminders of the later colonial city.

National Monument (Monas)

This 132-metre-high column towering over Merdeka Square is both Jakarta's principal landmark and the most famous architectural extravagance of Soekarno. Commenced in 1961, the monument was not completed until 1975, when it was officially opened by Soeharto. This phallic symbol topped by a glittering flame symbolises the nation's independence and strength (and, some would argue, Soekarno's virility). Monas is constructed 'entirely of Italian marbles', according to a tourist brochure, and the flame is gilded with 35 kg of gold leaf.

In the base, the **National History Museum** tells the history of Indonesia's independence struggle in 48 dramatic dioramas. The depictions of numerous uprisings against the Dutch are overstated but interesting, Soekarno is barely mentioned and the events surrounding the 1965 Untung coup are a whitewash.

The highlight of a visit is to take the lift to the top, for dramatic, though rarely clear, views of Jakarta. Avoid Sunday and holidays, when the queues for the lift are long.

Monas is open weekdays from 8.30 am to 5 pm, and until 7 pm on weekends and holidays. Admission is 500 rp to the museum in the base, or 2000 rp for both the museum and a ride to the top of the monument.

National Museum

On the west side of Merdeka Square, the National Museum, built in 1862, is the best museum in Indonesia and one of the best in South-East Asia.

The museum has an enormous collection of cultural objects of the various ethnic groups – costumes, musical instruments, model houses and so on – and numerous fine bronzes from the Hindu-Javanese period, as well as many interesting stone pieces salvaged from Central Javanese and other temples. There's also a superb

Top : Istana Merdeka, near Merdeka Square (GB)
Middle : National Museum, west of Merdeka Square (GB)
Bottom : National Monument, Merdeka Square (GB)

display of Chinese ceramics dating back to the Han Dynasty (300 BC to 220 AD). One of the best places to start a tour of the museum is the Treasure Room upstairs from the entrance. The gold exhibits are interesting, but the real attraction is the air-conditioning if you have walked to the museum. Collections include:

Archaeology – a truly stunning display of stone sculptures from the early Hindu-Buddhist empires. Some of the finest sculptures from Indonesia's major archaeological sites are on display here. One of the reasons the collection is so good is that a lot of the best sculpture ended up in the Netherlands, but after ministrations by the Indonesian government some of it has been returned to the National Museum. Household implements, jewellery, religious artefacts etc are also on display, including a big collection of Majapahit bronzes and pottery.

Ethnography – the collection includes a huge ethnic map of Indonesia, examples of ethnic costumes and architecture, household items and musical instruments – in fact a bit of almost everything from fishing nets to knives. This is a wonderful display of Indonesia's ethnic diversity.

Foreign Ceramics – over 4000 pieces dating back to the Han period in China. The pottery comes from throughout Asia, stretching from China and Vietnam to Persia, and all of it was found in Indonesia, reflecting Indonesia's extensive early trade networks.

Geography – various early maps and assorted bits and pieces ranging from fossils to stuffed animals. A big relief map shows all those volcanoes you may wish to climb.

Historical Relics – includes furniture, household goods, weapons etc from the colonial period, including Portuguese, Dutch, English and Chinese exhibits.

Numismatics – coins from early empires and Chinese traders to the present.

Painting – the museum also has a collection of later painting, with the 19th-century Javanese painter and former Jakarta resident Raden Saleh well represented.

Prehistory – a wide display of fossils and implements dating back to Java Man. Early bronzes are on display, including bronze drums from the very early Dongson culture.

Just outside the museum is a bronze elephant which was presented by the King of Thailand in 1871; thus the museum building is popularly known as the Gedung Gajah, or Elephant House. In return for the elephant the Thai king was given loads of Borobudur statuary.

The museum is open from 8.30 am to 2.30 pm Tuesday to Thursday and Sunday, until 11 am on Friday and until 1.30 pm on Saturday. It's closed on Monday. Entry costs 200 rp, and a 1000 rp camera fee applies. It's well worth a visit, for here you will find something of relevance to almost anywhere you have been or will go in Indonesia.

The Ganesha Society offers excellent guided tours in English (free) on Tuesday, Wednesday and Thursday at 9.30 am, and the last Sunday of the month at 10.30 am. Tours are also conducted in French (9.30 am Wednesday), German (10 am Thursday) and Japanese (10 am Tuesday).

Taman Prasasti Museum

North-west of the National Museum, this museum, also known as the Park of Inscription, is on Jalan Tanah Abang. This was once the Kebon Jahe Cemetery and a number of important figures of the colonial era are buried here, including Olivia Raffles, wife of British Governor-General Sir Stamford Raffles, who died in 1814. The cemetery is open from 9 am to 3 pm Monday to Thursday, until 1 pm on Friday and until 2 pm on Saturday. It's closed on Sunday and holidays.

Lapangan Banteng

Just east of Merdeka Square in front of the Hotel Borobudur Inter-Continental, Lapangan Banteng (formerly the Waterlooplein) was laid out by the Dutch in the 19th century and the area has some of Jakarta's best colonial architecture.

The **Catholic Cathedral** with its twin spires was built in 1901 to replace an earlier church. Facing the cathedral is Jakarta's principal place of Muslim worship. The modernistic **Istiqlal Mosque**, a Soekarno-inspired construction that was finally completed in 1978, is one of the largest in South-East Asia.

To the east of Lapangan Banteng is the **Makmah Agung**, the Supreme Court built in 1848, and next door is the **Ministry of Finance building**, formerly the Witte Huis (White House). This grand government complex was built by Daendels in 1809 as the administration centre for the Dutch government.

To the west on Jalan Merdeka Timur is the **Emmanuel Church**, another classic, pillared building dating from 1893. Just east along Jalan Pejambon from the church is the **Gedung Pancasila**, an imposing neo-classical building built in 1830 as the Dutch army commander's residence. It later became the meeting hall of the Volksraad (People's Council) but is best known as the place where Soekarno made his famous Pancasila speech in 1945, laying the foundation for Indonesia's constitution.

Other Buildings

The **Istana Merdeka** (Independence Palace), or Presidential Palace, stands to the north of Monas. It was built in 1879 and was Soekarno's official residence during his reign, but Soeharto has not lived in it. It holds special significance in the struggle for independence. On 27 December 1949, the Dutch flag was lowered for the last time and the red-and-white flag of independent Indonesia was raised. Hundreds of thousands of Indonesians gathered to witness the event and chant 'Merdeka' (Freedom). Every 17 August, Independence Day is celebrated with a flag-raising ceremony in front of Istana Merdeka when the President hands over the flag.

Istiqlal Mosque, near Merdeka Square (GB)

Behind Istana Merdeka facing Jalan Veteran, the older **Istana Negara** dates from the end of the 18th century and was the country house of J A van Braam. The colonial government bought the house in 1820 and it came the city residence of the governors-general, who by then were based in Buitenzorg (present-day Bogor). This fine two-storey mansion was surrounded by extensive gardens and had good views across the Koningsplein. The later Istana Merdeka was built when the Istana Negara became too small.

Other impressive buildings ring Merdeka Square on Jalan Medan Merdeka Barat and Jalan Medan Merdeka Selatan.

Emmanuel Church, east of Merdeka Square (GB)

Merdeka Square Walking Tour

Starting at the National Museum, you should head across to **Monas** and take the lift to the top for spectacular views of Jakarta. This is the place to get your bearings on Jakarta. Look south to the skyscrapers of post-independence Jakarta and north to the old city of Kota. In every direction the city sprawls in a haze to the horizon.

From Monas head across to the elevated Gambir railway station, facing the **Emmanuel Church**. Cross Jalan Medan Merdeka Timur (not always easy – otherwise a pedestrian bridge is a few hundred metres north of the station) and head along Jalan Pejambon to the **Gedung Pancasila**. You are now behind the Hotel Borobudur Inter-Continental, where you can take a drink or snack in the hotel. The hotel has some interesting, outrageously expensive antique/art shops.

The hotel faces **Lapangan Bateng**, the grassed square that was a fashionable strolling area in colonial times. In the centre is the enormous, tacky **Free Irian Monument**, commemorating Indonesia's takeover of Irian Jaya in 1963. The statue of a man breaking his chains was built when Soekarno's anti-imperialist rhetoric was at fever pitch. In colonial times a large pillar commemorated Waterloo and was a topped by the Dutch lion standing on an Edam cheese. It looked more like a dog and was known as 'Coen's Dog'. The statue was torn down by the Japanese, though probably not for reasons of good taste.

To the east of the square are the **Makmah Agung** and **Ministry of Finance building**, while to the north is the **Catholic Cathedral**, with its spires and massive organ inside. From here you can head across to the **Istiqlal Mosque** – visitors must remove their shoes and be conservatively dressed. It is best to visit outside prayer times.

From the mosque you can head east to the **Istana Merdeka** and **Istana Negara**, or an interesting side trip is to the Pasar Baru area to the north-east.

Head up past the post office and along to the **Gedung Kesenian**. Originally erected by Raffles, this theatre was built in 1814 but was replaced by a more substantial classical building in 1821 after the Dutch returned. It became the centre for high-brow entertainment from Dutch times right through to the present.

From the theatre cross the road (a pedestrian bridge is nearby) and take the small bridge across the canal to Pasar Baru. ■

PASAR BARU

This quiet precinct just north of the post office is almost free of traffic and is pleasant to wander around for shopping or to visit the quiet backstreets for a few sights of interest.

Pasar Baru itself is a paved pedestrian mall and one of Jakarta's more attractive shopping streets. It is a mixture of old and new, lined with slightly more upmarket shops, mostly clothes and shoe shops. The area is always active and has a traditional market as well as a multistorey shopping mall.

While on Pasar Baru, take a look at **Toko Kompak** at No 20, an old-fashioned shop selling nothing in particular. This magnificent building is a mixture of Dutch and Chinese styles with a cavernous roof, upper balconies and stained glass.

Pasar Baru is Jakarta's Indian area, and 5000 of Indonesia's 30,000 Indian community live here. Though not overwhelmingly Indian in character, a wander around the streets will take you to a **Sikh Temple** at Jalan Pasar Baru Timur 10, and on Jalan Pasar Baru Selatan are the **Gandhi Memorial School** and the **Sai Baba Centre**.

Also of note is the **Gereja Ayam** (Chicken Church) on Jalan Haji Samanhudi, an early 20th-century Dutch Reformed church.

TANAH ABANG

The busy market district of Tanah Abang lies about one km west of Jalan Thamrin. The large **Pasar Tanah Abang** is primarily a textile market but various bits and pieces are also on sale. Cloth is sold by the roll and the market is a favourite with Muslims for *peci* (Muslim caps), prayer mats, cheap clothes and other religious paraphernalia.

The **Textile Museum** is housed in a Dutch colonial house on Jalan Satsuit Tubun 4, a few hundred metres west of the market near the Tanah Abang railway station. It has a large collection of batiks and woven cloth from all over Indonesia, as well as looms and batik-making tools, and it's well worth a visit. This museum is open daily (except Monday) from 9 am until 4 pm Tuesday to Thursday, until 11.30 am on Friday, 1 pm on Saturday and 3 pm on Sunday. Admission cost is 150 rp.

JALAN THAMRIN

Jalan Thamrin is the most touristed street in the city. The street itself is designed for skyscrapers and cars, making it one of the most boring streets in Jakarta to walk down. But for many visitors Jalan Thamrin is one of the first ports of call because it has many of the luxury hotels and the tourist office for getting bearings, or visitors simply shop and browse in the welcome air-conditioning of the Sarinah department store and the Plaza Indonesia.

Jalan Thamrin starts at the south-west corner of Merdeka Square. On the roundabout is the **Arjuna Statue**, a tasteful classical statue compared with

Catholic Cathedral, near Lapangan Banteng (GB)

Soekarno's statuary dotted around the city. This scene from the Hindu epic, the *Mahabarata*, depicts Arjuna and Krishna going into battle astride a garuda chariot pulled by a team of horses.

On the corner of Jalan Wahid Hasyim is the **Jakarta Theatre** building, which houses the tourist office, and directly opposite is the **Sarinah department store**, inspired by Soekarno and named after his nursemaid. The 3rd floor is the place to browse for batik and handicrafts, and in the same building is Indonesia's first McDonald's and the new Hard Rock Cafe.

Farther down the street is the **Welcome Statue** in the middle of the fountain roundabout. This is the focus of Soekarno's Jakarta and was built for the Asian games in 1962 – the statue of two enthusiastic young Indonesians wave to visitors. The **Hotel Indonesia** on the roundabout was the pride of Jakarta, the city's first international hotel, and the **Plaza Indonesia** underneath the newer Hyatt hotel is Jakarta's ritziest shopping centre with a host of designer label shops, a supermarket and a good food centre on the top floor.

M H Thamrin

Mohammad Husni Thamrin, whose name graces Jakarta's most well-known street, was a rarity among Orang Betawi in that he received a modern education and went on to a position of importance in colonial Batavia. The son of a district official, he received a Dutch education and spoke fluent Dutch. He moved in colonial circles and had many Dutch friends, which helped him to establish a profitable real-estate business.

Thamrin became a Batavian councillor in 1919 and became active in the nationalist movement. He was prominent in the Kaum Betawi, formed in 1923 to promote the Orang Betawi and then was elected to the Volksraad in 1931. He was also involved in organisations formed by Soekarno and in 1935 joined the Parindra nationalist party.

Thamrin was the only nationalist leader from Batavia and died in 1941, after being arrested by the colonial government for alleged treasonous dealings with the Japanese. ■

MENTENG

Originally plantation land, Menteng was purchased by the city council in 1908 to make a planned, elite suburb. Spurred by development in the 1920s, it became a leafy colonial enclave of large bungalows and mansions. Conservation regulations protect many of the bungalows that make Menteng one of the most desirable pieces of

Menteng Walking Tour

You can do a pleasant tour of Menteng taking in the atmosphere of the suburb, interesting shopping and a couple of museums.

Start on Jalan Thamrin at the Welcome Statue and head down Jalan Imam Bonjol past the British Embassy. Turn left into Jalan Agus Salim, then immediately right into Jalan Pekalongan. At No 12 A is the **Jakarta Handicraft Centre**, an air-conditioned showroom featuring batik, jewellery and clothes. The selection and prices are generally not as good as nearby Sarinah department store, but worth a look.

From here on if walking does not appeal, you can take a *helicak*, one of the motorised becaks that hang out on Jalan Pekalongan. These unique vehicles have a two-wheeled passenger car mounted at the front of a motorbike. They are banned from the main roads and only drive the backstreets of Menteng – negotiate a price.

Head along the quiet residential backstreets of Jalan Pekalongan and Jalan Panarukan, which leads to the **Menteng shopping centre**. This trendy row of shops and restaurants on Jalan Cokroaminoto is a good place to browse. Batik Keris has a large collection of batik in its department store at No 87-89, and the large Menteng Plaza houses a number of shops.

Just south of the shopping centre, stroll down Jalan Besuki to the **Taman Suropati**, a village green surrounded by mansions. This area is a preservation zone for the colonial bungalows with art deco touches that flourished in Java in the 1920s. The park itself is a surprising patch of greenery amongst the traffic. It is dotted with modern statuary, and an art market sets up here with painters displaying their wares.

Across from Taman Proklamasi is the **Museum Permusan**, an imposing mansion that witnessed historic events as Indonesia proclaimed its independence at the end of WW II. This was the home of the Japanese naval commander Tadashi Maeda, where on 16 August 1945, Soekarno and Hatta composed the proclamation that was to be announced the following day. A brief message to the world, the proclamation was forced by the hand real estate in Jakarta. This is an old money suburb right in the centre of Jakarta, populated by many ambassadors and top-ranking government officials. Menteng Kecamatan extends up to Jalan Kebon Sirih and includes Cikini, but Menteng proper is the area around the fashionable Menteng shopping centre on Jalan Cokroaminoto, between Jalan Imam Bonjol and the canal to the north.

of youth groups, notably the Menteng 31 Asrama, whose members kidnapped Soekarno and Hatta until they agreed to a plan to declare independence. The final draft was worked out with the assistance of Admiral Maeda, who had always been sympathetic to the independence movement and helped the assumption of independence as the Japanese waited to surrender to Allied forces.

The museum features the meeting room of those present that night, but the best reason to come here is to wander around this large mansion. It is open every day except Sunday, from 8.30 am to 2.30 pm Monday to Thursday, until 11 am on Friday and 1.30 pm on Saturday.

From the museum, cross back to the park and head east down Jalan Diponegoro (or Jalan Syamsurizal, one street north, is quieter) to the **Adam Malik Museum** at Jalan Diponegoro 29, once the home of the former vice-president and foreign minister. This museum is crammed with Malik's private collection of Indonesian wood carvings, sculpture and textiles, a huge display of mostly Chinese ceramics and even Russian icons from when he was ambassador to Moscow. Wander around the house, another superb Dutch villa, and poke into his bedroom and even his bathroom, still much as he left it in 1984. This excellent museum is open from 9 am to 3 pm every day except Monday. Entry is 1000 rp.

From the Adam Malik Museum it is a short walk to the **Jalan Surabaya Antique Market**, a colourful string of stalls selling brassware, wood carvings, kris, some furniture – a bit of everything from around Indonesia. Arrive at a quiet time and see instant patina being applied to the 'antiques'. Most of the wares are churned out for the tourist trade and first asking prices can be outrageous, but some good pieces can be found if you pick through the many stalls and bargain hard.

South-west from Jalan Surabaya, Indonesia's independence was proclaimed at **Taman Proklamasi**, on the site of the former home of Soekarno at Jalan Proklamasi 56. A monument to President Soekarno and Vice-President Hatta marks the spot. ■

Top : A kampung near Jalan Jaksa (GB)
Bottom : Sculpture, Taman Surpati, Menteng (GB)

Top :   Free Irian Monument, Lapangan Banteng (GB)
Bottom : Vendor in a kampung near Jalan Jaksa (GB)

CIKINI

Bordering Menteng, Cikini is another later residential area that has lost its shine but still has some points of interest. Along Jalan Cikini Raya and parallel to Jalan Soeroso/Cik Ditiro are many of Jakarta's mid-range hotels. If you are in the area around breakfast time, start the day with the excellent value 4000 rp buffet breakfast at the Hotel Marcopolo. For dinner, at the other end of the scale in price and opulence is the Oasis Restaurant, housed in a Dutch villa and specialising in traditional *rijsttafel*, the Dutch 'rice table' version of Indonesian food served with many side dishes.

Kampungs

Jakarta's kampungs – the crowded city 'villages' that are home to millions of Jakarta's residents – have seen major improvements over the years. Over the last 20 years basic amenities have been provided to many of the kampungs, and the appalling conditions that shocked visitors in the 1960s and 1970s have been greatly alleviated. Though they are poor neighbourhoods, most kampungs are not the shantytown slums that visitors associate with the term, but are collections of simple dwellings with the amenities of any other village around the country: mosques, shops, schools, community associations etc. The real packing-case slums are now rare and well away from the centre of the city. Even many of the poorer kampungs are now paved.

Kampungs are found all over Jakarta, but right in the city centre a glimpse at the kampungs can be seen around Jalan Jaksa. Running off Jalan Jaksa's strip of backpackers' hostels and eateries, small alleyways lead through the Kebon Sirih kampung crammed with houses, neighbourhood shops and eating houses. The Kebon Sirih kampung is certainly not rock-bottom poverty, situated as it is on prime real estate, and many of the houses and shanties are being cleared as Jalan Jaksa goes more upmarket and becomes the bona fide tourist centre of Jakarta. Other large, central kampungs can be found around Pasar Baru and Tanah Abang.

To visit a kampung it pays to be able to speak some Indonesian, or ask an Indonesian friend to take you. Kampungs have a definite community feel to them, and as always in Indonesia hardship is tolerated with good humour, and a remarkable resilience and capacity to survive. Visitors are treated with great hospitality and interest, and to visit a kampung is to experience the Jakarta as lived by the majority of its residents. ■

Opposite the Oasis Restaurant on Raden Saleh is the **Cikini Hospital**, once the magnificent home of the Javanese painter Raden Saleh (1814-80). European educated, he went to the Netherlands to study art in 1829 and became Indonesia's most famous painter in the courts of Europe. He returned to Indonesia and settled in Jakarta in 1852, building his gothic-style mansion that would later become this hospital.

Around the corner on Jalan Cikini Raya, the **Taman Ismail Marzuki** (TIM) (☎ 322606) is Jakarta's cultural showcase, housing a number of theatres and an exhibition hall with rotating art and photographic exhibitions. There is a performance almost every night and you might see anything from Balinese dancing to poetry readings, gamelan concerts to overseas jazz groups or an Indonesian PKI film to a New Zealand film festival. The TIM monthly programme is available from the tourist office, the TIM office and major hotels, and events are also listed in the *Jakarta Post*. At the back of TIM is the Institute Kesenian Jakarta, one of the country's premier arts training institutes, with departments of drama, music, dance, fine arts and cinema. You may happen across some theatre or dance practice.

Jakarta's **Planetarium** is also housed at TIM, but shows are generally given in Indonesian. For information about shows in English, phone (☎ 337530). The whole TIM complex is open from morning until midnight, and there are good outdoor cafes here. The No 34 bus from Jalan Thamrin stops nearby.

Farther north is the **Museum Joang 45** at Jalan Menteng Raya 31, dedicated to the Menteng 31 Asrama, which figured so prominently in the independence movement. The asramas were youth groups set up by the Japanese for military training but they soon became the focus for those with independence aspirations. The Menteng 31 group was instrumental in forcing the declaration of independence and its members included Adam Malik and Chairul Anwar.

Housed in a neo-classical building are various exhibits relating to the independence movement and the key figures that played a role. The museum is open every day except Sunday, from 8.30 am to 4 pm Monday to Thursday, until 2.30 pm on Friday and 12.30 pm on Saturday.

At the southern end of Jalan Cikini Raya is the **Pasar Cikini**, a lively market featuring all sorts of household goods, fruit and vegetables. The gold market upstairs sells gold jewellery (always a cherished investment) by weight.

Top :   Taman Proklamasi, Cikini (GB)
Bottom :   Statue at TIM complex, Cikini (GB)

TAMAN MINI INDONESIA INDAH

In the south-east of the city, near Kampung Rambutan, Taman Mini is another of those 'whole country in one park' collections popular in Asia. The idea for the park was conceived by Mme Tien Soeharto, and in 1971 the families inhabiting the land were cleared out to make way for the project (then estimated to cost the awesome total of US$26 million) and the park was duly opened in 1975. The contentious project drew widespread criticism, though what seemed destined to become a tacky extravagance proved to be an impressive showcase of the archipelago and is Jakarta's most visited attraction.

This 100-hectare park has 27 full-scale traditional houses from the 27 provinces of Indonesia, with displays of regional handicrafts and clothing, and a large 'lagoon' where you can row around the islands of the archipelago or take a cable car across for a bird's eye view. There are also museums, theatres, restaurants, an orchid garden and a bird park with a huge walk-in aviary and attached museum. There's even a mini Borobudur. The park is good value and Indonesians will tell you that if you see this there's no need to go anywhere else in the country!

Other attractions include 'Indonesia Indah', a three-dimensional screen show of the Indonesian panorama which takes place at the **Keong Mas** (Golden Snail) Theatre, so called because of its shape. The theatre has the world's largest screen at 29.3 x 21.5 metres, according to the *Guinness Book of Records*. In 30 minutes the film packs a lot into a special effects travelogue. Admission is 2000 rp and screenings are from noon to 4 pm Monday to Friday, and 10 am to 5 pm Sunday. On Saturday an imported film screens.

You can walk or drive your own car around Taman Mini. Or go by horse and cart, or take the mini train service that shuttles around the park or the cable car that goes from one end to the other. The park is open from 8 am to 5 pm daily, the houses and Museum Indonesia are open from 9 am to 4 pm. Admission is 2000 rp (children 1000 rp). On Sunday mornings, there are free cultural performances in most regional houses from 10 am to 2 pm. Special cultural events from all over the country are also staged on Saturday nights from April to November. Check the Taman Mini monthly programme available from the Visitors Information Centre.

Taman Mini is about 18 km from the city centre; allow about 1½ hours to get there and at least three hours to look around. Take any bus to Kampung Rambutan terminal and then a T55 metro-mini to the park entrance. A taxi will cost around 12,000 rp from central Jakarta.

Museums

Taman Mini is a fertile hunting ground for museums, both within the park and just outside it. There's a **Stamp Museum** (Museum Prangko), **Museum Fauna**, **Oil & Gas Museum** (Museum Graha Widya Patra), **Sports Museum** (Museum Olah Raga), **Police Museum** (Museum Kepolisian) or the **Soldier's Museum** (Museum Preprajuritan), which is a Camelot-style building featuring warriors from around Indonesia. Two of the more interesting museums are the **Museum Asmat**, containing an excellent collection of woodcarvings from the famed Irian Jaya tribe, and the **Museum Indonesia**, the most important museum in the park with costumes and ethnographic exhibits from all over the country.

The **Museum Purna Bhakti Pertiwi**, before the main gate to Taman Mini, is the most impressive architecturally. Museum Soeharto would be a more apt name as the exhibits come from the Soeharto holdings, mostly gifts from foreign governments presented to the president and his wife over the years. It is certainly a varied collection, perhaps too varied, with everything from French glassware to paintings of the Soeharto family, all housed in an opulent, futuristic building. The 1st level is crammed with bits of everything – the magnificent jade bed is the pick of the diplomatic gifts. The highlight of the museum is the superb collection of Indonesian textiles on the 2nd floor. It is open from 9 am to 5 pm every day but is closed on the 2nd and 4th Monday of the month. Entry is 2000 rp.

LUBANG BUAYA

In the early hours of 1 October 1965, six generals and an army officer were taken from their Jakarta homes in an attempted communist coup and executed here at Lubang Buaya (meaning 'Crocodile Hole'). Indonesians flock to look down into a hole where the bodies lay, and view the large **Pancasila Sakti** memorial and museum dedicated to the generals. Highlights of the museum include the diorama showing the torture of the generals by the communists. Most famous of the generals is General Ahmad Yani, who may otherwise have passed into obscurity but has become a martyr under Soeharto's government. His name graces the streets of every city in Indonesia. This curious piece of pit tourism is one of the most visited memorials in Jakarta, while many of the more important independence monuments are largely ignored.

Lubang Buaya, just off Jalan Pondok Gede Raya, about one km north of Taman Mini, is open Tuesday to Sunday from 9 am to 4 pm.

TAMAN IMPIAN JAYA ANCOL

Along the bay front between Kota and Tanjung Priok, the people's 'Dreamland' is built on land reclaimed in 1962. This huge landscaped recreation park has hotels, nightclubs, theatres and a variety of sporting facilities. Ancol's main attractions are the Pasar Seni and Dunia Fantasi.

The **Pasar Seni** art market is a collection of stalls selling arts and crafts, and as it was designed as an artist's gallery you can see many of the craftspeople at work. A number of good painters work here and you can buy crafts from all over Indonesia. It also has sidewalk cafes and a gallery where there are often interesting exhibitions of modern Indonesian art and photography. On Friday and Saturday nights, live music is performed at the open stage. The Pasar Seni is very quiet during the day and gets most visitors in the cooler evenings during the week or on crowded Sunday.

Near the Pasar Seni, there's an **oceanarium** (*gelanggang samudra*) and an amazing **swimming pool complex** (*gelanggang renung*), including a wave pool and slide pool. The Ancol beach, so close to the city, is not the greatest place for a swim but you can take a boat from the marina here for day trips to some of Jakarta's Pulau Seribu islands.

The big drawing card at Ancol is **Dunia Fantasi** (Fantasy World), a fun park that must have raised eyebrows at the Disney legal department. Resemblances to Disneyland start at the 'main street' entrance, and the Puppet Castle is a straight 'it's a small world' replica. But the Indonesian influence prevails – Western World is the old west complete with a 'rumah jahil' for miscreants and a Sate Corner snack bar. Dunia Fantasi is actually very well done and great for kids, with a host of fun rides. It is open daily, on Monday to Saturday from 2 to 9 pm, Sunday and holidays from 10 am to 9 pm. Standard entry is 6000 rp, or including all rides it is 13,000 rp during the week, 14,000 rp on Saturday and 16,000 rp on Sunday and holidays.

Basic admission to Ancol is 800 rp during the week and 1000 rp on Saturday, Sunday and holidays (half price for children). The Pasar Seni is open from 9 am to 10 pm daily, and the swimming pool complex from 7 am to 9 pm daily. The oceanarium costs 6000 rp during the week and 8000 rp on weekends. The pool costs 2500 rp,

Top :   Keong Mas (Golden Snail) Theatre,
        Taman Mini Indonesia Indah (GB)

3000 rp on weekends and the slides are extra. Apart from
initial entry, discounts for children are virtually non-
existent at all Ancol attractions.

The park can be very crowded on weekends, but on
weekdays it's fairly quiet and a great place to escape
from the hassles of the city. From the Kota bus station
you can get there on a No 64 or 65 bus or an M15 minibus.
For more information, call ☎ 681511 in Jakarta.

RAGUNAN ZOO

Jakarta's Ragunan Zoo is about 10 km south of the city
centre in the Pasar Minggu area. The zoo has komodo
dragons, orang-utans, Sumatran tigers and a good collection of other Indonesian wildlife, as well as elephant
rides and horse-cart rides for the children. It's large and
spacious but the animal enclosures are not always well
kept and the landscaping consists of half-hearted
attempts to replace jungle with grass. It's open daily
from 7 am to 6 pm. Admission is 1000 rp, half-price for
children.

KEBAYORAN BARU

Kebayoran Baru is the start of the wealthy southern
suburbs and half a day can easily be spent wandering
around the Blok M shopping precinct. The bird market
(Pasar Burung) is also worth a visit.

Kebayoran Baru is approached by heading down
Jalan Jenderal Sudirman, which ends at the **Semangat
Pemuda Statue**. Representing the 'spirit of youth', the
muscular young man holding a flaming dish above his
head is commonly known as the 'Pizza Man' by Jakarta's
expatriate residents.

Start a tour of Blok M at the **Blok M Mall**, which has
a host of everyday shops and a good selection of food
stalls. It is right at the bus terminal if arriving by bus, or
take a taxi to Jalan S Hasanuddin and get dropped off at
the entrance to Blok M.

Across from the mall is the **Pasar Raya Big & Beautiful**,
a department store in the same mould as Sarinah with an
equally large selection of batik and Indonesian handicrafts.

Bird Market (Pasar Barung), Kebayoran Baru (GB)

Just north of the bus station is **Jalan Palatehan 1**, a small street with a few interesting antique shops. The street also has some well-known bars – Blok M is noted for its nightlife. Food stalls set up in the evening and the bars keep going for much of the night. Many bars are seedy hangouts crawling with bar girls, and for more nighttime lowlife there are also karaoke bars around Jalan Melawai 6, which are pitched at Japanese and Korean businessmen.

Across Jalan Panglima Polim is the **Blok M Plaza**, a multistorey shopping mall with more upmarket shopping possibilities.

If not exhausted from shopping, about half a km to the west is the colourful **Pasar Burung** bird market on Jalan Barito, where caged song birds and other animals are for sale.

About two km south-east of Blok M is **Kemang**, a fashionable residential area. The small shopping centre on Jalan Kemang has a few restaurants, a couple of hotels and Kem Chicks Supermarket, an expat favourite with goodies from all over the world. Also in Kemang are various antique shops, a couple of km farther south on Jalan Kemang Selatan.

OTHER ATTRACTIONS

Pasar Pramuka

To the east of the city centre on Jalan Pramuka is Jakarta's main bird market for captive birds from all over Indonesia. Wander around this dark covered market, which has an astonishing array of song birds, and bird cages are on sale to match the birds – tall pointy cages for tall birds, squat ones for short birds. Rare birds can fetch a small fortune. Other animals are also on sale, and you may well be offered a squirrel or civet cat.

Orchids

Jakarta has a number of gardens specialising in cultivating orchids. The **Taman Anggrek Indonesia Permai**, just north of Taman Mini, is the best place to see them and has hundreds of varieties. Entry is 1000 rp.

Other Museums

The **ABRI Satriamandala Armed Forces Museum**, on Jalan Gatot Subroto, has an enormous display of weapons and endless dioramas glorifying the Indonesian armed forces in their battles for independence. It's open from 9 am to 4 pm daily except Monday, and admission is 200 rp.

The **Museum Kebangkitan Nasional** (National Awakening Museum) is housed in the STOVIA medical school, where one of the first Indonesian national organisations, the Budi Utomo, was formed in 1908. It is at Jalan Dr Abdul Rahman Saleh 26, near Pasar Senen. It is closed on Monday.

The **Museum Mohammed Husni Thamrin** is dedicated to one of Jakarta's most famous sons. Thamrin was a leading Jakarta citizen and businessman, and was on the Batavia city council in colonial times. His former house at Jalan Kenari II No 15, across the Ciliwung River from Cikini, is now a museum, open Monday to Friday from 8 am to 5 pm and Saturday until noon.

The **Sasmitaloka Pahlawan Revolusi**, or the General A Yani Museum, Jalan Lembang D-58, is yet another memorial to the general murdered in the 1965 communist coup. His house in Menteng is now a museum, open every day except Monday from 9 am to 3 pm.

SPORTS

Many of the large hotels have fitness centres and pools, and some have tennis and squash courts. The Hotel Borobudur Inter-Continental is well set up for sports, as is the Hilton with its spacious grounds and jogging track. The Aryaduta, the Hyatt and Le Meridien also have tennis, squash and fitness centres. Ancol has a wide range of sporting facilities, and the Senayan Sports Complex, near the Hilton Hotel on Jalan Jenderal Sudirman, is the city's premier sports centre.

Bowling

Good venues for 10-pin bowling are the Jaya Ancol Bowl at Ancol, the Bowling Centre at the Kartika Chandra Hotel on Jalan Gatot Subroto, and the Kebayoran Bowling Centre, Jalan Melawai IX, in Blok M. These are well-equipped bowling alleys where all equipment can be hired and rates are very reasonable.

Diving

Indonesia has some superb diving sites, though those close to the city are not among the country's best. Nonetheless, Pulau Seribu is a popular diving destination close to Jakarta, and the west coast of Java also has some diving opportunities (see the Excursions chapter later in this book).

Good dive shops offering tours and renting equipment are: Divemasters (☎ 570 3600 ext 9006) and Jakarta Dive School (☎ 570 3600 ext 9008), both in the Indonesia Bazaar at the Hilton Hotel, and Stingray Dive Centre, in the Manggala Wanabakti building, Jalan Gatot Subroto.

Golf

No developing country in Asia can hold its head up in the international community unless it has a surplus of golf links. Jakarta is no exception and has some good courses, many designed by well-known pros.

Jakarta Golf Club (☎ 4891208), Jalan Rawamangun Muka Raya, is the city's oldest course, once the Batavia Golf Club. It is for members only, but has reciprocal rights with other clubs around the world.

Ancol has an attractive 18-hole golf course down by the sea. Jaya Ancol Golf Club (☎ 681511) is open to the public and a round costs 25,000 rp.

The Pondok Indah Golf & Country Club (☎ 748906), Jalan Metro, Kebayoran Baru, is one of the country's most prestigious and difficult courses, and is the site for international tournaments. Greens fees start at 150,000 rp.

Close to the city centre, the Senayan Golf Club (☎ 5710181) is at Jalan Asia Africa Pintu 9, near the Senayan stadium. It is an 18-hole course open to the public. Nearby, closer to the Hilton Hotel, is the Senayan Driving Range (☎ 5703063) on Jalan Pintu V.

Halim Golf Club (☎ 8080697), Jalan Skwadron, has two courses near the Halim airport, and the Fatmawati Golf Course (☎ 769867) is a nine-hole course closer to the city centre at Cilandek Barat.

Horse Riding

Jakarta has a few riding clubs, though most are for private members. Horses can be hired at the Djakarta International Saddle Club (☎ 798066), Jalan Warung Buncit Raya, Mampang Prapatan.

Swimming & Water Sports

If you are just after a swim, most of the hotels also let nonguests use the facilities. The Hotel Indonesia has a large pool costing 7500 rp for nonguests.

Ancol has a beach, of sorts, but the best place to swim is at Ancol's impressive swimming pool complex, which includes a wave pool. The Senayan Sports Complex also has an Olympic-size swimming pool, built for the ASEAN games back in the '60s.

Ancol is also the best spot for other water sports such as windsurfing and skiing, or the resorts of Pulau Seribu also have good facilities. The Horizon Hotel at Ancol rents windsurfers.

Tennis

The best place for playing tennis is at the hotels, and many will rent to nonguests on an hourly basis. The Senayan Sports Complex has a number of courts but they are usually booked weeks in advance.

Places to Stay

Jakarta is the most expensive city in Indonesia for hotels, though by world standards rooms are still moderately priced. The traditionally high rates of the top-end hotels are easing, while at the other end of the scale, a cheap bed can always be found in Jalan Jaksa, the centre for backpackers' hostels.

Accommodation can be tight in Jakarta in peak periods, but with so many new luxury hotels the squeeze is mostly at the bottom-end and mid-range hotels. The peak tourist season is August, when Jalan Jaksa can be almost full, but there are so many places that a room is always available somewhere. The better value mid-range hotels tend to fill up quickly and bookings are advisable.

Like most hotels in Indonesia, bargaining is possible when business is quiet. Rather than aggressive haggling, the trick is to enquire about discounts. Most luxury and mid-range hotels have excessive published rates and readily offer substantial discounts. The cheap hotels are less likely to give a reduction. As a general rule, if a hotel quotes its rates in US$ then a discount is probably available.

If arriving by air, hotel reservation counters at the airport offer discounted rates for many of Jakarta's hotels. These cover the top end and mid-range, though the cheapest hotel on their lists is the Djody Hotel.

PLACES TO STAY – BOTTOM END

Jalan Jaksa

One upon a time, so the story goes, a backpacker arrived at Jakarta's Gambir railway station and wandered off looking for a hotel, without success. He chanced down Jalan Jaksa, where a family took pity on him and gave him a bed for the night. The word spread and soon other backpackers started arriving at the house, so the family decided to open a hostel. Other guesthouses followed and now Jalan Jaksa is a lively strip of cheap hotels and restaurants, conveniently central near Jakarta's main drag, Jalan Thamrin, and only a 10 to 15-minute walk from Gambir railway station.

Wisma Delima, at Jalan Jaksa 5, was the original guesthouse and for long the only cheap place to stay. In fact, No 5 would actually be referred to as 'Jalan Jaksa' and as a consequence it was often hopelessly crowded and totally chaotic. Now, there are lots of alternatives and Wisma Delima is still popular but quieter. Dorm beds are 5500 rp (5000 rp for HI members), or small but spotless doubles are 12,000 rp. You can also get food and cold drinks here, and it has good travel information.

Moving down Jalan Jaksa from No 5, the *Norbek (Noordwijk) Hostel* (☎ 330392) is across the street at No 14 and has rooms at 9000/12,000 rp, most for around 12,000 to 15,000 rp, and up to 30,000 rp for its 'honeymoon' suite with fridge and air-con. It's a dark rabbit warren, but many of the rooms are air-conditioned. It is one of those places which likes to have lists of rules posted on every vertical surface.

Nick's Corner Hostel (☎ 336754) at No 16 advertises itself as the 'cleanest' in town, and it's hard to disagree. It's a mini version of the Hyatt – all mock granite and fresh paint – and a dorm bed costs 7500 rp in immaculate, if somewhat cramped, eight and 12-bed air-con dorms. Good doubles are 30,000 rp and 35,000 rp or 45,000 rp and 65,000 rp with bathroom. Breakfast is included.

Continue down the street to the *Djody Hostel* at Jalan Jaksa 27. This is another old standby with dorm beds for 7500 rp, and double rooms from 22,000 to 30,000 rp, but it is getting overpriced. A few doors farther up is the related *Djody Hotel* (☎ 332368) at No 35, where rooms without bath cost 15,000 rp and 20,000 rp. Rooms with bath and air-con cost 45,000 rp and 60,000 rp.

The *International Tator Hostel* (☎ 325124, 323940), Jalan Jaksa 37, is a small place and a notch above most of the others in quality. Rooms start at 17,500 rp with bath up to 35,000 rp with air-con, but renovations and extensions are planned.

More places can be found in the small streets running off Jalan Jaksa. Gang 1 is a small alley connecting Jalan Jaksa to Jalan Kebon Sirih Timur (running east off Jalan Jaksa). A short distance down are two small places: the *Kresna Homestay* (☎ 325403) at No 175 and the *Bloem Steen Homestay* right next door at No 173. They're a bit cramped but popular and good value for Jakarta. Rooms at these quiet places are 12,000 rp or 18,000 rp with bath at the Kresna or the Bloem Steen has singles/doubles for 9000/12,000 rp or larger rooms for 15,000 rp.

At Kebon Sirih Barat 35, running west off Jalan Jaksa, *Borneo Hostel* (☎ 320095) packs them in and has a lively cafe, despite the mediocre food. The dorm beds at 5000 rp are about the cheapest around. The rooms for 15,000 to 20,000 rp are well kept but no bargain. Still, it's popular, well run and friendly. Avoid the annexe next door, which is under different management – it's boring and the rooms are badly in need of maintenance.

There are more places dotted along this lane, such as the similarly priced *Bintang Kejora* (☎ 323878) at No 52, which has a small cafe and very clean rooms for 15,000/20,000 rp. Farther down, there's the *Hostel Rita* with rooms from 9000 rp, *Pondok Wisata Kebon Sirih* at No 16 with doubles for 12,000 rp and the *Pondok Wisata Jaya Hostel* at No 10, but these are less popular with travellers.

If you walk along Jalan Wahid Hasyim, at the southern end of Jalan Jaksa, and keep going across Jalan Thamrin, you'll come to the *Wisma Ise Guest House* (☎ 333463) at No 168. It has single/double rooms for 9900/15,400 rp, and some rooms with bath for 25,000 rp or with air-con for 35,000 rp. The basic rooms are fairly spartan but it's a clean and friendly place, and there's a pleasant balcony bar at the back where you can look out over Jakarta.

Other

Apart from Wisma Delima, Jakarta has other youth hostels popular with local school groups and university students, but they tend to be a long way from the city centre. The best and most convenient is the *Graha Wisata Mahasiswa* (☎ 516922), Jalan Rasuna Said, about four km south of Jalan Thamrin in Kuningan. Good dormitory accommodation costs 7500 rp (2500 rp for students) in six-bed dorms. Twin-bed, air-con rooms are about the best deal in Jakarta and cost 15,000 rp per person (7500 rp for students). The hostel has a cafeteria and sports facilities. To get there take bus P11 or 407 from Gambir railway station.

PLACES TO STAY – MIDDLE

Jalan Jaksa

Each year new hotels are being built and old ones renovated in the Jalan Jaksa area, pushing it slowly more upmarket. These middle-bracket hotels all charge 21% tax and service on top of the rates, but discounts of around 20% are readily available.

The *Hotel Karya* (☎ 320484), Jalan Jaksa 32-34, is undergoing big renovations but in the interim its older rooms cost US$35 and US$55. They are worn but comfortable enough with hot water, TV and telephone.

Jalan Wahid Hasyim has better hotels that are popular with local business people. They all have coffee shops

Plaza Indonesia & Hyatt Hotel, near Welcome Statue round-about, Menteng (GB)

and air-con rooms with hot water, minibar and TV. The *Cipta Hotel* (☎ 3904701) at No 61 is right at the southern end of Jalan Jaksa. Rooms for US$59 and US$66 are unexceptional for the price. The new *Arcadia Hotel* (☎ 2300050) at No 114 has a lobby with impressive modern decor and a pleasant coffee shop/bar. The rooms for US$69 and US$78 are very comfortable but quite small.

The best hotel on Jalan Wahid Hasyam is the *Cemara Hotel* (☎ 324417), on the corner with Jalan Cemara. The rooms and service are very good, and it is competitively priced with rooms for US$60 and US$70.

The larger *Sabang Metropolitan Hotel* (☎ 373933), Jalan H A Salim 11, is looking a little old but rooms have all the facilities; it has a swimming pool and it's in a good location. Rooms cost from US$60 to US$90.

Cikini

The Cikini area, east of Jalan Thamrin and close to the TIM Cultural Centre, has a selection of mid-range hotels and some good guesthouses.

The *Gondia Guest House* (☎ 3909221), Jalan Gondia Kecil 22, is in a quite side street off Jalan R P Soeroso. Comfortable air-con rooms around small garden areas cost 86,000 rp, including breakfast. It has a pleasant, homey atmosphere. Bookings are advisable.

Around the corner at Jalan Gondangdia Lama 28, the *Hotel Menteng I* (☎ 325208) is popular with Indonesian businesspeople. Rooms with TV, fridge and hot water showers start at 104,000/117,000 rp. Right next to the bar/restaurant is a tiny swimming pool where you are guaranteed a crowd of onlookers. Part of the same chain, the *Hotel Menteng II* (☎ 325543), Jalan Cikini Raya 105, is not quite as good and costs 115,000/127,000 rp. The other, more expensive, Menteng is the *Grand Menteng* (☎ 882153), farther south at Jalan Matraman Raya 21.

The big *Hotel Marcopolo* (☎ 325409) at Jalan Teuku Cik Ditiro 19 is better value than most in this range. Air-con rooms with fridge, TV and hot water cost 129,000 rp, single or double. The hotel has a good swimming pool and a reasonably priced restaurant with excellent buffet breakfasts for only 4000 rp.

Another good and very popular guesthouse near the TIM Cultural Centre is the *Yannie International Guest House* (☎ 3140012), Jalan Raden Saleh Raya 35. Spotless, bright rooms with air-con and hot water cost US$32/35, including American breakfast. It is good value for Jakarta and consequently often full. If so, try the *Karya II Hotel* (☎ 325078) next door at No 37. Comfortable air-con rooms range from 55,000 to 88,000 rp. Downstairs rooms are dark – the best value are the upstairs rooms with hot water, TV and phone for 66,000 rp.

At the top of this range are the three-star Sofyan hotels: the new *Sofyan Hotel Betawi* (☎ 3905011), Jalan Cut Mutiah 9, just east of Jalan Jaksa, and the *Sofyan Hotel Cikini* (☎ 3140695), Jalan Cikini Raya 79. The Betawi has well-furnished, classy rooms from US$59/85, but the singles are very small. The Cikini is slightly better value with rooms from US$57/69. A 21% tax and service charge is added, but a similarly sized discount is often available.

Other Areas

Kemang is a popular expat area, about nine km south of the city centre. It is too far out for most visitors, but the hotels here are worth considering if you have business in South Jakarta.

Close to Kem Chicks supermarket and popular with expats, the three-star *Garden Hotel* (☎ 7995808), Jalan Kemang Raya, is an older hotel with spacious grounds, a swimming pool and popular restaurants and bars. This good business hotel has rooms ranging from US$59/69 to US$161. A few small, always full apartments cost US$1500 per month. Nearby, the *Kemang Hotel* (☎ 7993208), Jalan Kemang Raya 2H, has an attractive swimming pool and rooms for US$68/76 but it's a dark, dull hotel. The large, new wing under construction should provide better accommodation.

A little closer to town, Kebayoran Baru has a few hotels. In the thick of things in Blok M, the *Interhouse Hotel* (☎ 716669), Jalan Melawai Raya 17-20, pitches itself to business clients on a budget. The rooms are getting a little old, but are comfortable and have air-con, fridge, TV and telephone. Rooms range from US$54 to US$93.

Of course Jakarta has hotels scattered all over town, most of which are isolated or too far off the beaten track to contemplate. For something different, you could stay in Pasar Baru, which is still close to the city centre in an area that has its own local character. *Hotel Pasar Baru* (☎ 3450280), Jalan Pasar Baru Selatan 6, is a well-run hotel north of the post office with fairly spartan but comfortable rooms from 63,000 to 100,000 rp. The air-con rooms are very clean and have hot water, TV and phone.

The Soekarno-Hatta Airport is such a distance from Jakarta's city centre that some travellers with flights in the wee, small hours of the morning might consider lodging at the nearby *Cengkareng Transit Hotel* (☎ 6191964), Jalan Jurumudi (Km 2.5 marker). Note that although it's just opposite the runways, it takes a while to reach the hotel by road. Basic air-con rooms cost from 65,000 rp and there is a 24-hour coffee house on the premises.

PLACES TO STAY – TOP END

City Centre

Most of the 'international-class' hotels are in the city centre, on or around the main boulevard of Jalan Thamrin. The Hotel Indonesia, built for the Asian Games which Jakarta hosted in 1962, heralded a new era for

Hotel List

The following hotel rates are the published rates before discount. Star classifications are given (with ✦✦✦✦✦ being the highest classification), though these don't always accurately reflect the quality of the hotel. An 11% service charge and 10% tax is added to the room rates.

Aryaduta Hotel (☎ 3861234; fax 380990), Jalan Prapatan 44-48. ✦✦✦✦✦ Pool, restaurants, shops, entertainment, business centre, health club, squash, tennis, conference facilities. Rooms US$180 to US$210. Suites US$230 to US$1350.

Borobudur Inter-Continental Jakarta (☎ 3804444; fax 3805555), Jalan Lapangan Banteng Selatan. ✦✦✦✦✦ Pool, restaurants, shops, entertainment, business centre, health club, squash, tennis, conference facilities. Rooms US$190 to US$200. Suites US$310 to US$750.

Citraland Hotel (☎ 5660640; fax 5681616), Jalan S Parman. ★★★★ Pool, restaurants, shops, entertainment, business centre, health club, conference facilities. Rooms US$110.

Dai-Ichi Hotel (☎ 3442828; fax 3442929), Jalan Senen Raya 135. ★★★★ Pool, restaurants, shops, entertainment, business centre, health club, conference facilities. Rooms US$160 to US$240. Suites US$400 and US$1200.

Grand Hyatt Jakarta (☎ 3901234; fax 3906426), Jalan Thamrin. ✦✦✦✦✦ Pool, restaurants, shops, entertainment, business centre, health club, squash, tennis, conference facilities. Rooms US$265 and US$295. Suites US$530 to US$5000.

Hilton Hotel (☎ 5703600; fax 5733089), Jalan Gatot Subroto. ✦✦✦✦✦ Pool, restaurants, shops, entertainment, business centre, health club, squash, tennis, conference facilities. Rooms US$180/200 to US$220/235. Suites US$310 to US$2000.

Hotel Atlet Century Park (☎ 5712041; fax 5712191), Jalan Pintu Satu Senayan. ★★★ Pool, restaurants, entertainment, business centre, health club, tennis, conference facilities. Rooms US$95/105 to US$130/140. Suites US$200 to US$500.

Hotel Horison (☎ 680008; fax 684044), Jalan Pantai Indah, Taman Impian Jaya Ancol. ★★★★ Pool, restaurants, entertainment, business centre, health club, tennis, conference facilities. Rooms US$135/145 to US$167/187. Suites US$325 to US$1300.

Hotel Indonesia (☎ 3140008; fax 3141508), Jalan Thamrin. ★★★★★ Pool, restaurants, shops, entertainment, business centre, health club, tennis, conference facilities. Rooms US$130/140 to US$150/160. Suites US$300 to US$800.

Hotel Kartika Plaza (☎ 3141008; fax 3905301), Jalan Thamrin 10. ★★★ Pool, restaurants, tennis, conference facilities. Rooms US$95/105 to US$125/135. Suites US$200.

Jayakarta Tower Hotel (☎ 6293000; fax 6295000), Jalan Hayam Wuruk 126. ★★★★ Pool, restaurants, entertainment, business centre, health club, conference facilities. Rooms US$85/95 to US$130/140. Suites US$145 to US$500.

Le Meridien Jakarta (☎ 5711414; fax 5711633), Jalan Jenderal Sudirman Kav 18-20. ★★★★★ Pool, restaurants, entertainment, business centre, health club, squash, tennis, conference facilities. Rooms US$180 to US$275. Suites US$300 to US$1500.

Mandarin Oriental Jakarta (☎ 3141307; fax 3148680), Jalan Thamrin. ★★★★★ Pool, restaurants, entertainment, business centre, health club, tennis, conference facilities. Rooms US$180 to US$235. Suites US$480 to US$1500.

President Hotel (☎ 2301122; fax 3143631), Jalan Thamrin 59. ★★★★ Pool, restaurants, entertainment, conference facilities. Rooms US$132/155 to US$215. Suites US$400 and US$480.

Putri Duyung Cottage (☎ 680108; fax 683614), Jalan Lodan Timur, Taman Impian Jaya Ancol. ★★★ Pool, restaurants, tennis, conference facilities. Rooms US$95 to US$175. Suites US$160 to US$600.

Sahid Jaya Hotel (☎ 5704444; fax 5733168), Jalan Jenderal Sudirman 86. ★★★★★ Pool, restaurants, entertainment, business centre, health club, tennis, conference facilities. Rooms US$170. Suites US$190 to US$3000.

Sari Pan Pacific Hotel (☎ 323707; fax 323650), Jalan Thamrin. ★★★★ Pool, restaurants, entertainment, business centre, health club, conference facilities. Rooms US$155/170 to US$185/200. Suites US$225 to US$1000.

Shangri-La Hotel (☎ 5707440; fax 5703531), Jalan Jenderal Sudirman Kav 1. ★★★★★ Pool, restaurants, entertainment, business centre, health club, tennis, conference facilities. Rooms US$220/250 to US$270/300. Suites US$380 to US$1800.

hotel development in Indonesia – at 14 storeys it was the first 'skyscraper' in the archipelago and it was to be the largest, most modern hotel in South-East Asia. A number of luxury hotels with superb facilities followed, spurred on in part by the boom that has brought troops of business travellers to the capital.

A hotel building boom in the early '90s has seen an easing of the staggeringly steep prices at Jakarta's luxury hotels. Occupancy rates are higher in Jakarta than in some of the tourist areas in Indonesia, but substantial discounts of 20% to 50% are on offer at Jakarta's hotels. More new hotels are being built, which could result in further discounting. New hotels due to come online are the Imperial Century Hotel and Holiday Inn, and the Regent may finally open its doors one day. 'Soft opening' rates (the Indonesian term for introductory offers) should be very competitive. Others are planned, including an airport Sheraton.

Most, but not all, hotels readily offer discounts for walk-in customers, usually around 20% if you ask, but this may increase if it looks like you will walk out the door. Other hotels have 'packages' that offer discounted rooms, including breakfast and sometimes free laundry, local telephone calls, cocktails etc, though these may be limited to weekends or for Indonesian residents only.

If arriving by air, hotel booking counters at Jakarta airport have a big list of hotels at the current discount rates. Travel agents in Jakarta and elsewhere also offer some of the best discounts. If booking by phone or fax, contact the sales departments of the hotel and enquire about discounts, packages or corporate rates – whichever phrase brings the biggest reduction.

The main centre for luxury hotels is the Welcome Statue roundabout on Jalan Thamrin. The Hotel Indonesia, Hyatt, Mandarin and President are all on the roundabout, and nearby on Jalan Thamrin are the Kartika Plaza and the Sari Pan Pacific. The main advantage of these hotels is that you can walk to many of the shopping centres and restaurants. Other hotels can be found farther south in the business district (but you'll need to catch a lot of taxis), and another hotel enclave is around the Banteng Square area to the north-east of the centre of the city.

The *Hotel Indonesia* is the first of Indonesia's international hotels and in the '60s was the refuge for foreigners surrounded by the turmoil of Soekarno's 'year of living dangerously'. It certainly has history and some nice '60s touches, like the mosaic mural in the main restaurant, but it is looking a little tired and the service in this government-run hotel is not always up to standard. Nonetheless, it has all the facilities, including a huge swimming pool, and the regularly offered big discounts make it a good buy.

Also on the Welcome Statue roundabout, the *Hyatt* is widely considered to be the capital's best and is favoured by many visiting dignitaries and VIPs. It is right on top of the Plaza Indonesia shopping centre and certainly has the best position in town, along with luxury rooms, a large, attractive swimming pool and almost as many tennis courts as Wimbledon.

Diagonally across from the Hyatt, the *Mandarin Oriental Jakarta* has no grounds but it is an excellent business hotel and the well-furnished rooms have good extras. The nearby *President Hotel* is a smaller and more old-fashioned looking hotel. The rooms are on the small side, especially the singles.

Just south from the welcome statue, the *Hotel Kartika Plaza* is also an older hotel without the gloss of its neighbours, but it has large rooms with balconies and a good pool. Substantial discounts often apply, making it a good deal.

The *Hotel Sari Pan Pacific* is conveniently located on Jalan Thamrin around the corner from the Jakarta Theatre building. It's popular for good service and good food, and the rooms are reasonably priced.

More hotels can be found heading south down Jalan Thamrin, which runs into Jalan Jenderal Sudirman. Just off Jalan Thamrin, one of the newest and most opulent hotels is the *Shangri-La Hotel*, with its impressive lobby of granite, glass and gold. Good service and excellent rooms with luxurious bathrooms make it one of the best hotels in Jakarta.

The *Sahid Jaya Hotel* on Jalan Jenderal Sudirman is a rambling hotel that seems to be designed around its conference facilities rather than the guests. The rooms are nothing special but the suites are better and the hotel has some good restaurants.

Farther south, *Le Meridien* is up there with the best. The rooms have nice touches and extras. Deluxe rooms are good, but the executive rooms with separate, walled sitting areas are worth the extra price.

The *Hilton Hotel* is at the bottom corner of the 'Golden Triangle' business district. It has large grounds and gardens, attractive decor and a good range of facilities, including a host of restaurants and bars.

Near the Hilton and the Jakarta Hilton Convention Centre, the *Hotel Atlet Century Park* is a three-star hotel, but it has good facilities and well-appointed rooms, and for the price it is a good alternative to some of the four and five-star hotels.

Around Jakarta

To the north-east of the city centre near Monas, the *Hotel Borobudur Inter-Continental* is one of the older generation of luxury hotels but is still one of the best. Copies of friezes from Borobudur, intricate wood-carved panels and antiques put it in a class of its own. For health freaks, it has an Olympic-size swimming pool, a jogging track, tennis and squash courts. Rooms have tasteful furniture and many have raised desk/office areas.

Near the Borobudur, the *Aryaduta Hotel* is hard to fault. This good business-class hotel has all the trimmings. Like many hotels it has a 'regency club', which for around US$20 more you get a room on the executive floors with extra trimmings like free local calls, discounted laundry and breakfast in the business lounge with spectacular views of the city.

Popular with Japanese and Singaporean visitors, the new *Dai-Ichi Hotel* in the busy Pasar Senen area certainly has good shopping in the nearby market and malls. It has very good rooms, excellent fitness facilities and an odd pool that looks like a Balinese car park.

Jayakarta Tower Hotel is in the bustling Chinatown district close to Kota. It is getting old and on a definite rung below the best, but the rooms are large, comfortable and very good value after the readily available big discounts are applied.

Farther north, *Hotel Horison* is the place to get away from it all. It is on the beach in Ancol, removed from the bustle of Jakarta, and close to Kota, Sunda Kelapa and Ancol's attractions, but is a long trip throughout the traffic jams to the city centre. Also by the water at Ancol, *Putri Duyung Cottage* is pitched at the holiday market with good sports facilities. Eclectically styled bungalows arranged around the garden are comfortable and quiet.

If you have business in West Jakarta, or want to be near the airport, the new *Citraland Hotel* is just off the toll road between the city centre and Soekarno-Hatta airport. The hotel sits on top of the huge Citraland Mall, which has plenty of shopping and eating possibilities.

LONG-TERM ACCOMMODATION

Jakarta house and apartment rentals are high for quality accommodation, which will cost from US$1000 per month to US$5000 or more depending on the size of the dwelling and position. The favoured areas for expatriate workers are the southern suburbs such as Kemang and Pondok Indah, where many properties are palatial houses with three or more bedrooms, large gardens and swimming pools. Such houses typically start at around US$2500 per month. Leases are long term, usually two years minimum, and rent is required in advance.

Perhaps as a hangover from Dutch times, employees of foreign companies are expected to have large numbers of servants. Most foreign companies and embassies that transfer staff to Jakarta include house, servants and car with driver as part of the conditions of employment. Essential reading for finding a house or apartment in Jakarta is *Introducing Indonesia: a Guide to Expatriate Living* by the American Women's Association.

Serviced apartments are becoming more popular, and new apartment blocks are springing up all over the city. Some require long leases, though some will rent on a per month basis. For your money you get the amenities of a hotel, laundry facilities and car parking, and the apartments will be suites with separate bedroom, small kitchens and a living/dining room. The cheaper places have essential furniture and cooking utensils, but are fairly bare.

The *Hilton Residence*, next to the Hilton Hotel, is an expat favourite, both with newcomers looking for a house, and long termers who prefer a sheltered existence. Two-bedroom apartments start at US$4500 per month or three-bedroom apartments cost from US$5000 per month. Leases start at six months. The *Hotel Borobudur Inter-Continental* also has one and two-bedroom serviced apartments in their Garden wing, starting at US$2000 for two weeks, less for longer rentals. Other popular apartment and town-house complexes include *Pondok Club Villas*, *Kemang Club Villas* and *Palm Court*.

Budget medium to long-term rental is difficult to find, and the hotels and guesthouses are the easiest option. Rooms for rent in a share house are sometimes advertised in the *Jakarta Post*.

Places to Eat

Jakarta has the best selection of dining possibilities of any major Indonesian city. They range from street food and air-conditioned food centres in the shopping malls to very chic and expensive restaurants in one of the many large hotels. In between are a lot of good moderately priced restaurants that represent the best value for a quality meal.

WHERE TO EAT

Food can be found all over Jakarta but there are concentrated areas of restaurants convenient to the main hotel areas where you can wander along the street and choose among a host of dining establishments.

Jalan Jaksa is the backpackers' centre, with a string of ultra cheap and convivial cafes serving a mixture of European and Indonesian food. One block west is **Jalan H A Salim** (still known by its old name of Jalan Sabang), famed for its sate and also crammed with budget and moderately priced restaurants. This whole block is a hive of new restaurant and hotel activity, and more restaurants can be found on Jalan Kebon Sirih and particularly Jalan Wahid Hasyim, at either end of Jalan Jaksa.

Jalan Thamrin is the centre of Jakarta for many visitors and has no shortage of eateries. The Jakarta Theatre building, Sarinah department store, Plaza Indonesia and any of the big hotels on this stretch have a number of well-known dining possibilities to suit most tastes and budgets.

About half a km east of the Welcome Statue roundabout on Jalan Cokroaminoto is the **Menteng shopping centre**, centred around Menteng Plaza. This chic shopping stretch has a number of very good restaurants for a moderately priced meal. Menteng has Indonesian, Chinese, Japanese, Thai, seafood and steak restaurants.

About five km south of Jalan Thamrin, Kebayoran Baru is a fashionable residential district centred around the **Blok M** shopping centre, which has plenty of choices from cheap street food to fine dining establishments. This is a popular area for Jakarta's expatriate community, as is **Kemang**, a couple of km to the south-east. A number of restaurants can also be found stretched out along Jalan Kemang, most of them close to the Kem Chicks supermarket.

The **Golden Triangle** business district to the south of Jalan Thamrin also has dozens of restaurants in the big hotels or tucked away in the office towers, though these are spread out over a few km. **Jalan Jenderal Sudirman**, the southern continuation of Jalan Thamrin, has plenty of moderate to expensive restaurants, and a few possibilities can be found on Jalan Rasuna Said and Jalan Gatot Subroto.

Other recommended restaurants can be found to the north of the city centre, along **Jalan Gajah Mada** heading towards the historic Kota district, and in **Pasar Baru** just to the north of the post office. Along Jalan Gajah Mada are numerous restaurants, bakeries, fast-food eateries and ice-cream parlours. Of course, the large hotels all have a selection of dining possibilities and house some of Jakarta's best restaurants.

CHEAP EATS

Jalan Jaksa

Jalan Jaksa's cafes are convivial meeting places dishing out the standard travellers' menu. They are certainly cheap and the breakfasts are very good value. Food is quasi-European or bland Indonesian, and coffee is never served with sugar, contrary to normal Indonesian practice. The cheapest eats on Jalan Jaksa are in the *warungs* (cheap restaurants) at the northern end and in the side alleys towards Jalan H A Salim, but some look remarkably dirty.

Topping the popularity polls on Jalan Jaksa is the *Asmat Cafe* at No 16-18, next to Nick's Corner Hotel. The food is only average, but people come here for the lively atmosphere, video movies in the evening and the disco at the back of the cafe.

On the opposite side of Jalan Jaksa, the *Anedja Cafe* at No 25 is a small place serving so-so Indian dishes and some Indonesian fare at moderate prices. *Angie's Cafe* at No 15 is another popular cafe, good for cheap Western breakfasts and fruit salads. Indonesian dishes are particularly bland here. *Memories Cafe* on the same stretch is similar. Many of the hostels, such as Borneo, also have their own cafes.

Romance Bar & Restaurant, Jalan Jaksa 40, is the fanciest restaurant in the street with air-conditioning and a small bar. The menu is a varied hodgepodge, including Mexican dishes, pasta and pizza for around 5000 rp, and while not outstanding, it is reasonably priced and a pleasant place to dine.

Top : Street stalls, Blok M (GB)
Bottom : Oasis restaurant, Cikini (GB)

Top :   Street vendors, Blok M (GB)
Bottom :   Cafe Batavia, Taman Fatahillah, Kota (GB)

Indonesian Food

Food in Indonesia – particularly meat dishes – is generally Chinese influenced, although there are a number of purely Indonesian dishes. Pork is not widely used since it is regarded by Muslims as unclean, but it appears in Chinese dishes. Javanese cooking uses fresh spices and a mixture of ingredients, the chilli mellowed by the use of sugar in many dishes. Sumatran cooking, on the other hand, blends fresh and dry spices to flavour the main ingredient.

Rice is the basis of the meal, with an assortment of side dishes, some hot (with chilli) and spicy, and some just spicy. Many dishes are much like soup, the water being used to moisten the large quantity of rice eaten. *Sambal* (a spicy relish) and *acar* (pickles) are common accompaniments. Many dishes are cooked in *santan*, the liquid obtained when grated coconut is squeezed. Other common ingredients are *terasi* (shrimp paste), *serai* (lemon grass) and *kecap* (soy sauce). *Bumbu* is a combination of pounded ingredients used to flavour a dish.

Some Indonesian dishes and important food words are:

ayam – chicken; *ayam goreng* is fried chicken

babi – pork
bakmi – rice-flour noodles, either fried *(bakmi goreng)* or in soup
bakso or *ba'so* – meatball soup
bubur ayam – Indonesian rice porridge with chicken

cap cai – Chinese fried vegetables (usually pronounced 'chop chai')
cumi cumi – squid

daging – meat

fu yung hai – a sort of sweet & sour omelette

gado-gado – another very popular Indonesian dish of steamed bean sprouts, various vegetables and a spicy peanut sauce
garam – salt
gula – sugar
gulai/gule – thick curried-meat broth with coconut milk

ikan – fish

kacang – peanuts or beans
kare – curry; as in *kare udang* (prawn curry)
kepiting – crab; features in quite a few dishes, mostly of Chinese origin

krupuk – shrimp crackers
kueh – cake

lontong – rice steamed in a banana leaf
lumpia – spring rolls; small pancake filled with shrimp and bean sprouts and fried

martabak – a popular street snack. A martabak is basically a pancake – and is either savoury or very sweet.
mie goreng – fried wheat-flour noodles, served sometimes with vegetables, sometimes with meat
mie kuah – noodle soup
mentega – butter

nasi campur – steamed rice topped with a little bit of everything – some vegetables, some meat, a bit of fish, a krupuk or two
nasi goreng – This is the most common of Indonesian dishes. Nasi goreng simply means fried (goreng) rice (nasi) – a basic nasi goreng may be little more than fried rice with a few scraps of vegetable to give it some flavour, but sometimes it includes some meat.
nasi gudeg – unripe jackfruit cooked in santan and served up with rice, pieces of chicken and spices
nasi Padang – Padang food, from the Padang region of Sumatra. It's usually served cold and consists of the inevitable rice, with a whole variety of side dishes
nasi pecel – similar to gado-gado, with boiled papaya leaves, tapioca, bean sprouts, string beans, fried soybean cake, fresh cucumber, coconut shavings and peanut sauce
nasi putih – white (putih) rice – usually steamed
nasi rames – rice with a combination of egg, vegetables, fish or meat
nasi rawon – rice with spicy hot beef soup, fried onions and spicy sauce

opor ayam – chicken cooked in coconut milk

pisang goreng – fried banana fritters; a popular streetside snack

roti – bread. The stuff you get in Indonesia is nearly always snow white and sweet.

sate – small pieces of various types of meat on a skewer served with a spicy peanut sauce; one of the best known of Indonesian dishes

---

sop – clear soup with mixed vegetables and meat or
    chicken
soto – meat and vegetable broth, often a main meal eaten
    with rice

tahu – tofu, or soybean curd; soft bean cake made from
    soybean milk
tempe – made of whole soybeans fermented into cake
telur – egg

udang – prawns or shrimps

Jalan H A Salim (Sabang)

The next street west of Jalan Jaksa has a string of cheap
to mid-range restaurants. Though Jalan Sabang was
renamed Jalan H A Salim years ago, everyone still knows
it as Jalan Sabang.

Though nasi goreng (fried rice) is the national dish,
Indonesia is best known for its sate, small morsels of
meat threaded on a skewer, charcoal grilled and served
with a peanut sauce. Goat meat is usual, though chicken,
mutton, various entrails or even snake can find their way
on to a sate skewer. Originally from Madura, sate is
found throughout Indonesia and on Java, Jalan Sabang
is famed as the sate capital of Indonesia. Dozens of sate
hawkers set up on the street in the evening and the
pungent smoke from their charcoal braziers fills the
air. Most business is takeaway, but benches are scattered along the street if you want to sit down and eat
there.

For standard Chinese fare, the *Lim Thiam Kie* at No 49
has air-con but the pretensions to being a fancy restaurant stop there. Most dishes are in the 5000 to 10,000 rp
range. Down a little alley close to the A&W is the *Paradiso
2001*, an interesting little Chinese vegetarian restaurant.
The restaurant is nothing fancy but the food is tasty,
healthy and cheap. It also serves good fruit juices. The
Kaharu at No 45 is a more upmarket Chinese restaurant
with hot plates, grills and fish dishes as well as the usual
lengthy Chinese menu.

Western-style fast food is also in evidence. The *Sizzler*
chain has hit Jakarta for expensive steaks and an all-you-
can-eat salad bar. Or you can try Japanese fast food at
Hoka Hoka Bento a few doors down. *KFC* and *A&W* also
have branches on Sabang, while *Sakura Anpan* is a Japanese bakery for cakes and pastries.

Jalan Thamrin

The *Sarinah* department store has a very good, if fairly expensive, food-stall area in the basement next to the supermarket. Try the excellent soto Betawi – thick coconut-based soup, a Jakarta speciality. Sarinah is also home to Indonesia's first *McDonald's* and the more expensive *Hard Rock Cafe* for grills. Across the road in the Jakarta Theatre building, there's a *California Fried Chicken* joint as well as a *Pizza Hut*.

Farther down Jalan Thamrin at the Welcome Statue roundabout, Plaza Indonesia under the Hyatt is the fanciest shopping mall in Jakarta. The *Happy Times Food Court* on the top floor is a salubrious, Singapore-style hawker's centre with a range of international food stalls. Excellent Indonesian, Chinese, Thai, Singaporean and Japanese dishes as well as pizza, French pastries and Western fast food can be enjoyed for around 5000 rp. Plaza Indonesia also has an abundance of fast-food emporia such as *Swenson's*, *Burger King* and *KFC*. *Cafe Oh La La* in the basement has good pastries and cappuccinos.

Elsewhere

Street Food Jakarta has plenty of street food, served from push carts called *kaki lima* (five feet) or slightly more permanent warungs with canvas overhangs. As Indonesia's melting pot, Jakarta's street food has specialities from all over the archipelago – delicious srabi (small pancakes with a coconut pudding centre topped with chocolate or banana) from Solo, sate from Madura or Sulawesi-style ikan bakar (barbecued fish). Those new to Indonesia should exercise caution with street food and gradually introduce themselves to the local microbes.

Jakarta's markets always have plenty of street-side warungs. Pasar Tanah Abang, west along Jalan Wahid Hasyim from Jalan Thamrin, has a collection of cheap and popular night warungs. South of the Welcome Statue roundabout, a string of stalls can be found along Jalan Kendal – walk south past the bars on Jalan Blora, and turn left (where the transvestites hang out) along Jalan Kendal, which runs parallel to the railway line.

When the shops close at 9 pm in the streets around Blok M, street stalls set up and rattan mats are laid out on the pavements for diners. This style of dining (called *lesahan*) is popular in Java, and many stall holders serve dishes from Central and East Java.

One of the fanciest and best warung areas is on Jalan Pecanongan, about one km directly north of the Monas monument. These night warungs start setting up large marquees around 5 pm and serve excellent Chinese seafood at moderate prices.

Food-Stall Centres Almost all Jakarta's shopping malls have food courts, which are collections of stalls housed in permanent, squeaky-clean surrounds. The stalls offer primarily Indonesian food with regional specialities from Java, but often include Chinese or even Western fast food. They are cheap and convenient.

As well as the already mentioned centres in the Plaza Indonesia and Sarinah department store on Jalan Thamrin, other malls with good food-stall centres are the *Gajah Mada Plaza*, to the north of the city centre on Jalan Gajah Mada, and *The Atrium*, on Jalan Senen Raya in the Pasar Senen area, which has a couple of Japanese stalls as well the usual fare. *Blok M Mall* in Blok M also has a large and cheap collection of food stalls.

RESTAURANTS

Indonesian

As the melting pot of Indonesia, Jakarta has restaurants with food from all over the archipelago. Javanese food tends to dominate, but a number of regional cuisines can be found. Indonesian restaurants are usually very reasonably priced.

Good Sundanese restaurants are typically built around a pond teeming with freshwater fish such as ikan mas (large 'goldfish' carp) and gurami. *Sari Kuring* (☎ 8583968), Jalan Matraman Raya 69 in East Jakarta, serves Sundanese food in pleasant surroundings. Try the excellent chicken dishes, such as ayam Kalasan or the sate which is served with a superb sauce, with a side dish of vegetables, or fresh fish out of the pond. You can eat very well for 10,000 rp or less, though the fish costs more. It also has branches just north of the city centre at Jalan Batu Ceper Raya 55A and at Jalan Kelapa Gading Blvd in Blok M.

The *Pondok Laguna* (☎ 3459991), Jalan Batu Tulis Raya 45-47, is a similarly styled restaurant specialising in grilled fish, fish curry and sea food lumpia (spring rolls)

Jalan Kebon Sirih, at the top end of Jalan Jaksa, has some interesting possibilities. At Jalan Kebon Sirih 31A on the corner of Jalan Jaksa, *Senayan Satay House* is a comfortable, air-con restaurant which serves superb sate. For dessert try the es kopyor (shaved ice with coconut and syrup). Other Senayan Satay Houses can be found at Jalan Cokroaminoto 78 in Menteng and Jalan Pakubuwono VI No 6 in Kebayoran Baru. Heading west along Jalan Kebon Sirih towards Jalan H A Salim, on the other side of the street at No 40, the *Ikan Bakar Kebon Sirih* specialises in that popular Sulawesi dish, Makassar-style ikan bakar.

At the southern end, Jalan Jaksa runs into Jalan Wahid Hasyim, where *Ayam Goreng Nyonya Suharti* is one of a chain of restaurants found throughout Java, featuring the famous Yogya-style fried chicken cooked in coconut milk. It's delicious and moderately priced.

Another Central Javanese speciality from Yogya is gudeg, jackfruit cooked in coconut milk, often including chicken. The most famous purveyor in Jakarta is *Bu Tjitro*, Jalan Cikajang 80, in Kebayoran Baru.

Padang food, from the Padang region of Sumatra, is popular all over Indonesia. Padang food consists of spicy, hot curries and rice, and is traditionally eaten with the right hand. In a Padang restaurant a number of dishes are laid out on the table, and only those that are eaten are paid for. It's usually served cold and consists of rice, with a whole variety of side dishes, including beef, fish, fried chicken, curried chicken, boiled cabbage, sometimes fish and prawns.

The award-winning *Natrabu*, Jalan H A Salim No 29A, in the Jalan Jaksa area, is Jakarta's most well-known Padang restaurant. This would have to be the classiest Padang restaurant in Indonesia, and if you only try Padang food once then do so here. It has tasteful decor, and the waiters are dressed in traditional costume, including hats styled like Minangkabau roofs. You can have a filling meal for 10,000 rp. If you prefer a classic no-frills Padang restaurant with laminex tables, the cheaper *Budi Bundo* and *Sederhana* are nearby on Jalan H A Salim.

The Menteng shopping centre on Jalan Cokroaminoto also has a few Indonesian restaurants, such as a branch of *Senayan Satay House* at No 78. The *Tan Goei* (☎ 3140829) at Jalan Besuki 1A, down a side street south of the Menteng Plaza, is an expat favourite and, though not strictly Indonesian (it features Chinese and steak dishes), it serves some classical Indonesian dishes. It has a pleasant garden area and is moderately priced. The *Menteng Kuring* at No 91 A, on the corner of Jalan Besuki, is another Sundanese restaurant with a pleasant garden.

Upmarket Indonesian dining can be enjoyed at the *Bengawan Solo* (☎ 5704444) in the Sahid Jaya Hotel on Jalan Jenderal Sudirman. It features Central Javanese dishes and serves rijsttafel. Prices are high.

Dutch/Indonesian

Rijsttafel (Dutch for 'rice table') is the Dutch equivalent of Indonesian food, with a big variety of Indonesian-influenced dishes laid out on the table. There is always more than you can eat, so start hungry.

The historic *Oasis Bar & Restaurant* (☎ 327818), on Jalan Raden Saleh 47 in Cikini, is housed in a large, old Dutch villa and has the feel of an extravagant 1930s Hollywood film set, with extravagant prices to match. More than a dozen waitresses serve up a traditional rijsttafel, while you are serenaded by a group of Batak singers from Sumatra. Reservations are recommended, and apart from the rijsttafel, continental a la carte meals are available. It's closed on Sunday. Many of the big hotels also serve rijsttafel.

Also in Cikini, the delightful *Art & Curio* (☎ 8322879), Jalan Cikini III No 8A, is Jakarta's answer to cafe society. Housed in a curio shop, it serves Dutch and Indonesian dishes.

Chinese

Bakmi Gajah Mada is a busy noodle-house chain with shops all over Jakarta. The original restaurant at Jalan Gajah Mada 92, just south of the Arsip building in Glodok, has been pumping out noodles since the '50s and is still a very popular, efficient place for cheap eats.

Cahaya Kota (☎ 3142434), Jalan Wahid Hasyim 9, just east of Jalan Jaksa, is a long-established restaurant which serves good Cantonese and Szechuan food, and some Indonesian dishes. It has traditional Chinese restaurant decor – dark and red – and its spicy Szechuan food is particularly good. It is moderate to expensive in price, and also has a bar.

For top-class Szechuan food at top prices, the *Spice Garden* (☎ 3141307) in the Mandarin Oriental Hotel on Jalan Thamrin has an elegant decor and an extensive menu.

If money is no object and you want to be seen with the high rollers, Jakarta has very expensive Chinese restaurants with very expensive cars parked outside. Try the *Halai International Executive Club* (☎ 689868) at Ancol, which used to be a casino. This huge complex is popular with Japanese and Chinese businessmen and features a restaurant, disco, bar, health club and hostesses. Bring a couple of credit cards. In Menteng, the *Summer Palace* (☎ 333899) in the Tedja Buana building, Jalan Menteng Raya 29, Menteng, is one of Jakarta's finest Cantonese and Szechuan restaurants where it's easy to blow

Traditional Padang cuisine, Jalan Jaksa area (GB)

US$100 or more, though more moderately priced options are available, such as the Sunday dim sum.

At the other end of the scale, very cheap Chinese restaurants such as the *Lim Thiam Kie* and *Paradiso 2001* can be found on Jalan H A Salim (see the Cheap Eats section earlier in this chapter).

Seafood

Jakarta has a particularly good selection of Chinese seafood restaurants, serving good prawn, crab and fish dishes.

Some say the *Jun Njan* (☎ 364063), Jalan Batu Ceper 69, at the northern end of Jalan Pecanongan, has the best seafood in Indonesia. Try the fried squid in oyster sauce or the fried prawns in butter sauce. Reservations are recommended. The decor is no frills and prices are very good for seafood. It also has a branch in South Jakarta at Jalan Panglima Polim Raya 77.

Lin's Garden Sea Food (☎ 330409) is in the Wisma GEHA, Jalan Timor 25, just behind the Sarinah department store in the Menteng area. It's a new, sparkling restaurant with cafeteria decor, good fish and crab dishes, and very reasonable prices.

A little more expensive, the *Nelayan Garden* (☎ 5254008), in the basement of the Wisma Argo Manunggal, Jalan Gatot Subroto, has excellent seafood prepared by a Hong Kong chef. It is very popular, which is understandable given the quality.

Seafood Senayan (☎ 712752), Jalan Paku Buwono VI No 6, Kebayoran Baru, is part of the Senayan Sate House chain and serves moderately priced Chinese-style seafood.

In Menteng, *Kuningan Seafood Restaurant* (☎ 331601), Jalan Cokroaminoto 122, has a wide variety of seafood and different styles of cooking.

Indian

The Pasar Baru area just north of the post office is home to Jakarta's Indian community, though Indian restaurants are in short supply. The *Rumah Makan Taj Mahal* (☎ 364754), Jalan H Samanhudi 10A, is a bare, basic Indian restaurant. The food is really imitation Indian, and while not top class it is certainly cheap. Most curries are around 6000 rp, and tandoori meats and breads and lassis are available. A much better Indian restaurant in Pasar Baru is the *Copper Chimney* (☎ 3865719), Jalan Antara 5-7, with a wide selection of curries at reasonable prices.

Hazara (☎ 3150424), Jalan Wahid Hasyim 112, near Jalan Jaksa, is a branch of the popular Singapore restaurant serving 'North Indian Frontier' cuisine. Tandoori meats and breads are available but the restaurant specialises in seafood and vegetarian dishes. The food is good but it is the chic Indian decor that makes this restaurant special. Small serves range from around 10,000 rp for vegetarian dishes to 35,000 rp for a leg of marinated lamb. Expect to pay 30,000 rp and up per person for a meal with side dishes and drinks.

For southern Indian cuisine served in banana leaves, *Mutu Curry* is adjacent to the Tanamur Disco on Jalan Tanah Abang Timur.

The *Shah Jahan* (☎ 5704444 ext 1444) in the Sahid Jaya Hotel, 86 Jalan Jenderal Sudirman, is another good North Indian restaurant, if a little expensive. It serves a good Sunday lunch buffet and you can dine on cushions in canopied areas.

Indian food also features on menus in a number of pubs and multi-cuisine restaurants. The best to try are the *Eastern Promise*, Jalan Kemang Raya 5 in Kemang, which serves an Indian buffet as well as Western dishes, and the *Akbar Palace Restaurant*, part of the Orient Express restaurant (see under Other International Cuisine later in this section) in Kebayoran Baru, which serves authentic Indian food at moderate prices.

Japanese

Jakarta has plenty of Japanese restaurants. They range from the *Hoka Hoka Bento* on Jalan Agus Salim, a popular fast-food chain with dishes that are Japanese in name only, to some excellent dining possibilities in the top hotels.

In general, you'll have to pay top dollar to get good Japanese food. Two good, moderately priced Japanese restaurants are *Kikugawa* (☎ 315 0668), Jalan Cikini IV No 13, or *Sushi-Sei* (☎ 711721) in the Ratu Plaza, Jalan Jenderal Sudirman, which serves sushi and standard Japanese dishes.

Some of the best Japanese food in Jakarta can be had at the *Sumire* in the Hyatt hotel on Jalan Thamrin. It is expensive but authentic.

Other Asian

Tamnak Thai (☎ 330409), Jalan Cokroaminoto 78, is a moderately priced Thai restaurant in the Menteng shopping centre. Like many Thai restaurants it has a heavy Chinese influence but the food and service are excellent, and it is one of the cheapest Thai restaurants in town. The speciality is seafood – good fish and prawn dishes, and the chilli crab is superb – but it has a varied menu with meat and vegetable dishes. Servings are large and with a good selection of dishes between two or more people, you can expect to pay 20,000 to 25,000 rp for an excellent feed. *Casablanca* (☎ 5254800) in the Kuningan Plaza on Jalan Rasuna Said has a mixed menu, but serves excellent Thai food. This expensive supper club also has live music and dancing.

Jakarta has its fair share of Korean restaurants. *Korea Garden* (☎ 322544), Jalan Teluk Betung 33, is just off Jalan Thamrin, immediately south of the Hotel Indonesia.

Top :   Market produce, Glodok (GB)
Middle :   Fruit market, Glodok (GB)
Bottom :   Street vendors, Blok M (GB)

This reasonably priced restaurant has BBQ grills set up on the table and the decor is pleasant.

Pare'gu (☎ 4212954), Jalan Sunan Kalijaga 65 in Kebayoran Baru, is in fact two Vietnamese restaurants, one more formal than the other. Good Vietnamese food is served and it also takes a stab at some Thai dishes. It's moderately priced and buffet lunches are served.

Italian

Maxi's Cucina Italiana is a very popular Italian bistro at Level 1, No 102 in the Plaza Indonesia on Jalan Thamrin. The decor is pleasant, the service good and a singer often performs in the evenings. The best bet is the pasta or pizzas for around 12,000 rp, plus a 21% service charge. Small main meals, such as veal and steak dishes, cost around 20,000 rp but the sauces are insipid, as is the house wine.

Pinnochio (☎ 5254736), on the top floor of the Wisma Metropolitan on Jalan Jenderal Sudirman, is another moderately priced Italian restaurant with good atmosphere.

One of the best places for reasonably priced Italian food is the *Napolina* (☎ 7996151), Jalan Kemang Raya 5, in the Kemang shopping centre. It is part of the Eastern Promise restaurant, which serves a number of cuisines (see Other International Cuisine later in this section).

For pizzas, *Pizza Hut* (☎ 3842049) in the Jakarta Theatre building on Jalan Wahid Hasyim serves its usual style of pizza, with a good salad bar. It has other outlets around Jakarta and will deliver.

The *Pizzaria* (☎ 5703600) at the Hilton hotel has a pleasant outdoor setting built over a pond. It has good pastas from around 10,000 rp, and pizzas, meat and seafood dishes from around 15,000 rp. A band plays on Friday and Saturday nights, when the place fills up. It pays to book.

For really top-notch Italian food, the *Ambiente* (☎ 3861234) in the Aryaduta Hotel is regarded as one of Jakarta's best Italian restaurants, and is one of the most expensive.

French

Jakarta has some surprisingly good French restaurants, though they tend to be expensive.

Le Bistro (☎ 3909249) is a moderate to expensive French restaurant tucked away in a small house at Jalan Wahid Hasyim 75, near Jalan Jaksa. The food is consistently good.

The *Café de Paris* has three outlets in Jakarta at Jalan Bulungan 24, behind the Blok M Plaza in Blok M, Jalan Kapt Tendean 1, near Jalan Gatot Subroto in Kuningan and Jalan Raya 90 in Kemang. It has French/continental dishes and is moderately priced.

More upscale and one of the city's best French restaurants is *La Rose* (☎ 5710800) in the Landmark Centre, Garden Plaza, Jalan Jenderal Sudirman 1.

Le Meridien Hotel also has some French dining possibilities, including *Le Brassiere*, with a mixed menu, and *La Boutique Gourmande*, a French delicatessan.

The *Margaux* (☎ 570440) in the Shangri-La Hotel is furnished with old-world opulence and has a mixed menu with an emphasis on French cuisine. It's expensive but the lunch meals are more reasonable.

Mexican

In the Jakarta Theatre building on Jalan Thamrin, the *Green Pub* (☎ 3159332) features Mexican food with a meal averaging about 20,000 rp and a happy hour from 3 to 6 pm with half-price drinks. In the evening, the place is jammed as Indonesians turn out to enjoy a local band perform in Mexican cowboy garb! This is a very popular expat hangout.

Under the same management, *Amigos* is another popular, moderately priced restaurant chain with live music. It can be found in the Artholoka building, Jalan Jenderal Sudirman 2, and in the Setiabudi building II, Jalan Rasuna Said.

For Mexican fast food, *Del Taco* in the Plaza Indonesia on Jalan Thamrin specialises in tacos.

Other International Cuisine

Right in the middle of historic Kota on Taman Fatahillah, *Cafe Batavia* (☎ 6926546) is the place to be seen. Housed in a tastefully renovated Dutch building, the restaurant is not cheap but not outrageously expensive for good food. The menu is mixed, with a Western menu and a Chinese menu with seafood and dim sum specialities. It is very popular in the evenings before the bands play, but is good anytime of day for a coffee or snack.

In Kemang, *Castelo Do Mar* (☎ 7994316), Jalan Kemang Raya 6A, is a chic grill, restaurant and wine bar opposite Kem Chicks supermarket. Paella is served, but despite the Portuguese name and decor, the food is international. Seafood and imported steaks dominate the menu; succulent lamb chops for around 15,000 rp are good value. Expect to pay 50,000 rp and up.

The wealthy southern suburbs are the favourite residential district for Jakarta's elite and expatriate community. An expat favourite is *Orient Express*, Wijaya Grand Centre, Block H37-39, Jalan Baramwangsa Raya in Kebayoran Baru. It serves a bit of everything – Indian, seafood, pizza, Mexican. The food is consistently good and the prices moderate.

The *Stage* (☎ 7397505), in the basement of Ratu Plaza on Jalan Jenderal Sudirman, has a bit of everything on its Indonesian and international menu, including passable Greek dishes. Prices are moderate and bands, mostly jazz, play in the evenings.

If you're hankering for sauerkraut and sausages, *Gastube* (☎ 251 2125) is a German restaurant, while adjoining *Memories* (☎ 2510402) serves Dutch food and rijsttafel in an old world setting. Both are in the Wisma Indocement, Jalan Jenderal Sudirman.

Orleans Restaurant (☎ 715695), Jalan Aditiawarman 67 in Blok M, serves gumbo, clam chowder, nachos and 20-oz T-bones from its Cajun/American menu. Homesick Americans can finish off their meal with the home-made apple pie.

The hotels on Jalan Thamrin have some of the fanciest, and most expensive, dining in town and the buffets can be good value. The *Ramayana Terrace* in the Hotel Indonesia has mostly Western fare and reasonable steaks on its menu, but best value are the buffets for 27,000 rp. The decor is very '60s with ceramic murals by Dharta and a strange collection of 'big' paintings. Farther south, the *Kartika Plaza* has a very cheap lunch buffet for 16,000 rp.

Grills & Pub Food

The *Hard Rock Cafe* (☎ 3902766) in the Sarinah building on Jalan Thamrin has very good steaks with ordinary vegetables for around 25,000 rp, or cheaper hamburgers and snacks. Food is served from 11 am to 11.30 pm, when the bands get going in earnest.

Also on Jalan Thamrin, the *Jaya Pub* (☎ 325633) at the back of the Jaya building, Jalan Thamrin 12, is another music venue that also puts on good grills and pub food.

Many of the international restaurants serve steaks, but the steak specialists tend to be chain restaurants. On Jalan Cokroaminoto in the Menteng shopping centre, two good steak houses to try are the *Gandy Steak House* (☎ 3102542) at No 90 and the *Black Angus* (☎ 331551) at No 86A. Other Gandy restaurants are at Jalan Melawai VIII No 2A in Blok M, and to the north of the city centre at Jalan Hayam Wuruk 73 and Jalan Gajah Mada 82A.

The *Sizzler* chain have their usual selection of grills for around 25,000 rp, including salad and dessert bars. Its most convenient restaurant is at Jalan Agus Salim 39 near Jalan Jaksa. There are others in the Pondok Indah Mall and Citraland Mall. *Ponderosa* is another chain with outlets around town, including one in the Artholoka building on Jalan Jenderal Sudirman.

Or try the popular *Planet Hollywood* recently opened in Jakarta at Jalan Gatot Subroto 16. International and local bands perform here also.

The *George & Dragon* (☎ 3102101), Jalan Talang Betutu 7, at the very southern end of Jalan Thamrin, has English-style pub food. You can even indulge yourself in sausage & mash here! The pub also serves some tasty Indian fare.

If money is no object, the swish *Toba Restaurant* in the Hotel Borobudur Inter-Continental is noted for its steaks. It's very expensive, and Batak musicians perform.

SUPERMARKETS

For self catering, almost every shopping centre has a supermarket. You can find one in the basement of the Sarinah department store, and a cheaper one across the road in the Jakarta Theatre building. The Sogo supermarket in the basement of the Plaza Indonesia on Jalan Thamrin is one of the best in the city centre and features Japanese groceries. Kem Chicks, beloved of expats, at Jalan Kemang Raya 14 in Kemang, is small but well stocked with imported groceries and variety goods ranging from Swiss chocolates to Australian barbeques. The range of cheeses and meats is impressive, as is the crusty, wholemeal bread.

Entertainment

Jakarta is the most sophisticated, broad-minded and corrupt city in Indonesia, and has nightlife to match. Hundreds of bars, discos, karaoke lounges and nightclubs range from the sleazy to the refined. Jakarta is also an excellent place to see traditional performing arts from all over the country. Look in the *Jakarta Post* for listings of special events, plays, films and lectures. The various tourist publications available from hotels, such as *Jakarta Now!*, also have a what's on section. Jakarta has interesting cultural events almost every day of the week.

A good time for the performing arts is during the Jakarta International Cultural Performance (JICP) held each year in May. This festival showcases Indonesian dance and music, with Betawi culture strongly represented in the past. Dancers and musicians from around Asia also perform. Events are free and held all around the city. JICP leads up to the annual Jakarta Fair in late June and July, when wayang and various other cultural events are held at the Jakarta Fair grounds in Kemayoran and around the city. On 17 August, Indonesia's independence is celebrated with food festivals, theatre and handicraft displays. The Jalan Jaksa Street Fair, also held in August, features traditional Betawi music and dance.

CULTURAL PERFORMANCES

Jakarta has some excellent venues for traditional theatre, dance and music. *Taman Ismail Marzuki*, commonly known as TIM, is the showcase for the arts in Jakarta. TIM is a theatre, gallery and arts school complex at Jalan Cikini Raya 73 in Menteng. TIM produces a monthly calendar of events, available from the Visitors Information Centre on Jalan Thamrin, and is one of the best places to see traditional and modern theatre, dance, film and music from all over Indonesia and abroad.

Taman Mini Indonesia Indah, the all-Indonesia theme park on the southern outskirts of the city, has an extensive programme of traditional performances. Free cultural performances are held on Sunday from 10 am to 2 pm. You might see dances from Kalimantan, a horse trance dance from East Java, a wedding ceremony from Sulawesi or keroncong music from Jakarta – all held in the pavilion of their origin. Special cultural events from all over the country are also staged on Saturday nights from April to November. Check the Taman Mini monthly programme available from the Visitors Information Centre.

The *Bharata Theatre* (☎ 4214937), at Jalan Kalilio 15 in Pasar Senen, has *wayang orang* (Javanese theatre) performances from 8 pm to midnight every evening. Housed in a large old theatre with a traditional Javanese facade, performances are held in Bahasa Indonesia and Javanese. Wayang orang is based on the Hindu epics, the *Ramayana* and *Mahabarata*, or Javanese legends associated with the courts of Central Java. Accompanied by gamelan, it is a mixture of dramatic and comic theatre, with some dancing and an inevitable battle scene as the noble characters vie for power or oppose the forces of evil. An all-evening performance is hard going if you don't speak the language or are unfamiliar with the stories, but tickets cost only 5000 rp or less, and you can sample Javanese theatre without having to stay for the entire performance.

Wayang orang and popular folk theatre, such as *ketoprak* (a less refined, comic theatre form), can also be seen every evening at 8 pm in the *Teater Populer* (☎ 3143041), Jalan Kebun Pala 1 No 295 in Tanah Abang. Performances are usually in Bahasa Indonesia.

Wayang kulit, the famous Indonesian shadow play, is well worth seeing if you haven't come across it elsewhere in Indonesia. The revered *dalang*, or puppeteer, is a kind of Indonesian renaissance performer, familiar with the ancient legends, music, dance and drama. He works the puppets, using different voices for each one, and directs the gamelan orchestra. Wayang kulit is performed around the city, or regular performances are held upstairs at the *Wayang Museum* on Taman Fatahillah in the historic Kota area. Wayang kulit or *wayang golek* (wooden puppet) performances are held every Sunday from 10 am to 2 pm. These are shortened tourist-oriented performances, rather than the traditional all-night plays, but are informative and well done.

The *Gedung Kesenian* (☎ 3808283), Jalan Gedung Kesenian 1, near the post office, is a delightful colonial theatre restored to its former grandeur. Various theatrical and music events are held, including many cultural events during the annual Jakarta Fair. With its domed ceiling and balconies, the Gedung Kesenian is an atmospheric venue for highbrow entertainment, such as the Jakarta Symphony Orchestra, which plays occasionally. Touring opera companies also perform in Jakarta.

Erasmus Huis (☎ 512321), Jalan Rasuna Said Kav S-3, is the Dutch cultural centre attached to the Dutch Embassy and sponsors chamber and choral music. Various lectures on Indonesian culture, history and society are also held at Erasmus Huis, including those organised by the Ganesha Volunteers, who run tours of the National Museum.

Gamelan music accompanies many traditional theatre and dance performances from Java and Bali. Gamelan orchestras also perform during the day in the lobbies at many of the hotels, such as the *Hilton* and *Hotel Indonesia*.

The *Hotel Borobudur Inter-Continental* puts on a buffet dinner with a choreographed glimpse of Indonesian dance and music at their Kintamani Pavilion every Friday evening.

CINEMAS

Jakarta has cinemas dotted over the city, and a few large well-appointed cinema complexes. Popular movies in Indonesia tend to be violent B-grade American adventure films or Hong Kong kung fu movies, but the latest Hollywood blockbusters are also screened in Jakarta. The dilapidated *Jakarta Theatre* on Jalan Thamrin shows the latest films. The ritzier main cinema complexes are the *Kartika Chandra* on Jalan Gatot Subroto, the *Empire* in the Wijaya Grand Centre, Jalan Wijaya II in Kebayoran Baru, and the *Megaria* at Jalan Cikini Raya 21, near Jalan Surabaya.

TIM also has regular film events, featuring everything from restrospectives on Japanese directors to New Zealand film festivals. The various cultural centres sometimes show films. The *British Council* (☎ 5223311) in the Widjojo Centre on Jalan Jenderal Sudirman has screenings once a fortnight. The *French Cultural Centre* (☎ 3908585), Jalan Salemba Raya, has regular screenings, and the *Goethe Institut* (☎ 8581139), Jalan Matraman Raya 23, screens German films on Wednesday.

DISCOS

Many discos are found at the big hotels, and dress requirements – no jeans, sneakers or T-shirts – usually apply. A first drink cover charge of around 15,000 rp is usual. Discos open around 9 pm, though they don't really get going until 11 pm and tend to peak in the early hours of the morning, especially on Saturday night or *malam panjang* (long night), the big night out in Jakarta.

The *Music Room* at the Hotel Borobudur Inter-Continental is popular with rich young Indonesians, and often has theme nights featuring fashion and dance shows. The slightly more casual *Pitstop* at the Sari Pan Pacific

Movie posters, TIM cultural complex, Cikini (GB)

Hotel and the *Oriental* at the Hilton are popular discos for locals and visitors alike. Another upmarket disco with impressive decor is *Ebony* in the Kuningan Plaza on Jalan Rasuna Said.

Fire, on the top floor of the Plaza Indonesia on Jalan Thamrin, is a high-tech disco, very popular with young Chinese. Singaporeans will feel at home – this is a clone of Singapore's Fire disco. Jalan Hayam Wuruk in the Glodok Chinatown area is also quite lively in the evenings, with large Chinese clubs and discos. The best is the large *Stardust* disco next to the Jayakarta Tower Hotel.

Jakarta's most infamous disco is *Tanamur* at Jalan Tanah Abang Timur 14. This long-running institution is jammed nightly with gyrating revellers of every race, creed and sexual proclivity, and innumerable ladies of the night. It's a popular straight and gay pickup spot, and is unbelievably crowded after midnight on Friday and Saturday nights. Try Thursday night to avoid the crush. Wear what you like here.

LIVE MUSIC

Local bands are found in profusion, doing everything from Beatles and Rolling Stones impersonations to jazz and the latest hits. European and American soul bands are definitely in vogue and provide the pick of the music. Jakarta also has plenty of Filipino bands, the blight of South-East Asian nightlife, invariably consisting of a trio of female singers dancing in coordination to bad covers of yesterday's songs.

Stained-glass Elvis, Hard Rock Cafe, Sarinah building,
Jalan Thamrin (GB)

The popularity of the venue depends on the quality of the bands, most of which play at the bars and pubs around town. Bands don't start until around 10 or 11 pm, and continue on until 2 or 3 am, sometimes later on the weekend. During the week many places close at 1 am.

Jakarta also gets a regular parade of well-known overseas acts that play at the *Jakarta Hilton Convention Centre*, or the real headliners pack them in at the *Senayan sports stadium*. Ticket prices are very high for famous acts – even Kenny Rogers can get them in at 350,000 rp minimum per seat.

Many places don't have cover charges, though a first drink cover charge sometimes applies. A beer or a mixed drink costs from 6000 rp in the pubs up to 12,000 rp in exclusive hotel bars.

The *Hard Rock Cafe* on Jalan Thamrin has the usual blend of rock memorabilia, music and food. It is always lively and has decent bands or occasional top line imports. The music starts around 11 pm, when dinner finishes, and keeps going until around 3 pm. The dance floor is dominated by a huge stained-glass portrait of the King, though this Elvis looks vaguely Indonesian.

Prambors Cafe in Basement II of Blok M Mall is more innovative than most venues and has some very good local and imported bands. Parking is not a problem – it's tucked away in the carpark.

The *Jaya Pub*, next to the car park behind the Jaya building, Jalan Thamrin 12, is a Jakarta institution that has live pub music most evenings. It is relaxed, very popular and frequented by an older clientele of expats and tourists. The crowd is always appreciative and honk applause on horns hanging from the bar.

Oreilly's in the Hyatt is a salubrious place for a business drink, but it also gets some very good bands on Friday and Saturday nights, when the ties come off, the crowds pack in and the place starts jumping.

The historic, restored *Cafe Batavia* at Taman Fatahillah is another upmarket venue and a popular spot to be seen. The music is mostly jazz and soul from imported bands. First drink cover charges are around 20,000 rp, depending on the band.

Casa Pub on Jalan Sidoarjo is just off Jalan Cokroaminoto, next to the Menteng Plaza in Menteng. It has a bar downstairs and bands play upstairs until 1 or 2 am. The bands aren't brilliant but you can usually get a seat and it's a convivial venue.

Dangdut music can sometimes be heard at Ancol's Pasar Seni on a Saturday night, and at numerous low-class bars around town. Dangdut is a very popular, modern Indonesian style of music, influenced by Indian pop music. Dance along to the bands with a sliding, 'get down' back beat. Other bands, usually jazz, play at the Pasar Seni on a Friday night.

Jakarta has a lively jazz scene, at its peak when the annual Jakarta International Jazz Festival is held in August. Keep an eye out for Java Jazz and the Jakarta All-Stars, two of Indonesia's top jazz bands. The number one jazz venue in Jakarta is *Jamz*, Jalan Panglima Polim Raya in Blok M. This salubrious jazz bar has the best local bands and gets some top name acts, when cover charges skyrocket.

PUBS/BARS

Jakarta has a profusion of bars and pubs. The more upmarket bars offer food, drinks and usually night-time entertainment, and many of the bars and pubs have video screens with sporting events beamed in from around the world, making them popular with expats. Jakarta also has plenty of lively and/or seedy places where bar girls and *kupu kupu malam* (night butterflies) abound, but even some of the more exclusive venues have their fair share of hostesses or high-class call girls.

The big hotels all have bars, which usually have resident singers, piano players or bands. The dark lobby bar at the Hotel Indonesia has a happy hour from 6 to 8 pm with discounted drinks, but it is a quiet affair compared with its heyday when Soekarno and friends used to party here. Better nearby alternatives across the Welcome Statue roundabout on Jalan Thamrin are the popular *Captain's Bar* in the Mandarin Oriental Hotel, which has entertainment in the evenings, or the ever-popular *Oreilly's* in the Hyatt hotel, a good place for lunch and it has good bands at night.

The Hilton has some good upmarket bars, including the *Kudus Bar*, with a magnificent carved wooden front courtesy of the Kudus artisans from Central Java, and the *Pendopo Lounge*, which has Batak singers. *The Tavern* in the Aryaduta Hotel is popular and lively. It is easy-going for a business drink and has sports telecasts during the day, and gets lively in the evening when the Filipino bands start playing. The *Lisoi Sports Bar* in the nearby Hotel Borobudur Inter-Continental also has a sports theme with satellite broadcasts. Downstairs in the Dai Ichi Hotel, Jalan Senen Raya 135, *Morgan's* is notable for the classic Morgan sports car in the bar.

Jakarta also has plenty of pubs offering pub fare, darts etc. The *Green Pub* in the Jakarta Theatre building on Jalan Thamrin is mostly a place to eat Mexican food, but it features bands, usually country and western, and the bar is always crowded on Friday and Saturday nights. The *Jaya Pub* nearby in the Jaya building, Jalan Thamrin 12, is another very popular hangout with live bands. *Casa Pub*, Jalan Sidoarjo 1, is just off Jalan Cokroaminoto next to the Menteng Plaza in Menteng. This Australian-run pub has a homey atmosphere and the bar is a favourite with journalists. The *George & Dragon*, Jalan Talang Betutu, at the very southern end of Jalan Thamrin, is a long-running place with pub fare, Indian food and a TV bar.

Blok M is a good place for a pub crawl. The *King's Head*, Jalan Iskadararsyah I No 9, is another English-style pub and meeting place for the Hash House Harriers, the jogging/drinking club that is a legacy of British colonial-ism. Jalan Palatehan I has a selection of bars, the pick of which is the *Sportsmans Bar & Grill* (☎ 7204731), Jalan Palatehan I No 6-8. It has a big range of beers from around the world and serves grills and other pub food. Sporting events are displayed on the big satellite screen, and this place pulls a large expatriate clientele. Across the street is *Top Gun* (☎ 7395436) at No 1, aptly named because of its contacts with top generals in the Indo-nesian military. This is a popular beer, billiards and bar girls venue, as is the slightly grungier *Oscar Restaurant & Pub* at No 25. Billiard tables in Jakarta are staffed by hostesses that are available for a game. They play a mean game of pool – under Indonesian rules you pot the balls in number order.

A few hundred metres away in Blok M, Jalan Melawai VI and the side streets running off it are crammed with

Japanese-style bars. Typical are the *Tokio* at No 7 and the *Koreana* at No 5. The mix of food, alcohol, karaoke and bar girls appeal to visiting Japanese and Korean business people.

For a walk on the wild side, Jalan Blora, just off the southern end of Jalan Thamrin, has a string of seedy bars and discos, such as the *Lone Star* at No 19. Popular music, dangdut and karaoke pump out of the bars and, of course, bar girls are in profusion. Just around the corner from Jalan Blora, Jalan Kendal is the hangout for Jakarta's famous *banci* (transvestites). As well as strutting their stuff in the evenings on Jalan Kendal, the never-shy banci appear in talent nights around town, miming and dancing to dangdut and other music. You may get to see them at the Jakarta Fair held in June and July.

Shopping

Jakarta has dozens of shopping malls and markets, and a large collection of antique and craft shops with artefacts from all over the country. Jakarta is a good place to get an overall view of Indonesian crafts and, if you have been travelling elsewhere in Indonesia, then it's always a last chance to find something that you missed. Naturally prices are higher than the region of origin, but Jakarta's range is impressive and prices are generally reasonable. Crafts and antiques are certainly the pick of Jakarta shopping, but clothes and shoes are very cheap, and other interesting bits and pieces can be picked up around the markets and malls.

Bargaining is the rule when shopping. Department stores and some shops are fixed price, but just because a shop displays prices doesn't mean that bargaining isn't possible. This is especially true in tourist-oriented arts & crafts shops, where hard bargaining is often required even in the most exclusive shops. In other outlets when shopping for electrical goods, clothes etc, it always pays to ask for a discount or bargain outright if you know that you can get the same goods cheaper elsewhere. In markets, street stalls and small shops where prices are not displayed, bargaining is almost always required. There is no rule as to what is a good price, and the first asking price may be 50% or even 500% higher than what the shopkeeper is prepared to accept. In the most touristed markets and shops, prices can be ridiculously high; elsewhere the first price is much more moderate.

The other rule for shopping in Jakarta is 'buyer beware'. Always check your goods thoroughly for quality and make sure you get what you buy. Larger, reputable shops may overcharge but are better at replacing faulty goods or honouring guarantees. Refunds or replacement goods are almost impossible to obtain in many of the smaller shops, but in any case check your goods when you buy them – there is nothing you can do about faulty goods when you are thousands of km away.

WHERE TO SHOP

Shopping Areas

For inveterate shoppers, Jakarta's shopping may well be the city's main attraction. **Jalan Surabaya** in Menteng is a colourful antique market that is included on most Jakarta itineraries. **Pasar Seni** at Ancol is another good craft market and can be combined with a visit to other attractions at Ancol. Other notable areas for antiques and crafts are **Jalan Kebon Sirih Timur**, just one street away from Jalan Jaksa, or collectors and those after antique furniture will want to browse through the large shops in **Ciputat**, on the southern outskirts of the city.

Perhaps Jakarta's best shopping area, **Blok M** in Kebayoran Baru has a huge array of shops and malls all within easy walk of each other, and most of the day can be spent browsing and buying. Here you'll find Pasar Raya Big & Beautiful, a department store with an excellent craft and batik selection. Nearby, Blok M Mall is a huge complex of everyday shops selling all manner of goods at reasonable prices. Jalan Palatehan I, just north of Blok M Mall, has a selection of antique shops, while Blok M Plaza is an upmarket multistorey mall. Blok M also has a large range of food stalls, restaurants and watering holes for a welcome break from shopping.

Pasar Baru, just to the north-east of the city centre near the post office, is a shopping precinct with a bit of everything, but clothes and shoes are the best buys. Jalan Pasar Baru is a pleasant pedestrian street, a rarity in Jakarta, with a variety of shops. The Marco Plaza is a large, air-conditioned shopping mall with shops and some food outlets. At the end of Jalan Pasar Baru on Jalan K H Samanhudi is the main Pasar Baru, which is a traditional market selling foodstuffs. If you take the pedestrian bridge across the street, you'll come to the Metro shopping centre with a department store and a host of Indian traders and others selling clothes and textiles. On Jalan Pintu Air Raya, just west of Jalan Pasar Baru, you'll find a few sports shops.

About one km south of Pasar Baru, **Pasar Senen** is a crowded local shopping area. The market area spreads out around the Matahari department store and is sprawling with stalls and shops selling foodstuffs and other household goods. Across the road, The Atrium is a modern, air-conditioned shopping mall housing the large Yaohan department store.

Jalan Thamrin is the city centre's main boulevard, where many of the large hotels are located. Shopping possibilities are limited, but almost everyone pays a visit to Sarinah department store for its good range of batik and crafts. Farther down the street, the large Plaza Indonesia is the city's fanciest shopping mall.

Jakarta has plenty of other shopping malls, department stores and traditional markets scattered all over the city.

Department Stores

A good place to start looking for crafts is **Sarinah** on Jalan Thamrin. The 3rd floor of this large department store is devoted to batik and handicrafts from all over the country. It's a little variable, and you might find some areas poorly represented, but items are generally good quality and reasonably priced. The batik floor is divided into different concessions sponsored by the big batik manufacturers like Batik Keris and Batik Danar Hadi. Handicrafts are souvenirs rather than true collectibles, but the quality is high.

In the same vein, but possibly even bigger, is **Pasar Raya Big & Beautiful**, Jalan Iskandarsyah II/2 in Blok M. The 3rd floor is devoted to batik with all the big batik companies represented, and some silk and cheap ikat are also on sale. The 4th floor is devoted to handicrafts and jewellery, and there is a big collection of precious and semi-precious stones. Like Sarinah, this is an all-round department store with other floors selling clothes, shoes, sporting goods etc.

Also worth looking at is the **Keris Gallery**, Jalan Cokroaminoto 87-89, in the Menteng shopping centre just east of Jalan Thamrin. This is the main outlet for Batik Keris, one of Indonesia's largest batik manufactures, and so batik and batik clothing tend to dominate, but it also has other fabrics and accessories, and a few craft items.

Sogo is a Japanese department store in the Plaza Indonesia on Jalan Thamrin, with three floors of expensive brand-name goods. The small craft section on the top floor has a few interesting items, but prices are very high. The best place to spend your money is in the well-stocked supermarket in the basement.

In a similar vein, though less ritzy, **Yaohan** is another large Japanese department store in The Atrium shopping centre, next to the Dai-Ichi Hotel on Jalan Senen Raya in Pasar Senen.

Lotus Department Store, Jalan Hayam Wuruk 28, is just to the north-west of the National Monument, heading towards Glodok. It stocks top imported and Indonesian brand-name goods. It is good for clothes, toys, sporting goods etc. In the same vein is the popular **Grand Duta** in the Barito Plaza, Jalan Melawai Raya 93. It's in Kebayoran Baru just west of Blok M.

The Indonesian chain department stores are well represented in Jakarta. These include Matahari, Metro and Robinson's. They are regular department stores stocking mostly better quality Indonesian-brand goods. They are cheaper than the fancier shops selling imported brands,

Top : Traditional massage, Kota (GB)
Bottom : Street scene, Blok M (GB)

though prices are much higher than in smaller shops and markets. The advantage is that they have a wide range, including larger sizes for clothes, and are fixed price.

Robinson's, Jalan Agus Salim 34, between Jalan Jaksa and Jalan Thamrin, is a smaller department store, stocking mostly clothes. **Matahari** has larger stores with a bit of everything. They are found around Jakarta, including Jalan Pasar Baru 52-56, Jalan Melawai III No 24 in Blok M and at Pasar Senen. **Metro** has a large store in the Pondok Indah Mall in South Jakarta, and in Pasar Baru.

Shopping Malls

The most obvious sign of Jakarta's new wealth are the huge shopping malls scattered all around the city. These multi-storeyed, air-conditioned edifices are as much a symbol of '90s Jakarta as the Soekarno statuary are of the '60s. Here the wealthy middle class shop for goods from all around the world, though most Jakartans wouldn't dream of shopping in the malls – they simply can't afford to. Shopping malls tend to be places to hang-out and browse, while the markets and cheaper shops get the biggest volume of trade.

The malls are like those anywhere in the world, with a wide selection of speciality shops, fast-food outlets and usually one or more large department stores. Many house Singapore-style hawkers' centres, with a cluster of good, reasonably cheap food stalls offering Indonesian, Chinese and Western food. Prices for goods are higher than elsewhere, but the quality is also usually higher and they stock imported goods not available in the markets.

Jakarta's most exclusive mall is the **Plaza Indonesia** in the centre of the city on Jalan Thamrin. It's a great place to browse at designer labels but the prices are very high. It houses the Sogo department store, a supermarket and has some good dining possibilities, including a great food centre on the top floor. It also has some expensive art & craft shops, a good film shop, the Times Book shop, a duty-free shop and plenty of banks and moneychangers.

Craft stall in Jalan Surabaya Antique Market (GB)

North of the city centre in the Glodok area, **Gajah Mada Plaza**, Jalan Gajah Mada 19-26, is a big, more old-fashioned mall. It has clothes and shoe shops, and Chinese jewellers with gold, precious and semi-precious stones. It also has plenty of food outlets, including the basement Food Court, a McDonald's and a Hero supermarket.

At the top end of Jalan Gajah Mada around Pasar Glodok, **Glodok Plaza** is noted for its computers and electronics, and also has some new furniture shops. Other shops around the mall sell household appliances and stereo equipment. Prices for electronics are as good as you'll find in Jakarta, if you bargain.

To the west of Merdeka Square in the Pasar Senen area, **The Atrium** on Jalan Senen Raya is a large mall dominated by the Japanese Yaohan department store, and the Food Court in the basement also has Japanese food stalls. Other shops include the Gunung Agung book shop on the 3rd floor and clothes, jewellery, sporting goods and music-cassette shops.

Heading south from the city centre down Jalan Jenderal Sudirman, the **Ratu Plaza** at No 9 is near the 'Pizza Man' statue. This five-storey centre has a Matahari department store, a Batik Keris batik outlet, a cinema centre and plenty of smaller shops for clothes, shoes, books and household items.

Farther south in Kebayoran Baru's Blok M, the **Blok M Plaza** on Jalan Panglima Polim is one of Jakarta's most upscale malls with plenty of exclusive outlets. In the centre of Blok M above the bus terminal, the large **Blok M Mall** is a modern centre that is half mall/half market. It has a host of small shops for clothes, shoes, cassette tapes and household goods. It is an interesting general shopping area with lower prices than most malls and a good selection of cheap food stalls on the lower levels.

About one km south of Blok M, the **Wijaya Grand Centre** on Jalan Wijaya II has plenty of shops but is notable for Toys' City, one of Jakarta's biggest outlets for children's toys.

Jakarta has plenty of other malls spread around the city. Though too far out for most visitors, two other malls of note are the **Pondok Indah Mall**, on Jalan Metro Pondok Indah in South Jakarta, and the **Citraland Mall**, on Jalan S Parman in West Jakarta. These are huge malls with hundreds of shops and food outlets, cinema complexes and department stores. The new Citraland Mall is topped by a multistorey hotel. You can't miss it coming in from the airport – it is next to the airport toll road.

Markets

Indonesia's markets are always fun to browse, and Jakarta has its fair share of large, everyday markets. For lots of local colour, the markets are crowded affairs selling meat, fish, vegetables, fruit, clothes, household items and lots of weird and wonderful bits and pieces you'll see only in Indonesia. These are where most householders in Jakarta shop, and though most visitors will find few shopping possibilities for souvenirs and the like, the markets are an interesting diversion and the place to hone your bargaining skills.

In the central city, good markets to explore are **Pasar Cikini** on Jalan Cikini, to the east of Jalan Thamrin and Menteng. Primarily a food market, it also has some Chinese shops and a gold section upstairs, selling gold jewellery by the gram. Next to it, behind the department store on the main road, the **Pasar Kembang** is a flower market. The already mentioned **Pasar Senen** and **Pasar Baru** to the east of Merdeka Square are lively traditional markets with other shopping possibilities nearby.

On a short walk to the west of Jalan Thamrin, **Pasar Tanah Abang** is a large general market with plenty of cheap clothes, prayer mats, *peci* (the Muslim felt hat) and other religious paraphernalia. This popular Muslim market is a favourite with visiting Malaysians.

Pasar Glodok, on Jalan Gajah Mada in Glodok, is in Jakarta's Chinatown and is the place to pick up some sharks' fins, birds' nests or traditional Chinese medicine.

Tucked away on Jalan Jenderal Sudirman in the Golden Triangle business district, **Pasar Benhil** is another traditional market between the Hilton and Le Meridien hotels. This market has a good fruit section at the back, everyday goods in the main building and electronic appliance shops to the side. A small night market is held here on the weekend.

Parkir Timur is a popular Sunday market held in the southern car park of the Senayan Sports centre, off Jalan Jenderal Sudirman. It is a general market, active in the morning, with all manner of goods, including some handicrafts. Food stalls sell snacks from all over Indonesia and buskers perform.

Pasar Pagi Mangga Dua is a huge multistorey wholesale market specialising in clothes, with plenty of stalls selling shoes, bags and other goods to the public. A lot of the clothes are rubbish and it may take some hunting to find your size, but prices here are the cheapest and the number of stalls is mind boggling. Pasar Pagi Mangga Dua is on Jalan Mangga Besar, a few hundred metres east of the Kota railway station in Kota.

Top : Brass & Copper stall in
Jalan Surabaya Antique Market (GB)
Bottom : Caneware stall, Pasar Cikini (GB)

Plaza Indonesia, Menteng (GB)

Antique & Craft Markets

Jakarta also has a few art & craft markets that are well worth visiting.

In Menteng, **Jalan Surabaya** is Jakarta's famous flea market. Here you'll find a whole string of shops selling woodcarvings, furniture, brassware, jewellery, batik and oddities like old typewriters and many (often instant) antiques. It is always fun to browse but bargain like crazy – prices may be up to five times their worth.

The **Pasar Seni** at Ancol recreation park is an excellent place to look for regional handicrafts and to see many of them actually being made. Whether it's woodcarvings, paintings, puppets, leather, batik or silver, you'll find it all here.

WHAT TO BUY

Arts, Crafts & Antiques

The best place to start looking for crafts and souvenirs is the department stores such as Sarinah and Pasar Raya Big & Beautiful, where the range is good and prices reasonable. The Jalan Surabaya antique market in Menteng is fun and Pasar Seni at Ancol also has a good range of crafts.

Menteng also hosts the small, air-conditioned Jakarta Handicraft Centre, Jalan Pekalongan 12 A, which carries handicrafts but mostly specialises in batik and clothes. Prices are OK but nothing special.

Jalan Palatehan I in Blok M has some good art & craft shops. Pura at No 43 is a Balinese craft shop stocked with woodcarvings and other items you see in Bali. Prigura next door at No 41 is more interesting and has a reasonable range of antique furniture upstairs. Jenta at No 37 also has Balinese crafts and souvenirs, or Urip at No 40 has a good and varied collection. Prices are fairly high.

Jalan Kebon Sirih Timur, the street east of Jalan Jaksa, has a number of shops for antiques and curios. The quality is high, but so are the prices, and some stiff bargaining is required. Try Djody at No 22 or Budaya at No 21, or there are plenty of other shops selling all sorts of crafts, such as kris, some ikat weavings, wood carvings, chests and some furniture.

A number of large shops specialising in antiques and particularly antique furniture are spaced out along Jalan Ciputat Raya in Ciputat, on the southern outskirts of Jakarta. Chinese beds and altar tables, chests from Madura and Sumatra, Jepara furniture and much more can be bought. It is a long way to go, but collectors and those after antique furniture will find probably the best range in Jakarta. Shops to try include Gallery 59 at No 22, Fine Art & Curio at No 23, Eko's at No 35H, Palembang at No 36, Nina's at No 38 and Indonesian Putra at No 86. Go there in the morning to avoid the afternoon traffic jams.

A couple of km south of Blok M, Kemang is another hunting ground for antiques and crafts. At the corner of Jalan Kemang Selatan and Jalan Kemang Timur is a cluster of half a dozen small shops selling furniture and wood carvings, including some interesting pieces from Sumatra.

Batik & Ikat

Jakarta has plenty of batik outlets. Sarinah and Pasar Raya Big & Beautiful have excellent selections of batik with all of the main styles and producers represented.

The biggest batik producers have their factories in Solo in Central Java and have retail outlets in Jakarta. Batik Keris has a large showroom at Jalan Cokroaminoto in Menteng, and a shop in the Plaza Indonesia, among others. Batik Semar is in the Plaza Indonesia and at the Blok M Plaza.

Irwan Tirta produces exclusive *batik tulis* (hand-worked batik) and is Jakarta's most famous batik designer. His showroom is at Jalan Panarukan 25 in Menteng, or there is a shop at the Hotel Borobudur Inter-Continental.

Jakarta also has a few batik factories where you can view the process, but prices are high. Batik Berdikari at Jalan Mesjid Al Anwar 7B is about four km west of the Hilton Hotel and the Senayan Sports Stadium. It is popular with tour groups that are able to see the process in the factory and then shop in the expensive showroom.

Ikat can also be bought in Jakarta. Ikat material are intricate weavings, whose threads are tie-dyed by a very painstaking and skilful process *before* they are woven together. Produced throughout Indonesia, ikat from the eastern islands is the most famous. Again, Sarinah and Pasar Raya have some examples, but the quality is often not that good. Better quality can be found in the antique shops, and those on Jalan Kebon Sirih Timur have some good pieces.

Books & Maps

Singapore's Times Bookshop chain has a branch in the Plaza Indonesia on Jalan Thamrin. It has the best stock of English-language books, and a good range of travel books. On the other side of the roundabout, the bookshop in the Hotel Indonesia lobby is expensive but has a very good range of books on Indonesia.

The big Indonesian book chains are good for maps, dictionaries and travel books, and have a few English and other-language books. Gramedia has shops at Jalan Gajah Mada 109 and Jalan Melawai IV No 13, Blok M, while Gunung Agung has a huge shop at Jalan Kwitang 6, just east of Jalan Jaksa. Many of the shopping malls also have branches. Sarinah department store also has a good book and map section.

Scientific Bookstore, Jalan Melawai IV, B-7/165 in Blok M, is crammed with imported text and scientific books.

Clothes & Shoes

Clothes and shoes are cheap, but it can take some hunting to find Western sizes and styles. Imported brand-name clothes are expensive, and no great bargain, but Indonesia is a growing exporter of clothes and shoes, producing some very good buys.

Pasar Pagi Mangga Dua, Jalan Mangga Besar, is a huge wholesale market with some of the cheapest clothes, accessories and shoes. Large sizes can be found if you sift through the hundreds of stalls here. More expensive but still very reasonably priced, Pasar Baru is another good area to hunt out clothes and shoes.

Every big mall and supermarket has a wide selection of clothes and shoes. Prices are higher but the selection and quality is usually good.

Jakarta has plenty of tailors, found all around the city, and rates are reasonable. Maxi, Jalan Teh 3B in Kota, is a leatherwear shop that will tailor to measure.

Jakarta is also a centre for Indonesian designers. Batik is a dress fabric and is required for many formal occasions in Indonesia. Irwan Tirta, Kisson Harto and Poppy Dharsono are well-known designers.

Computers & Electronics

Electronics are reasonably priced but not as cheap as in Singapore and the range is nowhere as large. Depending on your country of origin, prices may be attractive but in general prices are around the same as in many other countries. Glodok Plaza has the best range of computers, stereos and TVs. Some good buys can be found if you bargain. Pirated computer software is no longer openly on sale.

Duty-Free Goods

The airport has duty-free shops selling cigarettes and alcohol but not a lot extra. You can buy duty-free goods at the Duty-Free Shop on the 3rd floor of the Plaza Indonesia, which sells mostly alcohol, but you can also buy perfume and a few other odds and ends. You need to show your airline ticket and passport to buy, but there doesn't seem to be anything stopping you from enjoying your duty-free goods before departure.

Other duty-free shops cater mostly to the large expatriate community, some of whom are eligible to buy imported duty-free food and drink. Gunung Agung in the Wahana building on Jalan Rasuna Said is well stocked with everything from New Zealand lamb to Californian wine.

Jewellery & Gemstones

Jakarta has gold shops all over town, but gold jewellery is often more of an investment and not a lot of effort is put into the designs. The designs are usually thrown in for free and you pay for the weight only. Gemstones are also sold in some jewellery shops and there is a gemstone market, Pasar Rawabening, at Jalan Bekasi Barat Raya in Jatinegara, East Jakarta. Semi-precious stones are usually quite inexpensive, while precious stones should be left to the experts. Pasar Raya Big & Beautiful in Blok M also has a good range of gemstones.

Gajah Mada Plaza in Glodok has a number of Chinese jewellery shops. Crown Jewellery on the 2nd floor is one of the more interesting. F Spiro in the Hilton hotel has good quality work as does Joyce Spiro in the Hotel Sari Pan Pacific, but they aren't cheap.

Music

Pirated cassette tapes are a thing of the past, though under new copyright agreements tapes are widely available and still very cheap. The quality is reasonable though not always great, but at about 8000 rp who can complain? CDs are not as widely available and not as good a buy at around 30,000 rp. Duta Suara is a good shop at Jalan Agus Salim 26, between Jalan Jaksa and Jalan Thamrin. Otherwise most shopping malls and markets stock cassettes.

Excursions

If you are spending any time in Jakarta, then a trip outside the capital makes a welcome break from the congestion, noise and traffic. The province of West Java, which surrounds Jakarta, has a number of nearby points of interest that can be visited as a day trip or longer.

Pulau Seribu, the islands just off the north coast, have some great beaches and resorts right on Jakarta's doorstep. Java's west coast also has good beach resorts, and is the staging point for visits to Krakatau, Indonesia's most famous and destructive volcano. Pelabuhanratu on the south coast is another popular beach.

For an escape from the heat, head to the hills south of the city. Bogor and its world famous botanical gardens have long been a hill retreat from Jakarta, ever since the Dutch governors-general made Bogor their base. Farther on, the Puncak Pass and nearby hill towns are the most popular weekend destinations for Jakarta residents.

Though West Java doesn't have Java's famous archaeological sites like Borobudur in Central Java, you can visit the ruins of the old city of Banten that thrived in the days of the spice trade.

On the weekends, especially Sunday, anyone who can afford it gets out of Jakarta. The resorts and tourist spots are overrun, and the traffic getting in and out of Jakarta banks up for miles, so weekdays are the best time to visit the following points of interest. All can be reached by public transport, though you should allow for delays and some discomfort. Organised tours (see the Organised Tours section in the Getting There & Away chapter) are also arranged to many of these attractions, or you can rent a car and driver (see the Car section in the Getting Around chapter).

PULAU SERIBU (THOUSAND ISLANDS)

Scattered across the Java Sea to the north of Jakarta are the tropical islands of Pulau Seribu, or Thousand Islands, although they are actually only 105 in number. The area is a marine national park, though 37 of the islands are permitted to be exploited. Apart from a few inhabited islands and a handful of resorts, many islands are the private preserve of the Jakarta rich and famous.

Most of the islands have crystal-clear waters, good diving and beautiful white-sand beaches.

Jakarta's 'offshore' islands start only a few km out, in the Bay of Jakarta. The waters closest to Jakarta are murky – the better islands are found the farther you go from Jakarta. **Pulau Bidadari** is the closest resort island and popular for day trips with Jakarta residents. It is one of the least interesting resorts but from Bidadari you can visit other nearby islands like **Pulau Kahyangan**, **Pulau Kelor** (which has the ruins of an old Dutch fort) or **Pulau Onrust**, where the remains of an old shipyard from the 18th century can be explored.

Farther north, **Pulau Ayer** is another popular day-trip destination. It has a comfortable resort with a small stretch of good beach, though the waters are still cloudy. **Pulau Laki**, another resort island, is also close to the coast, being about 40 km west of Jakarta.

The entire island group has a population of 15,000, with the district centre on **Pulau Panggang**, about 15 km north of Jakarta, but most people live on just one island, **Pulau Kelapa**, farther north. These poor fishing communities have yet to share in the wealth generated by the resorts. Near Kelapa, **Pulau Panjang** has the only airstrip in the islands. Around this group of islands are two more resorts on **Pulau Kotok**, which has a good reef for snorkelling and diving, and the Matahari resort on **Pulau Macan Besar** . Some of the resorts have had to build retaining walls around their investments – Matahari is one. **Pulau Bira** has, believe it or not, a golf course, and it has recently been opened to the public.

The best resorts lie around four km north of Kelapa, all close to each other. **Pulau Putri** has good bungalows and a restaurant with a built-in aquarium. In fact, much of the island is an aquarium, with a huge range of tropical fish, sting rays, moray eels and even sharks. An underwater viewing tunnel is moored next to the island's dock. The island has plenty of white sand to lie around on, but it is separated from the water by a retaining wall.

Pulau Sepa is a small sandy island surrounded by wide stretches of pristine sand. While it has the one of best beaches, the accommodation is plain. Nearby, **Pulau Pelangi** also has some good stretches of beach and good accommodation. **Pulau Papa Theo** is a diver's island with a dive camp. **Pulau Antuk Timur** and **Pulau Antuk Barat** are separated by a small channel. Both house the fanciest resort on the islands with the best facilities.

Places to Stay

All the resorts have individual bungalows with attached bathrooms, and most are air-conditioned. While comfortable, none are international standard resorts despite the high prices. All the resorts have water-sport facilities, with diving and snorkelling equipment, windsurfers, boats for hire etc. Though not one of Indonesia's premier dive destinations, Pulau Seribu is one of the most popular because of its easy access from Jakarta.

All the resorts have offices in Jakarta for bookings and travel agents also sell packages. Most of the resorts offer packages that include all buffet meals and sometimes transport to the islands, and these work out to be

Top :   A fishing boat, Pulau Seribu (GB)
Bottom :   Resort, Pulau Antuk Timur, Pulau Seribu (PT)

slightly cheaper overall. Package rates are for twin share, and a single supplement of US$20 typically applies.

Pulau Bididari Resort, Marina Ancol (☎ 680048), Taman Impian Jaya Ancol. Simple cottages accommodating two to four people cost from 51,000 to 68,500 rp during the week, 61,000 to 84,500 rp on weekends. Day tours to nearby islands are arranged.

Pulau Ayer Resort, PT Sarotama Prima Perkasa (☎ 3842031), Jalan Ir H Juanda III/6. Spacious, very comfortable cottages range from US$92 to US$231, or US$137 to US$277 on weekends. The nicest cottages are those built over the water. All-inclusive packages start at US$70 per person.

Top :   Pulau Antuk Timur, Pulau Seribu (PT)
Bottom : Resort, Pulau Ayer, Pulau Seribu (PT)

Pulau Laki Resort , PT Fadent Gema Scorpio, (☎ 3144885), Jalan Cokroaminoto 116. Cottages range from US$70 to US$162 for three-bedroom cottages. Weekend rates are 50% more.

Kotok Island Resort (☎ 362948), 3rd floor, Duta Merlin Shopping Arcade, Jalan Gajah Mada 3-5. This resort is popular with Japanese tour groups and has packages for US$73 per person in non-air-con rooms or US$83 in air-con bungalows. Rates rise 30% on weekends.

Matahari Resort, PT Jakarta International Hotels Management (☎ 3800521), suite 103, Hotel Borobudur Inter-Continental, Jalan Lapangan Banteng Selatan. Rooms in attractive two-storey bungalows cost US$60 to US$80 per person, US$75 to US$90 on weekends, including all meals.

Pulau Putri Resort, PT Buana Bintang Samudra (☎ 8281093), Jalan Sultan Agung 21. Cottages start at US$60 and go up to US$110 for excellent, Balinese-style, thatched-roof cottages. Including meals, the package rate is US$70 per person. Weekend rates are US$10 higher.

Pulau Sepa Resort, PT Pulau Sepa Permai (☎ 6928828), Jalan Kali Besar Barat 29. Bungalows cost from US$78 to US$110. All inclusive packages cost from US$85 per person for one night to US$310 for six nights. The air-con bungalows are comfortable, though fairly basic for the price.

Pulau Pelangi Resort, PT Pulau Seribu Paradise (☎ 335535), Jalan Wahid Hasyim 69. Older bungalows cost US$85 to US$110, or full-board packages are US$80 per person.

Pulau Seribu Marine Resort, PT Pantara Wisata Jaya (☎ 5723161), Jalan Jenderal Sudirman Kav 3-4. Located on Palau Antuk Timur and Palau Antuk Barat, this is the most upmarket resort and is popular with Japanese groups. Full-board packages cost US$113/86/77 per person for single/double/triple occupancy. Bungalows are very comfortable, though not really luxurious. However, the restaurant and sporting facilities are the flashest in Pulau Seribu. Antuk Barat has the better beaches while Antuk Timur has most of the facilities, but it doesn't matter which island you stay on as a regular shuttle connects the two.

Getting There & Away

The resorts have daily boats for guests and day trippers, usually leaving around 8 or 9 am and returning around 3 am Jakarta's Ancol Marina is the departure point, but boats to Laki leave from Tanjung Kait, 40 km to the west of Jakarta. *KM Betok* is a new ferry service that operates from Ancol and runs to the villages on Tidung (3500 rp) and Kelapa (4000 rp), but from these islands it is necessary to charter boats to other islands. If you want to rent a speed boat from Ancol, expect to pay around 750,000 rp for a day. No regular flights operate to the islands and planes have to be chartered, usually from Jakarta's Halim airport.

Return day-trip rates to the resorts include: Pulau Bididari (20,000 rp plus 5000 rp entry), Pulau Ayer (48,000 rp, including lunch), Pulau Laki (US$25, including lunch), Pulau Putri (US$55, including lunch), Pulau Sepa (US$45, including lunch), Pulau Pelangi (US$55, including lunch) and Pulau Seribu Marine Resort (US$63 plus US$6 entry). Transport rates for guests are slightly cheaper. The resorts provide fast speed boats, and even the farthest islands take only a little over two hours.

BANTEN

West of Jakarta, on the coast, are the few fragments of the great maritime capital of the Banten sultanate, where the Dutch and English first landed on Java to secure trade and struggle for economic supremacy. Banten reached its peak during the reign of Sultan Ageng (1651-83) but he unwisely clashed with rising Dutch power in Batavia. In 1680, Ageng declared war on Batavia but, before he could make a move, internal conflict within the royal house led to Dutch intervention on behalf of the ambitious crown prince. Ageng fled from Banten but finally surrendered in 1683 and his defeat marked the real beginning of Dutch territorial expansion in Java. Not only was Banten's independence at an end but its English East India Company rivals were driven out, which effectively destroyed British interests in Java.

The Dutch maintained trading interests in Banten for a time but they did a good job of demolishing the place in the 19th century. At some point too this coastline silted up and Banten became a ghost town, a small dusty fishing village, which is really all that Banten is today.

The chief landmark of a prosperous era is the 16th-century **Mesjid Agung** mosque, which dominates the village, and this is the most interesting part of a visit to Banten. It's a good example of early Hindu-Islamic architecture, but the mosque's great white lighthouse of a **minaret** was reputedly designed by a Chinese Muslim. A narrow staircase spirals up through the thick walls of the minaret to two high balconies; from the top you have a fine view of the coastline.

Adjoining the mosque are the **royal tombs**, where the leaders of Banten and their families are buried, including Sultan Mauluna Hasanudin, the first ruler of Banten. Just to the right inside the door is the small gravestone of Hors Kwadil, a Dutchman who converted to Islam

Top :   Mesjid Agung, Banten (PT)
Bottom :   Tower Mesjid Agung, Banten (PT)

and was accorded the privilege of burial in the royal tombs by Sultan Hasanudin.

The **alun alun**, or main square, was once the centre of Banten. Pride of place here was the Ki Amuk (Raging Fury) cannon, the partner of Si Jagur, which stands in Jakarta's Taman Fatahillah. Legend has it that when the two cannons were reunited Banten's power would be restored (though another legend has Si Jagur's partner in Solo). The cannon has now been moved to the front of the museum, partly to stop visitors' sitting astride the cannon, which is reputed to have spiritual power and is a symbol of fertility.

Next to the mosque is an **archaeological museum** (open from 9 am to 4 pm, closed Monday) with a modest collection of mostly clay artefacts found in the area and weapons, including a few of the long, iron, chained spikes which the 'Debus players' are famous for. Banten has long been a centre for practitioners of the Debus tradition, which is supposed to have come from India. These Islamic ascetics engage in masochistic activities such as plunging sharp weapons into their bodies (without drawing blood!), and are able to control pain and fear by the strength of their faith. It's said that in Banten this was originally part of the training of the invincible special soldiers to the court.

Directly across from the mosque is the large grass-covered site of Hasanudin's fortified palace, the **Surosowan Palace**, which was wrecked in the bloody civil war during the reign of Sultan Agung and rebuilt, only to be razed to the ground by the Dutch in 1832.

Other points of interest around the mosque include the massive ruins of **Fort Speelwijk** to the north-west, which now overlook an expanse of sand-silt marsh, although at one time it stood on the sea's edge. The fort was built by the Dutch in 1682 and finally abandoned by Governor-General Daendels at the beginning of the 19th century. Opposite the entrance to the fort is a **Chinese temple**, dating from the 18th century, which is still in use.

Back along the road to Serang are the huge crumbling walls and archways of the **Kaibon Palace** , which was inhabited by the mother of the last sultan of Banten in the 19th century. Farther south is the **Pakalangan**, tomb of Maulana Yusuf, the second ruler of Banten who died in 1580. Nearby the **Kasunyatan** is a restored mosque dating from the 16th century.

The **Tasikardi** was once a water palace, which are found in most Javanese royal cities. Here the sultan and his family relaxed, and the small artificial lake was once surrounded by royal pavilions. Just to the south-east is the **Kenari** royal cemetery. Through the split gateway, a Hindu-influenced architectural detail common in Java and Bali, lie the tombs of Sultan Abulmaali and Sultan Abulmafakhir.

Just offshore from Banten, the islands of **Pulau Dua** are one of Indonesia's major bird sanctuaries.

Getting There & Away

By car, Banten is about a 1½-hour drive from Jakarta, via the western toll road to Merak.

By public transport, take a bus to Serang, 10 km south of Banten, and then a minibus (500 rp, half hour), which will drop you right by the Mesjid Agung. A slightly quicker alternative is to take any bus between Jakarta and Merak and get off at the mosque in Kramatwatu village on the main highway, from where ojek motorbike riders can take you the five km to Banten for 2000 rp.

WEST-COAST BEACHES

This picturesque coast has masses of coconut palms and banana trees, and because of its easy access by toll road from Jakarta, it is a popular weekend beach strip. Though not really world beaters, the beaches are good and make a fine escape from Jakarta's heat and crowds.

The road between Cilegon and Labuan runs along a flat green coastal strip bordered by a rocky, reef-lined coast that is punctuated by stretches of white-sand beach.

Anyer, 12 km south of Cilegon, is an upmarket beach resort and the closest to Jakarta. Anyer was the biggest Dutch port in Selat Sunda before being totally destroyed by tidal waves generated by the eruption of Krakatau. The Anyer lighthouse was built by the Dutch at the instigation of Queen Wilhelmina in 1885 after the disaster.

There's another good beach at **Karang Bolong**, 11 km south of Anyer and 30 km north of Labuan, where a huge stand of rock forms a natural archway from the land to the sea.

Carita Beach is a popular base for visits to the Krakatau islands and the Ujung Kulon National Park. The wide sandy beach has good swimming, and there are plenty of opportunities to go wandering along the beach or inland. About two km from Carita across the rice paddies see the village of Sindanglaut ('End of the Sea'), where the giant tsunami of 1883 ended. Adjoining Carita village, the Hutan Wisata Carita is a forest reserve with walks through the hills and jungle.

Places to Stay

Because of the easy access from Jakarta, the resorts along this stretch of coast are expensive, but standards are generally high. Dozens of hotels and villas (many private but some for rent) are spaced out along the 30-km stretch from Anyer to Carita, and more are being built. Prices drop the farther south you head from Anyer, and the only cheap accommodation is found in Carita.

On weekends the hotels fill up and prices rise. Prices quoted here are the weekday rates. Weekend rates at the more expensive hotels are usually 20 to 30% more, and 21% tax and service is charged on top of the room rates. However, most hotels are simply overpriced and it pays to ask for a discount or just bargain. During the week, you can often get big discounts if you push hard, especially at the mid-range hotels.

Anyer Most hotels in Anyer have swimming pools, restaurants and rooms with air-con, TV and hot-water showers. They are spaced out over a five-km stretch. Heading south, the better places start just past the Anyer lighthouse. The first one you come to is *Mambruk Quality Resort* (☎ 601602), with large gardens, a swimming pool, tennis courts and diving facilities. It is the best in Anyer and prices range from US$80 for excellent rooms with all the trimmings to US$165 for the big cottages. They have manufactured a small beach, but the coast is still rocky here and unsuitable for swimming.

A little farther south, *Marina Village* (☎ 601288) also suffers from a lack of beach, though it does have a boat marina and a dive shop. Speed boats can be hired for a mere US$500 per day. Facilities are almost the same as at the Mambruk, but the rooms, costing US$70 up to US$370 for four-bedroom suites, are not as good.

Keep heading south until you reach *Ancotte* (☎ 601556), right on a fine stretch of sandy beach, the best in Anyer. This hotel is moderately priced and very popular with expats. It has a pool and good rooms from US$50 or large, attractive cottages, many with kitchens, for US$85 to US$120.

Putra Jasa (☎ 601376) is also on this good beach, but the older rooms starting at US$70 are overpriced. A new section with swimming pool is being built across the road.

Karang Bolong Coming in to Karang Bolong from Anyer, *Anyer Beach Hometel* (☎ 629224) is on the beach and has a pool. Rooms range from US$75 up to US$200 for three-bedroom cottages. Some need maintenance but this is still one of the best places in Karang Bolong.

Lalita Cottages (☎ 7806514) is on the beach right next to the recreational park. Large two-bedroom cottages with kitchen are quite simple but very comfortable and reasonably priced at 125,000 rp, before discount.

Three km farther south, *Puri Retno II* (☎ 201228) has extravagant Balinese-style cottages with extravagant prices – US$125 and US$200 – but no beach. A good beach can be found half a km south and the villas there are worth trying.

Three km south of its sister hotel, the *Puri Retno I* is built in the same style and is even more expensive. At least it has a thin stretch of beach. Next door, the friendly *Matahari Park Resort* (☎ 42167) has well-appointed, air-con rooms facing the beach. They start at 100,000 rp but with a big discount they are reasonable value for this part of the world.

Carita Heading north from Labuan, at the Km 5 marker, the first big hotel you come to is the four-star *Carita Beach Resort* (☎ 202222). It is the most luxurious on the coast with a swimming pool, tennis courts, diving and windsurfing facilities, restaurants, bars etc. Excellent rooms start at US$75 and bungalows cost from US$85, less after discount. The only drawback is that the beach fronts a rocky reef that is unsuitable for swimming.

One km farther north, *Mutiara Carita* (☎ 5720360) has an attractive swimming pool and large cottages with kitchen for US$70 to US$140, but the beach is also rocky.

After you pass through Carita village, the sweeping bay here has one of the best beaches on the coast with good swimming. This is also the area for budget and mid-range accommodation. Bargaining is usually required.

The *Hotel Wira Carita* (☎ 200016) has rooms with mandi for 40,000 rp or 65,000 rp with air-con; cottages are 140,000 rp. The rooms are simple but large and comfortable, and there is a good swimming pool.

Around the Km 9 marker is the *Carita Beach Bungalow* (☎ 81126). Three-bedroom bungalows with kitchens are way overpriced at US$100, but you can rent a large room in the bungalows (shared bathroom) for 30,000 rp and the restaurant on the beach is good.

A little farther on, *Desiana Cottages* (☎ 201010) has clean rooms with mandi for 37,500 rp or overpriced cottages from 150,000 rp. Try bargaining. Opposite, the *Karang Sari Cottages* are more upmarket.

Just past the Hutan Wisata Carita, across from the beach park, is the popular *Black Rhino* (☎ 81072), the only really cheap place in Carita. Rooms with shared mandi are very basic but cost only 5000 rp and 7000 rp. This friendly place also organises tours to Krakatau, Ujung Kulon and other attractions in the area.

Right next door is the good *Sunset View* (☎ 81075), where clean rooms with mandi cost 15,000 rp, after bargaining.

The road continues north past a number of villas and cheaper mid-range places. At the Km 11 marker, *Nerida Beach Inn* (☎ 81465) has a variety of cottages from 60,000 to 160,000 rp but they rent out 'tourist class' rooms to travellers for 15,000 rp, including breakfast.

Places to Eat

Restaurants are few and dining is usually at the hotels. In Carita, *Rumah Makan Nyenil*, opposite the Carita Krakatau Beach Hotel, is a pleasant budget restaurant with a wide range of Indonesian dishes and traveller-oriented fare. Farther north, the *Cafe de Paris* is an oddity – air-conditioning, European food and it accepts credit cards.

Getting There & Away

To get to Carita, take a bus from Jakarta's Kalideres bus station to Labuan (2700 rp, 3½ hours) and then a Colt or *angkot* (public minibuses) to Carita (500 rp). Overcharging is common.

Most visitors to Anyer go by car from Jakarta, which takes 2½ to three hours via the toll road and the turn-off at Cilegon. By bus from Jakarta, take a Merak bus (2500 rp) and get off at Cilegon, from where infrequent buses run to Labuan via Anyer and Karang Bolong. Minibuses are much more frequent and run to Anyer market, from where you can catch other minibuses farther south. It usually takes three minibuses to get to Carita and Labuan from Cilegon.

Organised Tours from Carita The Black Rhino (☎ 81072) and the privately run Tourist Information Service (☎ 81330), opposite the Desiana cottages, have almost identical tours to Krakatau (40,000 to 65,000 rp per person), Ujung Kulon National Park (US$150 per person for four days/three nights), Pulau Dua (US$125) and other destinations. They can also arrange boat hire to nearby coral reefs and islands. The Carita Beach Resort (☎ 202222 ext 8364) also rents out speed boats and arranges quite expensive diving tours and trips to Krakatau.

KRAKATAU

The legendary Krakatau lies only 50 km from the West Java coast. Today only a small part of the original volcano remains but when Krakatau blew itself apart in 1883, in one of the world's greatest and most catastrophic eruptions, the effects were recorded far beyond Selat Sunda and it achieved instant and lasting infamy.

For centuries Krakatau had been a familiar nautical landmark for much of the world's maritime traffic which was funnelled through the narrow Selat Sunda. The volcano had been dormant since 1680 and was widely regarded as extinct but from May through to early August in 1883 passing ships reported moderate activity. By 26 August Krakatau was raging and the explosions became more and more violent. At 10 am on 27 August Krakatau erupted with the biggest bang ever recorded on earth. On the island of Rodriguez, more than 4600 km to the south-west, a police chief reported hearing the booming of 'heavy guns from eastward'; in Alice Springs, 3500 km to the south-east, residents also reported hearing strange explosions from the north-west.

With its cataclysmic explosions, Krakatau sent up a record column of ash 80 km high and threw into the air nearly 20 cubic km of rock. Ash fell on Singapore 840 km to the north and on ships as far as 6000 km away; darkness covered Selat Sunda Straits from 10 am on the 27th until dawn the next day. Far more destructive were the great ocean waves triggered by the collapse of Krakatau's cones into its empty belly. Giant tsunamis more than 40 metres high swept over the nearby shores of Java and Sumatra, and the sea wave's passage was recorded far from Krakatau, reaching Aden in 12 hours over a distance 'travelled by a good steamer in 12 days'. Measurable wave effects even said to have reached the English Channel. Coastal Java and Sumatra were devastated: 165 villages were destroyed and more than 36,000 people were killed.

The following day a telegram sent to Singapore from Batavia (160 km east of Krakatau) reported odd details such as 'fish dizzy and caught with glee by natives'! Three months later the dust thrown into the atmosphere caused such vivid sunsets in the USA that fire engines were being called out to quench the apparent fires, and for three years it continued to circle the earth, creating strange and spectacular sunsets.

The astonishing return of life to the devastated islands has been the subject of scientific study ever since. Not a single plant was found on Krakatau a few months after the event; 100 years later – although the islands are virtually bereft of fauna except for snakes, insects, rats, bats and birds – it seems almost as though the vegetation was never disturbed.

Krakatau basically blew itself to smithereens but, roughly where the 1883 eruption began, Anak Krakatau (the 'Child of Krakatau') has been vigorously growing ever since its first appearance in 1928. It has a restless and uncertain temperament, sending out showers of glowing rocks and belching smoke and ashes, but boats can land on the east side and it is possible to climb right up the cinder cones to the caldera. It is a hard scramble up the loose slopes to the outer rim with fine views of the fuming caldera and the surrounding sea and islands. You can venture farther to the very lip of the crater, but be careful. In 1993, Krakatau belched a load of molten rock on one unfortunate tourist who ventured too close. Krakatau is still a menacing volcano, and in its more active phases Krakatau's intermittent rumblings can be heard on quiet nights from the west-coast beaches.

A Guide to Krakatau, by zoologist I W B Thornton, has detailed maps and information and is available at the Carita Krakatau Beach Hotel or from the Krakatau Foundation, PO Box 4507, Jakarta 10001.

Getting There & Away

The islands of Krakatau are about 50 km from the nearest point on Java and getting out there can be a real hassle. During the rainy season (November to March) there are strong currents and rough seas, but even during the dry season there are sometimes strong south-east winds that whip up the swells and make a crossing inadvisable. When weather conditions are fine it's a long one-day trip, four or five hours there and four or five hours back, but having visited Krakatau we'd say it's definitely worth the effort – *if* you can hire a safe boat.

By far the easiest way to reach Krakatau is to take a tour from Carita. The tour operators (see under Organised Tours from Carita in the previous West-Coast Beaches section) charge 40,000 rp per person (minimum of 10) for a day drip to Anak Krakatau, with two hours on the island. During the peak July/August tourist season a boat goes every day or two. Put your name down with one of the operators when you arrive in Carita and they will tell you when they have a full complement. There is no difference between the operators as they pool their resources to fill a boat, which is usually a small boat but is equipped with radio and life jackets. If there is enough demand, a larger, faster boat

Top :   Dutch graves, Botanical Gardens, Bogor (PT)
Bottom : Botanical Gardens, Bogor (PT)

will be chartered and these provide a more comfortable journey in the swells. In the quieter periods, it can take longer to fill a tour and the cost is 50,000 rp per person for eight people or 65,000 rp per person for a group of six. To charter a whole boat from the tour operators costs 400,000 rp for a small boat carrying 10 to 12 people and taking four to five hours; a large boat costs 700,000 rp (maximum 25 people) and takes around three hours, and the fast boats cost 900,000 rp, take 15 people and complete the trip in just over two hours.

The large hotels also have tours. The Carita Beach Resort has expensive tours by speed boat for US$99, depending on demand, and the Wira Carita rents large boats for 750,000 rp. In Anyer, Marina Village rents high-speed launches carrying 10 or more people for around US$500 per day.

It is cheaper to charter a boat yourself from Labuan or Carita, but make sure you get a seaworthy vessel. The PHPA office in Labuan can be helpful in arranging a larger boat, or you can haggle with the fishermen on the beach and get a much smaller boat. Be forewarned that many of these smaller fishing boats have a history of engine trouble when they get into the strong currents of Selat Sunda. If you do decide to take one of the fishing boats, be sure to take along a food reserve, some water and warm clothes in case you go adrift. In 1986, two foreigners and their Indonesian crew drifted for nearly three weeks before washing up near Bengkulu, Sumatra. In 1988, Lonely Planet almost lost one of its researchers, Joe Cummings, who spent the night adrift on such a boat in high swells along with 10 other travellers.

BOGOR

Bogor, 60 km south of Jakarta, is most famous for its botanical gardens. In the days before independence this was the most important Dutch hill station, midway between the mountains and the heat-ridden plains. Governor-General van Imhoff built a large country estate here in 1745 and named it 'Buitenzorg' ('Without a Care'), but it was not until 1811 that it was first used as a country residence by Sir Stamford Raffles, during the British interregnum. It was not until many years later that Bogor became the semiofficial capital.

Raffles judged it as 'a romantic little village' but Bogor has grown and, except for the gardens, its beauty has faded somewhat. Nevertheless, Bogor has become an important centre for scientific research, including botany, agronomy and forestry.

Though Bogor stands at a height of only 290 metres, it's appreciably cooler than Jakarta. But visitors in the wet season should bear in mind the town's nickname: the 'City of Rain'. Bogor has probably the highest annual rainfall in Java and is credited with a record 322 thunderstorms a year.

Bogor can easily be visited as a day trip from Jakarta, or can be used as a base for exploring the surrounding region.

Orientation & Information

The bus station south of town is about 10 minutes' walk from the botanical gardens entrance. Many of Bogor's losmen and hotels are closer to the railway station, roughly two km north-west of the bus station.

Bogor's Tourist Information Centre (☎ 321075) is on the west side of the gardens at Jalan Ir H Juanda 10, and it also has a branch at the entrance to the gardens.

Kebun Raya (Botanical Gardens)

At the heart of Bogor are the huge, world-class botanical gardens, known as the Kebun Raya (Great Garden), covering an area of around 80 hectares. They are said to be the inspiration of Governor-General Raffles, but the spacious grounds of the Istana Bogor were converted to botanical gardens by the Dutch botanist Professor Reinwardt, with assistants from Kew Gardens, and officially opened by the Dutch in 1817. It was from these gardens that various colonial cash crops such as tea, cassava, tobacco and cinchona were developed by early Dutch researchers during the so-called Forced Cultivation Period in the 19th century. The park is still a main centre for botanical research in Indonesia.

The gardens contain streams and lotus ponds and more than 15,000 species of trees and plants, including 400 types of magnificent palms. The garden's orchid houses are reputed to contain more than 3000 orchid varieties but are not open to the general public. Close to the main entrance of the gardens is a small monument in memory of Olivia Raffles, who died in 1814 and was buried in Batavia, and farther behind, near the palace, is a cemetery with Dutch headstones. The cafeteria on the eastern side of the gardens has a fine view across the lawns and is a pleasant place for a snack or drink.

The gardens are open between 8 am and 5 pm and although they tend to be very crowded on Sunday, on other days they are very peaceful and a fine place to escape from the hassles and crowds of Jakarta. The entrance fee is 1500 rp during the week and 1000 rp on Sunday and holidays. The southern gate is the main entrance; other gates are open only on Sunday and holidays.

Zoological Museum

Near the botanical gardens entrance, this museum has a motley but interesting collection of zoological oddities, including the skeleton of a blue whale and a stuffed Javan rhinoceros. If you ever heard about the island of Flores having a rat problem, one glance at the stuffed Flores version in the showcase of Indonesian rats will explain why. Admission to the museum is 400 rp, and it's open from 8 am to 4 pm daily.

Istana Bogor (Presidential Palace)

In the north-west corner of the botanical gardens, the summer palace of the president was formerly the official residence of the Dutch governors-general from 1870 to 1942. The present huge mansion is not 'Buitenzorg' though; this was destroyed by an earthquake and a new palace was built on the site a few years later in 1856. In colonial days, deer were raised in the parklands to provide meat for banquets, and through the gates you can still see herds of white-spotted deer roaming on the immaculate lawns. The Dutch elite would come up from the pesthole of Batavia and many huge, glamorous parties were held there. Following independence, the palace was a much favoured retreat for Soekarno, although Soeharto has ignored it. It was recently used to host the APEC conference, attended by heads of state from the Asia-Pacific region.

Today the building contains Soekarno's huge art collection of 219 paintings and 156 sculptures (which is reputed to lay great emphasis on the female figure), but the palace is open to the public only by prior arrangement. Contact the tourist office in advance or write directly to the Head of Protocol at the Istana Negara, Jalan Veteran, Jakarta.

Other Attractions

The huge **Batutulis** is an inscribed stone dedicated to Sri Baduga Maharaja by his son King Surawisesa in 1533. Sri Baduga Maharaja (1482-1521) was a Pajajaran king accredited with great mystical power. The stone is housed in a small shrine visited by pilgrims – remove your shoes and make a small donation before entering. Batutulis is 2½ km south of the gardens

One of the few remaining gongsmiths in West Java is Pak Sukarna, and you can visit his **gong factory** at Jalan Pancasan 17. Gongs and other gamelan instruments are smelted over a charcoal fire in the small workshop out the back. A few gongs and wayang golek puppets are on sale in the front showroom. The gong foundry is a one-km walk south from the garden gates down Jalan Empang and west across the river. Look for the 'Pabrik Gong' (Gong Factory) sign.

Places to Stay

Bogor has plenty of hotels available for an extended stay.

For budget accommodation, *Abu Pensione* (☎ 322893), near the railway station at Jalan Mayor Oking 15, is clean, attractive and pleasantly situated. Dorm beds cost 5000 rp or doubles are 15,000 rp in the rickety old section. Rooms with bath in the new section cost 25,000 to 45,000 rp.

Facing the west side of the gardens at Jalan Ir H Juanda 54, the very colonial *Wisma Ramayana* (☎ 320364) is a family-run, Dutch-style homestay. Singles/doubles start at 18,000/19,000 rp without bath, and better rooms with bath are from 29,000 to 44,000 rp. Around the corner at Jalan Paledang 48, *Pensione Firman* (☎ 323426) is the cheapest around with dorm beds at 6000 rp, and rooms for 10,000/13,000 rp or 15,000/20,000 rp with bath, all including breakfast.

About one km north of the gardens, the *Hotel Pangrango* (☎ 328670) at Jalan Pangrango 23 has a small pool and is the best hotel in Bogor. Most air-con rooms with TV cost 75,000 rp, plus 21% tax and service charge, or suites cost 120,000 rp. Tariffs include breakfast. Next to the Hotel Pangrango, the *Sriguntung Guesthouse* (☎ 324160), Jalan Pangrango 21, has well-appointed rooms in a comfortable house with a large garden. Rooms cost 65,000 to 72,500 rp, plus 15%.

Places to Eat

Among its many restaurants, Bogor has a couple of particularly good places to try Sundanese food. For budget dining, *Jongko Ibu* is opposite the west side of the gardens at Jalan Ir H Juanda 36. Meals are served buffet style so you can try a number of dishes. *Rumah Makan Si Kabayan* (☎ 311849), Jalan Bina Marga I No 2, is one of Bogor's most pleasant restaurants. You can dine on mats in individual bamboo huts arranged around an attractive garden. You'll need to order a number of dishes to get your fill, but this restaurant is reasonably priced. The restaurant is in a side street south-east of the bus station, near the end of the toll road.

Getting There & Away

Bogor is easily reached by a good train service. The *Pakuan* express train (2000 rp, one hour) leaves Jakarta's Gambir station at 7.30, 10.30 am, 2.15 and 4.40 pm, and departs from Bogor for the return journey at 6.20, 9.20 am and 3.25 pm, with extra services on Sunday and holidays. This train is comfortable and roomy, but without air-conditioning. Otherwise, ekonomi trains operate every 20 minutes until 8.20 pm and take 1½ hours, but are crowded, especially during peak hours when they are jam-packed with commuters.

Buses from Jakarta depart every 10 minutes or so from the Kampung Rambutan bus station, and can do the trip in a little over half an hour via the Jagorawi Highway toll road. The only problem is that it takes at least double that time to travel between Kampung Rambutan and central Jakarta.

Getting Around

Efficient angkot shuttle around town, particularly between the bus and railway station. Metered taxis are non-existent, but you can haggle with the minivan drivers that hang out near the entrance to the botanical gardens. Becaks are available but are banned from the main road encircling the gardens.

AROUND BOGOR

Purnawarman Stone (Batutulis)

From the village of Ciampea, which is about 12 km north-west of Bogor, you can take a Colt to the village of Batutulis, where sits a huge black boulder on which King Purnawarman inscribed his name and footstep around 450 AD. His inscription, in the Palawa script of South India, reads: 'This is the footstep of King Purnawarman of Tarumanegara kingdom, the great conqueror of the world.'

Another stone inscription of the Taruma kingdom, the Prasati Tugu, can be seen in the National Museum in Jakarta. It refers to the digging of an 11-km-long canal in the Jakarta area during the reign of Purnawarman – which may have been the first of many efforts to solve

Jakarta's flooding problem! The canal was dug by Brahmans in only 21 days and for their labours they were rewarded with 1000 cows. The Ciampea boulder has been raised from its original place, embedded in the shallow water of Sungai Ciaruteun. The inscription on the stone is still remarkably clear after more than 1500 years.

PUNCAK PASS AREA

Between Bogor and Bandung you cross over this beautiful 1500-metre-high pass on a narrow, winding mountain road which passes through small resort towns and tea plantations. At high altitudes it's cool and often misty but in the early mornings the views across the valleys can be superb.

The resort strip with its hotels and villas starts about 10 km out of Bogor at Ciawi and continues up through Cibogo, Cipayung and Cisarua to the Puncak Pass and over the other side to Cipanas. While somewhat over-developed, the area has fine scenery, a refreshing climate and some good walks, especially from Cisarua on the Bogor side of the pass or Cibodas on the other side. Avoid weekends when the crowds and traffic jams are horrendous.

In the foothills just before the Puncak summit, you can stop at the huge **Gunung Mas Tea Estate** for a free tour of the tea factory, a couple of km from the highway. Almost at the top of the pass, the Rindu Alam Restaurant has either fine views of the surrounding tea estates or is surrounded by ethereal mist. From here you can walk down through the tea plantations to **Telaga Warna**, a small 'lake of many colours' just below the top of the pass which reflects different colours with changing daylight (if you're lucky).

Cisarua

Ten km from Bogor on the slopes of the Puncak, there are good walks to picnic spots and waterfalls around Cisarua, which has good budget accommodation. **Curug Cilember** is a waterfall about 30 minutes' walk from Cisarua.

To reach Cisarua, take a bus or Colt from Bogor (700 rp, 45 minutes) or a bus from Jakarta (1500 rp, 1½ hours).

Taman Safari Indonesia

Just east of Cisarua is the turn-off to this wildlife park. As well as indigenous and African 'safari' animals in the drive-through game park, there is a bird park, white tiger pavilion, children's rides and a programme of animal shows, and for 1000 rp you can get your photo taken with an orang-utan or panther. This spacious park with its well-tended animals is streets ahead of any of Indonesia's zoos.

Though best explored with your own car, any Bogor-Bandung bus can drop you at the turn-off, from where minibuses go to the park (500 rp, 2½ km). Entry is 5000 rp for adults, 4000 rp for children; cars are 5000 rp or a minibus is 10,000 rp. A park bus does tours of the safari park if you don't have your own car. Park facilities include a swimming pool, restaurants and accommodation.

Cibodas

At Cibodas, over the Puncak Pass, is a beautiful high-altitude extension of the Bogor botanical gardens, the **Kebun Raya Cibodas**, surrounded by thick tropical jungle on the slopes of the twin volcanoes Gunung Gede and Gunung Pangrango. The 80-hectare gardens were originally planted in 1860. Entry to the gardens is 1500 rp.

Right next to the entrance to the gardens is the entrance to the Gede Pangrango National Park (for details see the following entry). Cibodas has limited facilities and is just a little more difficult to reach than the resort strip along the Puncak Highway. Consequently, it gets much fewer visitors, but it has fine scenery and excellent walks.

The turn-off to Cibodas is on the Bogor-Bandung Highway, a few km west of Cipanas. The gardens are then five km off the main road. Angkot run from Cipanas (500 rp, ½ hour), or coming from the west you can catch them at the turn-off (300 rp).

Gede Pangrango National Park

The Cibodas gardens are also at the main entrance to the Gede Pangrango National Park, the highlight of which is the climb to the 2958-metre peak of volcanically active **Gunung Gede**. From the top of Gede on a clear day you can see Jakarta, Cirebon and even to Pelabuhanratu on the south coast – well, Raffles reported he could! To make the climb you must first get a permit for 4500 rp from the PHPA office (Indonesia's national parks body) just outside the garden entrance. The office has an information centre and pamphlets are available on the park.

A rhinoceros, Taman Safari Indonesia, Cisarua (PT)

It is open from 7 am to 2.30 pm Monday to Thursday, until 11.30 am on Friday and 1.30 pm Saturday.

From Cibodas, the trail passes **Telaga Biru** (15 minutes), a blue-green lake, **Cibeureum Falls** (one hour) and another place where the falls drop deep into a steaming gorge (another hour) fed by a hot-water stream. Many visitors to the park only go to the waterfall. The 10-km hike right to the top of Gunung Gede takes at least 10 hours there and back, so you should start as early as possible and take warm clothes (night temperatures can drop to 5°C). Most climbers bring sleeping bags and camping equipment to camp out on the mountain, allowing them to be at the summit for dawn when the views are spectacular. There is also a steeper trail to the top of **Gunung Pangrango** (3019 metres), which requires an extra one to two hours. Dense fog is common on the mountain so take extra care when on the steeper trails – hikers have been known to walk off into unseen gorges during foggy conditions. The best time to make the hike is from May to October. Gede is only marginally less rainy than Bogor and the climb isn't recommended during the rainy season. An alternative approach is to climb Gede from Selabintana to the south.

Cipanas

Cipanas, five km beyond the Cibodas turn-off, has hot springs noted for their curative properties. The **Istana Cipanas** is another seldom-used summer presidential palace favoured by Soekarno. Built in 1750, it is an elegant country house in beautiful gardens but, like the

Bogor palace, it is not normally open to the public. Apart from that, Cipanas is another resort town with plenty of hotels and a few restaurants.

Places to Stay & Eat

Scores of hotels and villas are spread out along the highway from Ciawi to Cipanas. Many of the villas are private, some owned by large corporations and foreign embassies, but some are for rent and worth looking into for longer stays.

For budget accommodation, the area has two very good youth hostels. The *Kopo Hostel* (☎ 4296), Jalan Raya Puncak 557, on the main road in Cisarua, is excellent value: the four or six-bed dorms cost 6000 rp per person or comfortable rooms cost from 22,000 to 34,000 rp, including breakfast. The hostel has quiet garden grounds and a small restaurant, and maps of walks and information on places of interest in the area is available.

In Cisarua, the *Pondok Pemuda Cibodas* (☎ 512807), near the Cibodas PHPA office, has large dorms costing 4600 rp per person. It's a friendly comfortable place in a superb location. It caters mostly to groups, but outside of weekends and holidays you'll probably have the place to yourself. There's cheap food at the warungs near the gardens and in the village, 500 metres down the hill

A truly tranquil place to lodge is right within the gardens themselves at the colonial *Cibodas Botanical Gardens Guesthouse* (☎ 512233). You certainly can't beat the surrounding ambience and large, if somewhat rundown, rooms costing 30,000 to 45,000 rp. Food is also served. Bookings are essential and you can make reservations at the Bogor botanical gardens as well as the Cibodas gardens.

The top hotel, in terms of facilities and elevation, is the *Puncak Pass Hotel* (☎ 512503), right near the pass itself. Mostly modern bungalows are scattered over the hillside below the old colonial central building. Rates range from US$47 a room up to US$175 for two-bedroom bungalows, 20% less during the week. Not far away, the *Bukit Indah* (☎ 512903) is another older hotel with good facilities, but is slightly cheaper.

Along the main road, in the various towns, there are numerous sate places and restaurants. For big and beautiful kitsch, keep an eye out for the *DC6 Airport Restaurant* in Cisarua. As the name suggests, the restaurant is an old DC6, perched above the highway. The Puncak is also an excellent place for fruit, which is sold along the roadside – pineapples, melons, durian and delicious mangosteens (in season around November, December).

Getting There & Away

From Jakarta's Kampung Rambutan station any Bandung bus can drop you off at any of the resort towns on the highway (but not on Sunday when they aren't allowed to use this highway). From Bogor frequent buses and Colts (which travel on Sunday) also ply the highway.

SELABINTANA

Selabintana is much less developed but also much less crowded than the Puncak Pass resort area to the north of Gunung Gede. It is possible to walk up the hillside to **Sawer Waterfall** and on to **Gunung Gede**, but there is no PHPA post in Selabintana. Selabintana has a golf course, swimming pools and a selection of mid-range hotels. Otherwise Selabintana is simply a quiet place to relax and soak up the mountain air. Selabintana is just seven km north of the city of Sukabumi, which can be reached by bus from Bogor.

Places to Stay

Minibuses from Sukabumi to Selabintana run straight up to the foot of Mt Gede and terminate at the old fashioned, slightly faded *Hotel Selabintana* (☎ 221501), Jalan Selabintana Km 7 marker. Set on 36-hectare grounds, it has a golf course, tennis and volley ball courts, three swimming pools and three restaurants. Small, dark rooms opposite the golf course cost 40,000 rp, rooms in the hotel section are good value at 50,000 rp, or bungalows are 75,000 to 150,000 rp for those with three bedrooms.

The Hotel Selabintana is *the* place to stay, and there is not a lot to do if you stay elsewhere. Nevertheless, Selabintana has plenty of other hotels. Just below the Hotel Selabintana is the *Pondok Asri Selabintana*, under the same management. Modern, well-appointed flatettes cost 70,000 rp, or flatettes with kitchens and two to three bedrooms cost 140,000 to 300,000 rp, plus 20% tax and service.

Next down the hill is the good value *Hotel Pangrango*, with large, musty rooms for 20,000 rp up to 45,000 rp for two-bedroom bungalows, plus 21% and a 5000 rp premium on weekends. The public swimming pool next door is free for guests.

The main village, around the Km 6 marker, has cheaper hotels, including the *Pondok Mandari* and *Melinda Hotel*. Cheapest of all is the *Hotel Intan* at 22,000 rp for good, clean rooms with bath.

Anther good mid-range hotel at the Km 6.3 marker is the *Sukabumi Indah*, a relatively new, 80-room hotel with a swimming pool. Good rooms cost 45,000 rp and 60,000 rp, or cottages are available.

PELABUHANRATU

Pelabuhanratu, 90 km south of Bogor, is a seaside resort popular with Jakarta residents. On a large horseshoe bay, this small fishing town has black-sand beaches and lush scenery, with rice paddies coming almost to the water's edge. Though quiet during the week, it can be crowded at weekends and holidays, and accommodation is quite expensive.

Swimming is possible when the sea is quiet, but like most of Java's south coast, the crashing surf can be treacherous. Drownings do occur in spite of the warning signs which went up after the Bulgarian ambassador disappeared here some years ago. If you want to enter the realms of legend, Pelabuhanratu (Harbour of the Queen) actually witnessed the creation of Nyai Lara Kidul, the malevolent Goddess who takes fishermen and swimmers off to her watery kingdom. Don't wear green on the beach or in the water (it's her colour), and in the Samudra Hotel a room is set aside for offerings to the Queen of the South Seas.

Orientation & Information

Pelabuhanratu is essentially a two-street town – Jalan Siliwangi, which leads into town and to the harbour, and Jalan Kidang Kencana, which runs around the harbour and out to the western beaches. The bus station is near the intersection of these two streets. The beach road continues on to Cisolok, 15 km to the west, and a number of places to stay are scattered along this road.

Bank Central Asia on Jalan Siliwangi will change cash and travellers' cheques. For telephone calls, there is a wartel on Jalan Kidang Kencana near the Queen restaurant.

Things to See & Do

Pelabuhanratu town has little of interest, but the harbour is dotted with brightly painted prahu and the fish market is lively in the morning. The beaches to the west

Rice paddies, Pelabuhanratu (PT)

hold the main interest and some have good surfing. **Cimaja**, eight km west of Pelabuhanratu, has a pebble beach and the best surf when it is working.

Thirteen km west of Pelabuhanratu, at **Pantai Karang Hawu**, is a towering cliff with caves, rocks and pools which were created by a large lava flow that pushed over the beach. According to legend, it was from the rocks of Karang Hawu that Nyai Lara Kidul leapt into the mighty ocean to regain her lost beauty and never returned. Stairs lead up to a small *kramat* (shrine) at the top.

Farther west, about two km past Cisolok, are the **Cipanas** hot springs (not the Cipanas described earlier). Boiling water sprays into the river, and you can soak downstream where the hot and cold waters mingle. It is a very scenic area, and you can walk a few km upstream through the lush forest to a waterfall. Cipanas has changing sheds, warungs and crowds on the weekend.

Goa Lalay bat cave, about four km south-east of Pelabuhanratu, is of limited interest except at sunset when thousands of small bats fly out.

Places to Stay & Eat

Pelabuhanratu has a plenty of mid-range accommodation, and a few vaguely cheap options. The only major hotel is the big Samudra Beach Hotel. The beach, and the nicest accommodation, start one km west from the town.

Two cheap losmen can be found in town on Jalan Siliwangi, a few hundred metres before the harbour. *Penginapan Laut Kidul* at No 148 has simple but clean rooms with bath for 12,500 rp. *Wisma Karang Nara* at No

Pantai Karang Hawu, Pelabuhanratu (PT)

82 is a notch up in quality and priced at 15,000 rp for a room. Nearby, *Restoran Sanggar Sari* at No 76 has good, cheap Chinese food.

Just west of the bus station on Jalan Kidang Kencana, *Penginapan Gunung Muliu* (☎ 41129) has clean but over-priced rooms for 20,000 to 40,000 rp. A string of good restaurants are just along from the Gunung Mulia, including the *Queen Restaurant*, the best in town. It serves excellent food, including Western breakfasts, Chinese food and seafood. Lobster will set you back 15,000 rp, and other dishes are moderately priced.

The *Pondok Dewata* (☎ 41022) is the first place in town on the beach. Balinese-style cottages (all air-con) are comfortable but expensive at US$25 to US$45, plus 20% tax and service. Rates are up to 100% more in holiday periods.

Next along on a headland, *Buana Ayu* (☎ 41111) has some rooms for 45,000 rp, though most cost 60,000 rp. The very comfortable rooms and the good seafood restaurant have fine sea views. Farther around the headland is *Bayu Amrta* (☎ 41031), run by the same proprietor. The rooms, costing 25,000 to 40,000 rp, are a little run-down but the cliff views and the gardens are pleasant. Two nearby mid-range hotels are the *Karang Sari* (☎ 41078), with cottages and air-con bungalows, and the *Bukit Indah* (☎ 41331), perched high up on the cliff.

In Citepus village, three km from Pelabuhanratu, *Losmen Asry* is a friendly budget place and the owner speaks excellent English. Rooms with bath cost 15,000 rp, less when it's quiet, or the one cottage has three bedrooms for 20,000 to 25,000 rp per room. At the Km 4 marker in Citepus, *Hotel Cleopatra* (☎ 41185) has a pool, restaurant and landscaped gardens. Good rooms cost 40,000 to 75,000 rp, while two-bedroom cottages are 150,000 rp and 300,000 rp. Many warung and seafood rumah makan are found on the foreshore here.

About five km west of town, the *Samudra Beach Hotel* (☎ 41023) is a modern high rise with several restaurants and a good swimming pool. Singles/doubles cost US$65/75 for slightly faded rooms or those for US$75/90 are better. All rooms face the sea. Add 21% tax and service, but substantial discounts are available.

Eight km out, Cimaja, the surfing beach, has a couple of very basic penginapan (cheap hotels). The *Andrias* and *Kamboja* both have rooms with bath for 15,000 rp – try bargaining. The *Mustika Rata* is much better and has rooms from 15,000 to 25,000 rp plus 20% tax and service but rates rise substantially on weekends and holidays. Farther along near the river, *Bumi Pasundan* is a large place but nothing special. Rooms cost from 48,000 to 60,000 rp.

A few km farther towards Cisolok is the *Wisma Tenang* on the beach. It is reasonable value with comfortable rooms for 30,000 rp and 50,000 rp. On the other side of the road, the *Pantai Mutiara* (☎ 41330) is one of the best places. It has a swimming pool, fitness centre and restaurant. Standard rooms with bamboo decor cost 30,000 to 50,000 rp, deluxe rooms are 60,000 rp and 90,000 rp, or a family room is 135,000 rp, plus 15.5% tax and service.

The last of the beach places is at Pantai Karang Hawu. *Awina Cottage* (☎ 0226 223363) has ordinary one/two/three-room cottages for 50,000/100,000/150,000 rp – 50% more on weekends and holidays.

Getting There & Away

The road from Bogor cuts south over the pass between Gunung Salak and Pangrango through valleys and hillsides of rubber, coconut, cocoa and tea plantations and terraced rice fields. By car, Pelabuhanratu can be reached in four hours from Jakarta. Local buses run throughout the day from Bogor (2000 rp, three hours) and Sukabumi (1500 rp, 2½ hours). Buses from Sukabumi continue on to Cisolok from Pelabuhanratu.

Getting Around

Angkot run between Pelabuhanratu and Cisolok for 500 rp, less for shorter journeys. They occasionally continue on to Cipanas, otherwise charter them from Cisolok to Cipanas for around 1500 rp. Ojek at the Pelabuhanratu and Cisolok bus stations can be hired for around 3000 rp per hour for sightseeing. Bicycles (1000 rp per hour) and motorbikes (30,000 rp per day) can be hired at Losmen Asry in Citepus.

OTHER

Java has plenty of other interesting attractions for trips farther afield. For full details, Lonely Planet's regional guide to *Java* covers Java in depth, or *Indonesia* covers all of Indonesia.

Ujung Kulon National Park is the best national park on Java. On the remote south-western tip of Java, access is difficult and so Ujung Kulon has remained an outpost of primeval forest and untouched wilderness in heavily developed Java. The park presents some fine opportunities for hiking and wildlife spotting (including the rare one-horned rhinoceros), and has some good beaches with intact coral reefs.

The normal access point is Labuan, from where boats go to the park. To reach the park involves a full day's travel from Jakarta, so at least four days is needed for the return journey and time to enjoy the park. Secure your permit and book accommodation at the PHPA office in Labuan, just south of Carita, or contact PT Wanawisata Alamhayati (☎ 5710392) in Jakarta, which manages accommodation and transport in conjunction with the PHPA. Tours can also be arranged from Carita (see under Carita in the West-Coast Beaches section earlier in this chapter).

Good train connections from Jakarta can get you in Cirebon or Bandung in around four hours.

Cirebon is a court city on the north coast in West Java, near the border with Central Java. Though it attracts few tourists, it has well-preserved royal palaces and is an interesting town for a short visit.

Bandung is Java's third-largest city, but is less congested than Jakarta and cooler because of its position in the central highlands. Bandung has some good architectural reminders of the Dutch occupation and, as the capital of West Java, is a centre for Sundanese culture. The hills around Bandung are dotted with hot springs, volcanoes and small resorts.

Java's most popular tourist destination is **Yogyakarta**. Yogyakarta is a centre for the still strongly Hindu-influenced court culture of Central Java. The city has a host of attractions and is the main base for visiting Indonesia's most awe-inspiring archaeological sites – Borobudur and Prambanan. Regular flights connect Jakarta with Yogyakarta.

Index

Maps

MAP LEGEND

ROUTES

	Freeway
	Highway
	Major Road
	Unsealed Road
	City Road
	City Street
	Railway
	Walking Track
	Walking Tour
	Ferry Route
	Cable Car

AREA FEATURES

	Park, Gardens
	National Park
	Built-Up Area
	Pedestrian Mall
	Market
	Cemetery
	Beach

HYDROGRAPHIC FEATURES

	Coastline, River
	Lake, Swamp

SYMBOLS

✈	Airfield	P	Parking
✈	Airport	★	Police Station
⊖	Bank	✉	Post Office
⊖	Bus Station	🍺	Pub, Bar
☕	Café		Railway Station
⚠	Camping Ground	▼	Restaurant
☯	Capital City	33	Route Number
⌗	Caravan Park	⚜	Ruins
†	Cathedral	◈	Shopping Centre
⌒	Cave	⊞	Stately Home
†	Church	▱	Swimming Pool
	Cliff	✿	Synagogue
✺	Gardens	☎	Telephone
✚	Hospital	⊥	Temple
▪	Hotel, Pension	▣	Tomb
☀	Lookout	❶	Tourist Information
♟	Monument		Tunnel
▲	Mountain		Wall
⚸	Mosque		Waterfall
⛪	Museum	⌂	Youth Hostel
←	One Way Street	🐄	Zoo

Note: not all symbols displayed appear in this book

MAP 2

Sunda Kelapa

Jl Luar Batang

Pelabuhan Sunda Kelapa

Sunda Kelapa

Jl Maritim Raya

Jl Baruna 2

Jl Baruna 1

▼ Phinisi Cafe

Jl Baruna Raya

Luar Batang Mosque

Jl Pinisi

Jl Sunda Kelapa

Jl Ancol 4

Harbour Gate

Museum Bahari 🏛

Pasar Ikan

Jl Lodan Raya

Watchtower ●

Jl Krapu

Jl Pakin

Jl Kambing

Jl Ekor Kuning

Jl Kakap

VOC Shipyards ●

Jl Tongkol

Harbour Tollroad

🏹

lp

Bendera

Chicken Market Bridge ●

Jl Tiang

Sunda Kelapa & Kota

Jl Kali Besar Timur

Jl Cengkeh

0   250   500

••••• Walking Tour

Jl Tiang Bendera 2

Jl Kopi

Jl Besar Timur 3 Kunir

Toko Merah ●

Kali Besar

Jl Kali Besar Barat

Wayang Museum 🏛

Cafe ▼ Batavia

Jl Kemukus

Cilitung

Jl RM Selatan

Jl Kali Besar Timur

Taman Fatahillah

🏛 Balai Seni Rupa

Jakarta History Museum 🏛

Jl Ketumbar

Jl Pos Kota Lada

Jl Pintu Besar Utara

MAP 3

Jl Malaka

Kota

Jl Bank

Jl Telepon Kota

Jl Pasar Pagi

Jl Kota

Jl Stasium

Kota Railway Station

Jl PS Pagi Flyover

Jl Pintu Kecil

Jl Asemka

•••• Jl Jembatan Batu ••••

Jl Timur

Jl Pintu Kecil

Jl Pintu Besar Seltan

Jl Pinangsia Timur

Jl Pangeran Jayakarta

✝ Gereja Sior

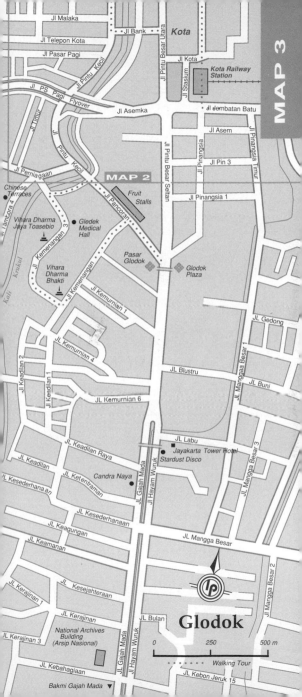

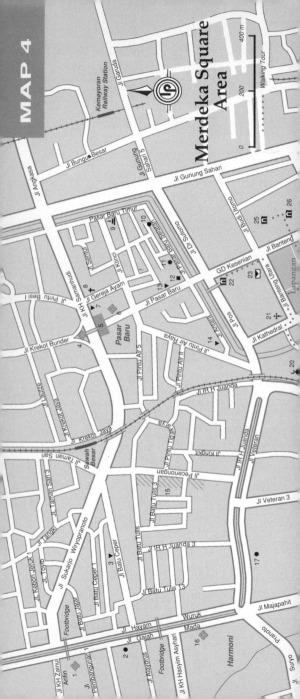

Map 4
Merdeka Square Area

PLACES TO STAY

12 Hotel Pasar Baru
28 Hotel Borobudur Inter-Continental
37 Dai-Ichi Hotel

PLACES TO EAT

3   Sari Kuning
7   Rumah Makan Taj Mahal
13 Toko Kompak
14 Copper Chimney
15 Seafood Warungs

OTHER

1   Gajah Mada Plaza
2   Pelni Head Office
4   Metro Department Store
5   Pasar Baru
6   Marco Plaza
8   Gereja Ayam
9   Sikh Temple
10 Sai Baba Centre
11 Gandhi Memorial School
16 Duta Merlian
17 Istana Merdeka
18 Taman Prasasti Museum
19 Istana Negara
20 Istiqlal Mosque
21 Catholic Cathedral
22 Gedung Kesenian
23 Post Office
24 Free Irian Monument
25 Makmah Agung
26 Ministry of Finance Building
27 Bharata Theatre
29 Gedung Pancasila
30 Imanuel Church
31 National Monument (Monas)
32 National Museum
33 Tanamur Disco
34 City Hall
35 US Embassy
36 Museum Kebangkitan Nasional
    (STOVIA Building)
38 The Atrium
39 Pasar Senen Market

Top :	Old Dutch warehouses, VOC Shipyards,
	Kota (GB)
Middle :	Boats moored at Sunda Kelapa (GB)
Bottom :	Wayang Museum, Kota (GB)

MAP 5

Jalan Jaksa Area

Map 5
Jalan Jaksa Area

PLACES TO STAY

- 5 Sabang Metropoltan Hotel
- 22 Sari Pan Pacific Hotel
- 25 Wisma Ise Guesthouse
- 34 Bali International Hotel
- 36 Arcadia Hotel
- 38 Pondok Wisata Jaya Hostel
- 40 Pondok Wisata Kebon Sirih
- 41 Hostel Rita
- 42 Bintang Kejora
- 47 Wisma Delima
- 49 Bloem Steen Homestay
- 50 Kresna Homestay
- 51 Jusran Hostel
- 52 Norbek (Noordwijk) Hostel
- 53 Nick's Corner Hostel
- 56 Borneo Hostel
- 60 Djody Hostel
- 61 Djody Hotel
- 62 International Tator Hostel
- 63 Hotel Karya
- 64 Hostel 36
- 69 Cipta Hotel
- 71 Cemara Hotel

PLACES TO EAT

- 6 Ayam Goreng Jakarta
- 7 Hot Pot Garden
- 8 Bakwan House
- 9 Sakura Anpan Bakery
- 10 Natrabu Padang Restaurant
- 11 KFC
- 12 Sederhana Padang Restaraunt
- 13 Sizzler
- 14 Kantin 43
- 15 Hoka Hoka Bento
- 16 Kaharu Restaurant
- 17 Paradiso 2001
- 18 A&W
- 20 Dunkin Donuts
- 21 Lim Thiam Kie Restaurant
- 30 McDonald's
- 35 Warung Bali
- 37 Hazara Restaurant
- 43 Shalimar & Ikan Bakar Kebon Sirih Restaurants
- 46 Senayan Satay House
- 48 Angie's Cafe
- 54 Asmat Cafe
- 57 Memories Cafe
- 59 Anedja Cafe
- 66 Romance Bar & Restaurant
- 67 Mbak Merry
- 68 Le Bistro
- 70 Ayam Goreng Nyonya Suharti
- 73 Cahaya Kota Restaurant

OTHER

- 1 Bank Indonesia
- 2 Bangkok Bank
- 3 Airlines: Garuda, Qantas, Thai, Ansett & Continental
- 4 BDN Building
- 19 Robinson Department Store
- 23 ATD Plaza
- 24 Jaya Pub
- 26 Jaya Building
- 27 Skyline Building
- 28 Jakarta Theatre
- 29 United Nations
- 31 Hard Rock Cafe
- 32 Sarinah Department Store
- 33 Police Station
- 39 Mosque
- 44 Bank Duta
- 45 Lippobank
- 55 Kencana Travel
- 58 RTQ Warparpostal
- 65 Seabreeze Travel
- 72 Media Taxis

MAP 6

Menteng

MAP 5

Cikini

Cikini

River

Walking Tour

Gondangdia
Railway
Station

Jl Kramat Raya
Jl Salemba Raya
Jl Raden Saleh
Jl Ciliwung
Jl Cisadane
Jl Cimandiri
Jl Cikini
Jl Cikini 6
Jl Cikini 5
Jl Cikini 4
Jl Cikini 2
Jl R P Soeroso
Jl Soeroso T Cik Ditiro
Jl Cut Nyak Dien
Jl Sawo
Jl Jambu
Jl Teuku Umar
Jl Teuku Umar
Jl Cut Meutia
Jl Cut Meutia
Jl Gondangdia Kecil 1
Jl Johar
Jl Kenari
Jl Cendana
Jl Cemara
Jl Kamboja
Jl Dr Sam Ratulangi
Jl Yusuf
Jl Sultan Syahrir
Jl Prof Moch Yamin
Jl Suwiryo
Jl Hos Cokroaminoto
Jl Lombok
Jl Maluku
Jl Sumbawa
Jl Gereja Theresia
Jl Lombok
Jl Ulim
Jl Yusuf Adiwinata
Jl Wahid Hasyim
Jl Sumatera
Jl Haji Agus Salim
Jl Riau
Jl Biliton
Jl Timor
Jl Sunda
Jl MH Thamrin
Jl Kebon Kacang
Jl Indramayu
Jl Pekalongan
Jl Panarukan
Jl Imam Bonjol
Jl Betung
Jl Banyuwangi
Jl Bintaro
Jl Kediri
Jl Bromo
Jl Sidoarjo
Jl Tasikmalaya

500 m
250
0

PLACES TO STAY

13 President Hotel
15 Grand Hyatt Jakarta
17 Hotel Indonesia
20 Mandarin Oriental Hotel
25 Kartika Plaza Hotel
39 Solyan Hotel Betawi
40 Gondia Guest House
42 Hotel Menteng I
46 Solyan Hotel Cikini
48 Yannie International
   Guest House
49 Karya II Hotel
52 Hotel Marcopolo
53 Hotel Menteng II

PLACES TO EAT

7 Lin's Garden Sea Food
24 Korea Garden
28 Jalan Kendal Food Stalls
32 Tan Goei
33 Menteng Kuring
36 Black Angus
37 Tamnak Thai
44 Kikugawa
45 Art & Curio
50 Oasis Bar & Restaurant

OTHER

1 Skyline Building
2 Jakarta Theatre
3 United Nations
4 Sarinah Department Store
5 Bank Surya
6 French Embassy
8 Studio 21 Building
9 Bank International
   Indonesia
10 Russian Embassy
11 Japanese Embassy
12 Bank Niaga
14 Nusantara Building
16 Plaza Indonesia
18 Welcome Statue
19 British Embassy
21 German Embassy
22 Thai Embassy
23 Jakarta Handicraft Centre
26 Lone Star
27 George & Dragon Pub
29 Museum Permusan
30 Taman Suropati
31 Philippines Embassy
34 Keris Gallery
35 Menteng Plaza
38 Casa Pub
41 Immigration Office
43 Taman Ismail Marzuki
47 Cikini Hospital
   (Raden Saleh's House)
51 Museum MH Thamin
54 Pasar Kembang
55 Pasar Cikini
56 Adam Malik Museum
57 New Zealand Embassy
58 Italian Embassy
59 Austrian Embassy
60 Taman Proklamasi

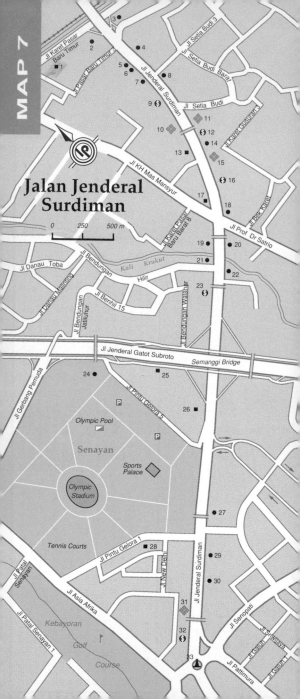

Map 7
Jalan Jenderal Surdiman

PLACES TO STAY

1	Shangri-La Hotel
13	Sahid Jaya Hotel
17	Le Meridien
25	Jakarta Hilton
26	Hilton Residence
28	Atlett Century Park Hotel

OTHER

2	BNI Bank Tower
3	Landmark Centre
4	Wisma Indocement
5	Artholoka Building
6	Prince Centre
7	Toyota-Asta Building
8	Bumiputra
9	Bank Pacific
10	Mid Plaza
11	Chase Plaza
12	BCA Bank
14	Tamara Centre
15	Lippo Plaza
16	Bank Bali
18	Wisma Metropolitan
19	Wisma Rajawali
20	Danamon Square
21	Wisma Benhil
22	Pasar Benhil
23	Bank Perdania
24	Jakarta Hilton Convention Centre
27	Widjojo Centre
29	Sudirman Tower
30	Summitmas Tower
31	Ratu Plaza
32	Panin Bank
33	Semangat Pemuda ('Pizza Man') Statue

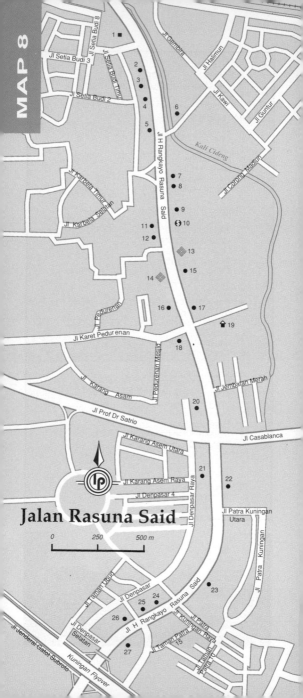

Map 8
Jalan Rasuna Said

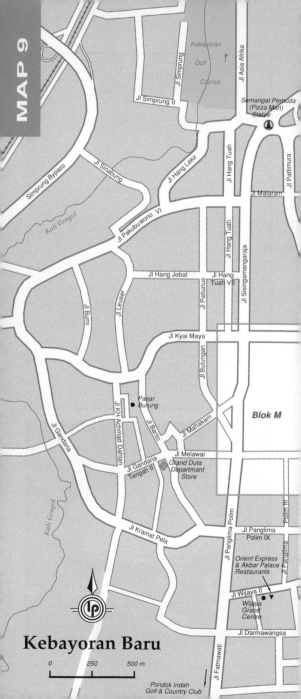

MAP 9

Kebayoran Baru

Kebayoran Golf Course

Jl Simprung II

Jl Simprung

Jl Asia Afrika

Semangat Pemuda (Pizza Man) Statue

Jl Pattimura

Simprung Bypass

Jl Sinabung

Jl Hang Lekir

Jl Hang Tuah

Jl Mataram

Kali Grogol

Jl Pakubuwono VI

Jl Hang Tuah

Jl Hang Jebat

Jl Hang Tuah VII

Jl Patunus

Jl Leuser

Jl Bumi

Jl Kyai Maya

Jl Sisingamangaraja

Jl Bulungan

Pasar Burung

Blok M

Jl KH Achmad Dahlan

Jl Barito

Jl Mahakam

Jl Gandaria

Jl Gandaria Tengah II

Jl Melawai
Grand Duta
Department
Store

Kali Grogol

Jl Kramat Pela

Jl Panglima Polim

Jl Panglima Polim IX

Polim III

Orient Express & Akbar Palace Restaurants

Jl Panglima

Jl Wijaya II

Wijaya Grand Centre

Kebayoran Baru

Jl Darmawangsa

0   250   500 m

Jl Fatmawati

Pondok Indah
Golf & Country Club

Map 9 (see previous page)
Kebayoran Baru
(Blok M inset)

1 Top Gun
2 Sportsman's Bar & Grill
3 Prigura Art Shop
4 Tambora Hotel
5 Pare'gu Restaurant
6 Golden Truly Supermarket
7 Blok M Plaza
8 Tokio
9 Blok M Mall
10 Blok M Bus Terminal
11 Gandy Steakhouse
12 Jamz
13 Interhouse Hotel
14 Matahari Department Store
15 Pasaraya Big & Beautiful
16 Rencana Hotel
17 King's Head Pub

Dutch architecture, Kota (GB)

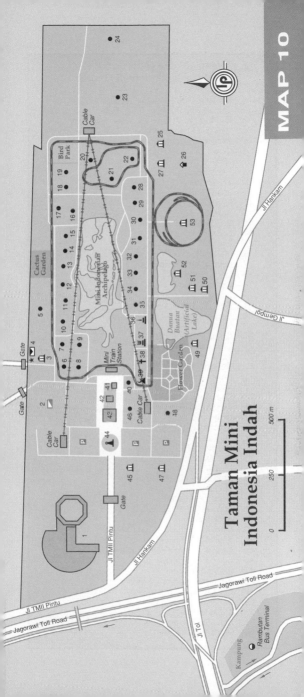

MAP 10

Taman Mini
Indonesia Indah

24

23

25

26

Cable Car

20 Bird Park

18 19

17 16 15 14 13 12 11 10

Cactus Garden

21 22

27

28

29

30

31

32

33

34 35

36

37 38 39

53

52

51 50

49

Damu Buatan (Artificial Lake)

5

7

6 8 9

Mini Indonesia Archipelago

Mini Train Station

Gate

4

3

2

Gate

Cable Car

40 41

42

43

46

48

Cable Car

44

45

47

P

P

P

Flower Garden

1

Gate

Jl TMII Pintu

Jl Hankam

Jagorawi Toll Road

Jl TMII Pintu

Jagorawi Toll Road

Jl Tol

Jl Hankam

Jl Gempol

Jl Hankam

Rambutan Bus Terminal

Kampung

0   250   500 m

Map 10 (see previous page)
Taman Mini Indonesia Indah

1   Museum Purna Bhakti Pertawi
2   Taman Renang (Swimming Pool)
3   Information Museum
4   Police \ Post Office
5   Childrens Playground
6   Jambi
7   Riau
8   Bengkulu
9   South Sumatra
10 West Sumatra
11 North Sumatra
12 Aceh
13 West Kalimantan
14 South Kalimantan
15 East Kalimantan
16 Maluku
17 Central Kalimantan
18 North Sulawesi
19 Central Sulawesi
20 Irian Jaya
21 Childrens Palace
22 East Sulawesi
23 Science Centre
24 Graha Widya Patra
25 Stamps Museum
26 Youth Hostel
27 Komodo Museum
28 South Sulawesi
29 Tenggara Sulawesi
30 East Nusa Tenggara
31 West Nusa Tenggara
32 Bali
33 East Java
34 Yogyakarta
35 Central Java
36 Buddist Temple
37 Hindu Temple
38 Protestant \ Catholic Church
39 Mosque
40 Borobudur Relief
41 Enquires \ Information
42 Administration Offices
43 Main Building
44 Tugu Api Pancasila
45 Telecommunications Museum
46 Handicrafts Centre
47 Sports Museum
48 Keong Emas (Imax Theatre)
49 ASMAT Museum
50 Museum Serangga
51 Museum Pasaka
52 Museum Keprajuritan
53 Transport Museum

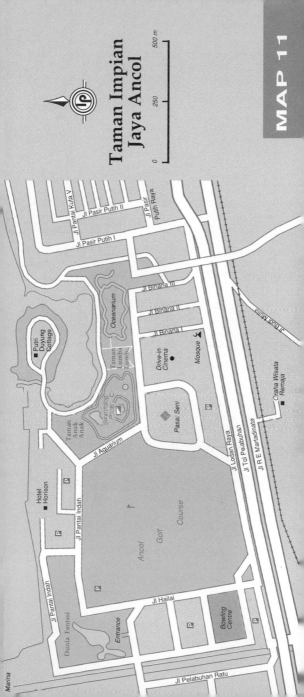

MAP 11

Taman Impian
Jaya Ancol

0   250   500 m

MAP 12

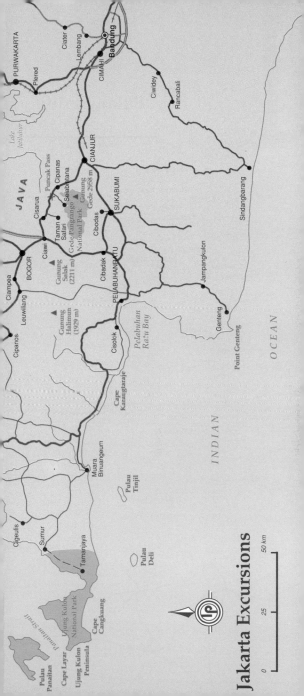

Jakarta Excursions

MAP 13

Pulau Seribu

```
0        5        10       15      20 km
```

P Satu - Pulau Satu

P Dua Barat

P Dua Timur

P Pancalirang Besar

P Gosong Rangat

P Pancalirang Kecil

P Jagung

P Ringgit

P Sebaru Besar

P Sebaru Kecil

P Antuk

P Laga

P Sabtu

P Sepa

P Papa Theo

P Melinjo

P Melintang

P Pelangi

P Putri

P Genting

P Bira

P Macan Besar

JAVA

P Panjang
(Airstrip)

P Kelapa

P Opak

P Kotok

P Karang

P Panggang

SEA

P Simpit

P Lang

P Ayer

P Sekati

P Tidung

P Payung

P Tikus

P Pari

P Lancang Beasr

P Laki

P Lancang Kecil

P Bokor

P Damar Besar

P Rambut

P Untung Java

P Ayer Kecil

P Damar Kecil

Tanjung Kait

Tanjung Pasir

P Ayer Besar

P Nyamuk Kecil

P Ohrust

P Kelor

Mauk

P Kahyangan

P Bidadari

P Nyamuk Besar

Kamal

Jakarta Bay

Ancol Marina

Soekarno-Hatto International Airport

TANGERANG

JAKARTA

Top :   Pulau Sepa, Pulau Seribu (PT)
Bottom :   Pulau Antuk Timur, Pulau Seribu (PT)

MAP 14

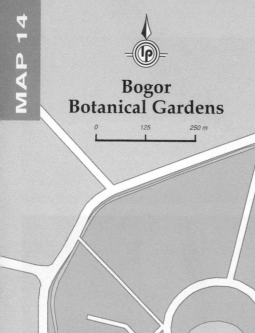

Bogor Botanical Gardens

0   125   250 m

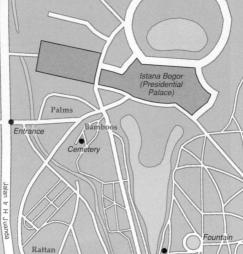

Istana Bogor
(Presidential
Palace)

Palms

Entrance

Bamboos

Cemetery

Jalan Ir H Juanda

Rattan

Fountain

Olivia
Raffles
Memorial

Laboratory

Office

🏛 Zoological
Museum

Main Entrance

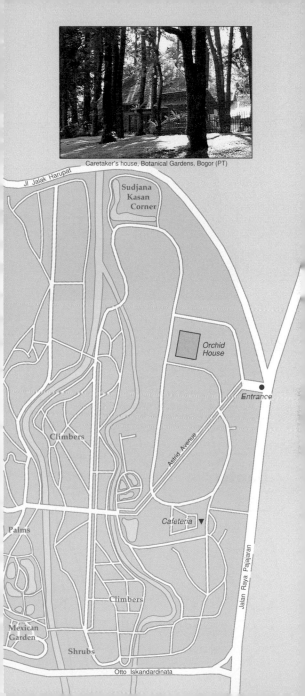

Caretaker's house, Botanical Gardens, Bogor (PT)

MAP 15

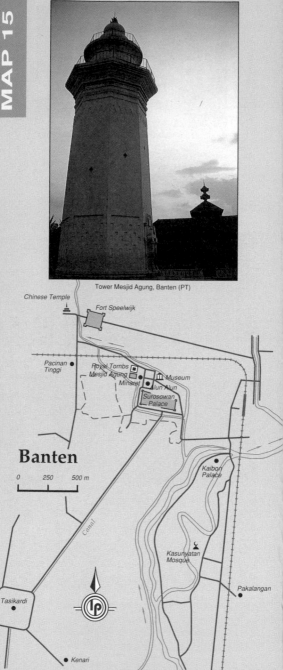

Tower Mesjid Agung, Banten (PT)

Chinese Temple

Fort Speelwijk

Pacinan Tinggi

Royal Tombs

Mesjid Agung

Minaret

Museum

Alun Alun

Surosowan Palace

Banten

0   250   500 m

Canal

Kaibon Palace

Kasunyatan Mosque

Tasikardi

Pakalangan

Kenari

Top :   Fruit vendor (PT)
Bottom : Chinese terraces (PT)